THE STRANGE DEATH
OF VINCENT FOSTER

AN INVESTIGATION

CHRISTOPHER RUDDY

THE FREE PRESS

New York   London   Toronto   Sydney   Singapore

THE FREE PRESS
A Division of Simon & Schuster Inc.
1230 Avenue of the Americas
New York, NY 10020

THE FREE PRESS and colophon are trademarks
of Simon & Schuster Inc.

Designed by Carla Bolte

Manufactured in the United States of America

10   9   8   7   6   5   4   3

Library of Congress Cataloging-in-Publication Data
Ruddy, Christopher.
    The strange death of Vincent Foster : an investigation / Christopher
Ruddy.
      p. cm.
    Includes index.
    1. Foster, Vincent W., d. 1993—Death and burial.   2. Clinton,
Bill, 1946–   —Friends and associates.   3. Homicide investigation—
Virginia—Arlington—Case studies.   4. Governmental investigations—
United States—Case studies.   5. Political corruption—United
States—Case studies.   6. Suicide—Virginia—Arlington—Case
studies.   I. Title.
E840.8.F69R83   1997
364.15′22′09755295—dc21   97-22737
                                                   CIP

ISBN 0–684–83837–0

1

It was Wednesday afternoon, July 21, 1993, and the White House briefing room was humming with tension. A crisis was at hand, and the press corps was waiting for details. This much was known. White House deputy counsel Vincent Walker Foster, Jr., one of the nation's highest federal officers and First Family confidant, was dead. His body had been found some twenty-one hours before in Fort Marcy Park, Virginia, just across the Potomac River from Washington, D.C., seven miles from the White House.

For a Clinton administration that was still struggling to find its footing, this was just the latest in a long line of crises running from Nannygate to Travelgate. If, as the U.S. Park Police suspected, the forty-eight-year-old Foster had died by suicide, it was the first death of a high official since Secretary of Defense James Forrestal leaped from the sixteenth floor of the naval hospital in Bethesda, Maryland, in 1949. If, on the other hand, he had been killed, he would be the highest-ranking White House official to be slain since President John Kennedy was assassinated in Dallas's Dealey Plaza on November 22, 1963.

At 3:38 P.M. eastern standard time, White House Chief of Staff Thomas "Mack" McLarty and Communications Director Mark Gearan entered the briefing room. McLarty hesitantly began his statement.

> Good afternoon. As I'm sure you can appreciate, this is one of the hardest things I've ever had to do. Like the president and myself, Vince Foster was from Hope, Arkansas, and for more than forty years was my friend. . . .

McLarty went on to describe how Foster had been a highly successful litigator for Arkansas's powerhouse legal organization, the Rose Law Firm, which was sometimes referred to, reverentially, as "The Firm." The troika he formed with Rose partners Hillary Rodham Clinton and Webster Hubbell was respected both in Arkansas and Washington.

McLarty then turned to the matter that was foremost on everyone's mind: the death itself. McLarty never mentioned the word "suicide," and his statement offered no details. "[T]ry as we might, with all of our reason, all of our rationality, all of our logic, we can never answer the questions raised by such a death." McLarty continued, "We really can never fully know a person's private pain and what might lead them in their thought process, even a person we have known all our lives." The press corps began peppering McLarty with questions. "Mack, did you know of any personal reason why he might have done this?"

At that point Gearan interrupted to explain how the White House had learned of the death. U.S. Park Police, he said, had called White House security and administrative officers "about a body being found" in a Virginia park; Secret Service then informed administrative officers at the White House, including White House personnel security chief Craig Livingstone, at 8:30 P.M. McLarty was notified of the unconfirmed report "soon after" the president had begun his appearance on CNN's *Larry King Live* at 9:00 P.M., which that night was being broadcast from the White House library.

At the end of that hour, just before 10:00 P.M., Gearan said, "We had the confirmation that indeed Vince had been confirmed as deceased."

During a commercial break, McLarty informed the president there was bad news, causing Clinton to withdraw his offer to King to continue for an additional half hour.

Those in the room pressed their questions:

"Is there any doubt . . . as to the apparent suicide?" Although he had admitted there was an ongoing investigation, Gearan quickly dismissed its significance, saying it was "standard operating procedure."

"Do you know anything about the weapon that was used?" Gearan did not know.

"Was there a note?"

Gearan responded tersely, "There was not."

"What accounts for the lapse in time . . . between 6:00 P.M. [when the body was found] and 9:15 P.M. before you or the White House was notified, and who made that positive identification? . . . It just seems like an inordinate amount of time. . . ."

Gearan was at a loss to explain the gap. "I don't know if it was inordinate or not," he said.

"What is the evidence that this is a suicide?"

"The Park Service report indicated that," he replied, adding, "We have no reason to dispute it."

"Did his wife know he owned a gun?"

"I don't know."

"Are you looking for . . . financial problems or blackmail or something that's unseen at this point?"

Gearan's response was cryptic. "No, we're looking just to ensure that the standard procedure is followed in the sense of the counsel's office here because some of it may require the broadened focus of the Justice Department only in the sense of the counsel's office. . . . I don't want to confuse anyone here. The Department of Justice has been asked by the counsel's office, Bernie [Nussbaum], to coordinate this from the Park Service to any of the other procedural investigatory authorities on behalf of the White House."

Gearan's odd reply prompted another question. "Is it standard procedure for the White House, despite the fact that the victim worked here, to be involved in directing how the investigation is coordinated or having the federal authorities do that?"

Gearan promised to "provide additional details on the specific legalities. . . ." He suggested the inquiry was being directed solely by "the Park Service." His response became muddled: "Another part of the investigation would be any information that would provide background that also involves his place of work or whatever."

Gearan could not explain who was in charge of the investigation. The reporter posed the question a second time. This time Gearan admitted he had not been "prepared fully on this" but believed that the Department of Justice had been asked to coordinate the investigation. He said he would get back to them when he knew for sure.

"Do you have any details about how he was found or who found him?"

"I don't know the answer to that."

"Do you know if [Foster and Hillary Clinton] had any other business relationship other than being law partners?"

"I'm not aware of any other business relationship, no."

The details that Wednesday afternoon were sketchy. It was clear that to those in the White House, Vince Foster's death was not simply another crisis; it was a personal loss that had to be absorbed.

By the end of the week, Vince Foster's body was returned to Hope for burial. Soon after he made his final journey home, two new pieces of information helped provide answers to the many questions that remained about his death.

White House lawyer Stephen Neuwirth disclosed that while in Foster's office on July 26, packing belongings to be shipped to Foster's widow, he had stumbled on something. As he turned Foster's soft-leather bag on its side, scraps of yellow paper fell out. Neuwirth took the pieces into Nussbaum's office.

The contents of the note were soon released to the public. While the note made no explicit mention of suicide, it seemed clear that it was, in fact, a sort of suicide note that revealed a man deeply disturbed by the intense scrutiny of public life and disappointed with his own actions in damaging the president. The note was not coherent, but rather a series of statements apparently scrawled in his own handwriting.

I made mistakes from ignorance, inexperience, and overwork.

I did not knowingly violate any law or standard of conduct.

No one in the White House, to my knowledge, violated any law or standard of conduct, including any action in the travel office. There was no intent to benefit any individual or specific group.

The FBI lied in their report to the AG [Attorney General].

The press is covering up the illegal benefits they received from the travel staff.

The GOP has lied and misrepresented its knowledge and role and covered up a prior investigation.

The Ushers Office plotted to have excessive costs incurred, taking advantage of Kaki [Kaki Hockersmith, the Clintons' decorator from Little Rock] and HRC.

The public will never believe the innocence of the Clintons and their loyal staff.

The WSJ [*Wall Street Journal*] editors lie without consequence.

I was not meant for the job or the spotlight of public life in Washington. Here ruining people is considered sport.

Almost at the same time the note surfaced, the press was reporting that the Park Police had found another note in Foster's wallet in his handwriting with the names and phone numbers of two Washington area psychiatrists.

All the pieces were coming together: Vince Foster was a man battling depression, loneliness, and a sense of failure. He had sought to fight that battle with help from professionals, but clearly it was a fight that he did not win.

By August 5, the Park Police had completed their investigation into the death. The report concluded that, based on the "facts and circumstances," the case should be closed and the death ruled a suicide.

On August 10, Park Police Chief Robert Langston, together with two prominent officials, Deputy Attorney General Philip Heymann and Metropolitan Washington FBI Special Agent Robert Bryant, appeared at a press conference at the Justice Department to announce these findings. Heymann began by saying that he had received the Park Police report on Foster's death. He would leave it to Langston and Bryant to explain the results of the inquiries. Instead, Heymann focused on the torn note. For the first time, he announced, he was authorizing the release of the full text of the note to the public. Photocopies of the note, however, would not be distributed to the press, at the Foster family's request.

After Heymann's brief remarks, Chief Langston and Special Agent Bryant took the podium. Langston gave the results of the Park Police inquiry that concluded suicide while Bryant dutifully assisted. But few were satisfied with the Park Police's work.

Within six months, enough new questions were raised about Foster's death, the White House's response, the investigation, and related matters that Attorney General Janet Reno appointed longtime Republican and noted attorney Robert Fiske to give the government's definitive account of the death of Vincent Foster. In a detailed and documented fifty-eight-page report issued on June 30, 1994, Fiske concluded that Foster "committed suicide by firing a bullet from a .38 caliber revolver into his mouth. . . . [T]he evidence overwhelmingly supports this conclusion and there is no evidence to the contrary." His report provides the foundation for what has come to be accepted as the "official" version of the Foster death.

The Fiske report began by detailing Foster's early life: He was born on January 15, 1945, in one of America's prototypical small towns, Hope, Arkansas. His next-door neighbor and childhood friend Bill Clinton would turn out to be governor and then president. Another childhood friend, Thomas "Mack" McLarty, would go on to run Arkla, a natural gas company that is one of Arkansas's major industries, and later become Clinton's chief of staff.

Foster was raised in a prosperous family. His father, Vincent Sr., was the owner of a local real-estate firm, and his mother, the attractive Alice Mae, was socially active in the town.

Clinton left Hope at the age of seven when his mother, Virginia, moved to Hot Springs, Arkansas. Young Vince Foster's roots, however, were deeply embedded in tiny Hope, where everything seemed to revolve around family, school, or church. His father was an elder at the First Presbyterian Church, and Vince was active in the church's youth association.

After graduating from North Carolina's Davidson College, a school affiliated with the Presbyterian church, in 1967 with a degree in psychology, Foster married his sweetheart, Elizabeth "Lisa" Braden, a Catholic from Nashville. Foster worked hard and advanced rapidly. He graduated first in his 1971 class at the University of Arkansas Law School, took the highest mark on the state bar exam, and was hired by the prestigious Rose Law Firm. There, he worked for top clients like Tyson Foods and Stephens, Inc., Little Rock's huge financial conglomerate.

There Foster also became a friend and confidant of Hillary Rodham Clinton. She was a Yankee outsider to Little Rock, but the wife of the soon-to-be governor. At the Rose firm she became a rainmaker, one who brought in business. Foster was the firm's chief commercial litigator, and a steely one at that.

Outside the firm, Foster and Mrs. Clinton shared some common interests, including their support for legal services for the poor. President Jimmy Carter had appointed Mrs. Clinton chairwoman of the Legal Services Corporation. Foster was active in the local Legal Services office and in 1982 was appointed chairman of its advisory council by Governor Clinton. Foster was remembered for being extremely civic-minded. He chaired the board of the Arkansas Repertory Theater and was active in a number of community organizations.

Foster's office at the Rose firm came to be lined with plaques and awards he received for his public service. His mother complained that her unpretentious son would never tell anyone, including her and her husband, about his accomplishments. For Foster, virtue was something to be practiced, not talked about.

Neither glib nor a backslapper, Foster liked interacting with people. He was noted for his wry sense of humor, one that developed at an early age. His family still talks of the time when, as a young boy, he asked his mother how old she was. When she told him she was forty he responded, "You don't look like forty." His mother felt deeply complimented and asked him how old he thought she was. He said, "Umm, let's see, about thirty-nine."

Friends who knew Foster from his boyhood in Hope and through his adult life in Little Rock describe him as normal, if somewhat vain. One friend likened him to Cary Grant. He was a tall, distinguished-looking man who worked out regularly and always looked his best, every hair in place.

While Foster was a man concerned about his reputation, he was also a man of real substance. In a speech he gave to graduating law students in Arkansas shortly before his death Foster stressed the importance of the family. "Balance wisely your professional life and your family life. . . . God only allows us so many opportunities with our children to read a story, go fishing, play catch, say our prayers together. Try not to miss a one of them."

Foster had lived by those words. He had even avoided becoming an avid hunter or golfer so that he could be at home with his three children, Vincent III, Laura, and Brugh.

On his last birthday in January 1993, Foster's mother sent him a birthday card. It read, "I'm proud of you for so many things, but first of all for being a wonderful father, second a wonderful husband, and third a wonderful son." She and her husband knew of his devotion to them. His mother recalls that when Vince's father moved to Little Rock to be treated for prostate cancer and, later, terminal lung cancer, her son visited or was in contact with his father every day. And when his father returned to Hope, Vince would come to Little Rock for days at a time to be with him.

Around Christmas after the 1992 presidential election, Foster and his wife and children, his mother, and other family members gathered at the Little Rock home of his sister Sharon. Foster called them all together in the living room and told them that the president-elect had asked him to join the new administration. Foster was elated, though his wife and mother had misgivings.

His selection as deputy White House counsel was widely perceived to be Hillary Clinton's choice, and he became one of her key players in the new administration.

Foster temporarily left his family behind in Little Rock because his younger son was finishing his junior year in high school. The separation was said to be the cause of some of Foster's stress. In Washington, Foster took up residence with his sister Sheila, a Clinton appointee to the Justice Department, and her husband Beryl Anthony, a former congressman turned lobbyist from El Dorado, Arkansas.

By early summer, Foster was reunited with his family, and things seemed to be going well. But the stress of the job was almost unfathomable. Like many of his colleagues, Foster was immersed in his White House duties. According to the Fiske report, Foster's work schedule had him on the job "from between 7:30–8:30 in the morning until 9:30 or later at night, either six or seven days per week."

The Fiske report said that during this period Foster "showed signs of stress" and appeared "exhausted much of the time, his face drawn and gray." It "was obvious to many that he had lost weight," added the report, although "no one noticed a loss of appetite." The conclusion was that these were the symptoms of something deeper, and Fiske called attention to two significant items his investigation believed had contributed to Foster's depression and ultimate suicide.

First, there was the travel office matter. The firestorm over the travel office had begun in mid-May 1993, when White House officials sought to remove seven longtime employees of the office whose main function was to provide travel arrangements for White House staff and journalists accompanying the president on his trips. The pretext for this change was the allegation that the travel office employees had "mismanaged" the office and some employees may have "embezzled funds or received kickbacks," according to Clinton staffers.

The move was quickly suspected by some in the press to be a power grab whose real purpose was to provide jobs and travel contracts for Clinton loyalists. This became obvious when, shortly after the firings, the new travel office staff moved to give all the travel business to World

Wide Travel of Little Rock, a firm with links to Clinton's Arkansas friend and Hollywood producer Harry Thomason. World Wide Travel had handled the travel business for the 1992 Clinton/Gore campaign.

Though not as well known as the rest of the controversy, the most serious infraction may have been the summoning to the White House of FBI agents by Associate White House Counsel William Kennedy to begin a criminal probe of the fired travel office employees—contravening all rules prohibiting the use of the FBI for political purposes. The White House had never consulted with the FBI director, William Sessions, who learned about the involvement of the FBI from a radio news broadcast on the day of the firings.

For improperly involving the FBI, Kennedy (another Rose Law Firm alumnus) came under scathing criticism and received an official reprimand from his White House superiors. Kennedy eventually resigned in November 1994.

According to Fiske, the impropriety came back to haunt Foster since he "felt responsible for Kennedy's situation because he had assigned Kennedy to the matter." The travel office mess was "the single greatest source of [Foster's] distress," said the Fiske report, adding that Foster was "deeply disturbed" about it and had told Webster Hubbell that he "thought the matter would never end."

The most significant indication of the impact of the matter on Foster, Fiske concluded, was that out of ten items mentioned in the suicide note, five were apparently related to the travel office.

The second significant cause of Foster's distress, according to Fiske, was a series of critical *Wall Street Journal* editorials. Fiske cited one in particular, that of June 17, 1993, headlined WHO IS VINCENT FOSTER? wherein Foster was chided for his refusal to turn over a photograph of himself for use with an editorial. The *Journal* noted that it had taken the unusual step of filing a Freedom of Information Act request to obtain the photo. "No doubt Mr. Foster and company consider us mischievous (at best)," the editorial stated, accompanied as it was with a silhouette of Foster in lieu of the picture.

The *Journal* expressed outrage at the White House's claim that the

Freedom of Information Act did not apply to the counsel's office. "Does the law mean one thing for critics and another for friends?" the *Journal* demanded to know. "Will we in the end have to go to court to get a reply, or will even that work? Does it take a $50,000 a day fine to get this mule's attention? . . . Who ensures that this administration follows the law, or explains why not? A good question. While Constitutional law may not have been a big part of the Rose firm's practice, it seems to us that a good man for the job would be Deputy Counsel Foster."

Fiske cited a second editorial that appeared a week later headlined VINCENT FOSTER'S VICTORY—a sarcastic tribute to Foster for having won his case to keep secret the health care reform task force headed by Hillary Clinton. Fiske cited one particular part of the editorial:

> As for Iran-Contra, we suspect that Vince Foster and Ollie North might hit it off. After all, we're supposed to believe that the health task force "officially" disbanded on May 30, and so FACA's requirements are moot. [The Federal Advisory Committee Act requires public hearings whenever private individuals are appointed to commissions by the president.] That is, we're supposed to believe that Mrs. Clinton and her associates will never hold off-the-books meetings with "non-government" advisers to get the reform plan finished.

In the closing days of the previous week, several major media sources were reporting that the president had decided to fire FBI Director William Sessions. The *Wall Street Journal*, citing these reports, criticized the impending move, noting that "the gang that pulled the great travel office caper is now hell-bent on firing the head of the FBI," and commenting that the "mores on display from the Rose alumni are far from confidence-building."

According to Fiske, these public criticisms had a profound impact on a man who had spent his whole life outside of media scrutiny. The criticism was just too much for Foster to bear because his "professional reputation was of paramount importance to him, particularly among colleagues in Arkansas"—even more so because he was "a man of honesty and integrity, respected for his intelligence and judgment."

Two and a half months before his death, Foster had given a commencement address at the University of Arkansas Law School on the very topics of honesty and integrity. Foster laid great stress on the importance of one's reputation: "There is no victory, no advantage, no fee, no favor, which is worth even a blemish on your reputation for intellect and integrity."

On the weekend before his death, according to Fiske, Foster, feeling the need for a break from the White House, went on a weekend getaway with his wife to Maryland's Eastern Shore. It was their first trip together since Lisa Foster came to Washington.

At the same time, Webster Hubbell and his wife were visiting with Washington insiders Michael and Harolyn Cardozo, who also had a home on the Eastern Shore. Upon hearing that the Fosters were in the vicinity, the Cardozos invited Vincent and Lisa to join them. According to Fiske, "Foster jogged, went boating, hit some golf balls, read the newspaper and ate fresh crab for the first time." It seemed to Hubbell, at least, that Foster was having a relaxing, happy weekend.

On Monday Foster returned to work at the White House, where perhaps the most significant thing he did, according to Fiske, was to leave three personal letters on his desk that he himself had sealed and stamped. This was "unusual," said his secretary, Deborah Gorham; he normally left letters unsealed. Fiske's report indicated that the letters appeared to be mundane. One was addressed to his mother. It included oil leases that his mother had inherited from her husband, along with a typed note from her son providing instructions for the documents. Fiske said another was a letter to an insurance company, and the third was a bill Foster was paying at his wife's request.

On that day, Foster also contacted Dr. Larry Watkins, his family physician in Little Rock. According to the report, he "told Watkins that he was under a great deal of stress and was depressed, that he had a loss of appetite and was losing weight. Watkins prescribed an antidepressant drug called Desyrel, which is a brand name of the generic drug trazodone." A Washington pharmacy filled the prescription that day and delivered it to his home.

Another unusual occurrence that Monday—one that was not mentioned in the Fiske report—was a lengthy, closed-door meeting in Foster's office between Foster and Marsha Scott, a longtime Clinton aide from Arkansas. Gorham told FBI agents working for Fiske that Scott's visits to Foster were typically brief ones that took place with the office door open.

Soon after Foster arrived at his Georgetown home that Monday night, Clinton called to invite him to a private showing of Clint Eastwood's thriller *In the Line of Fire*. Clinton told him that two longtime associates from Arkansas, Bruce Lindsey, then a presidential aide, and Webster Hubbell, the associate attorney general, would be there. Foster declined and instead agreed to meet Clinton on Wednesday to discuss "White House organizational changes." According to President Clinton's deposition to Robert Fiske, Clinton asked for the meeting with Foster because the president needed Foster's "advice on some organization issues." Neither Clinton nor Fiske elaborated on what these issues were.

The following day, July 20, Foster left his home about 8:00 A.M. His wife remembers him standing "stiffly," drinking his coffee before he departed. Foster, his daughter Laura, and son Vincent III got into a 1989 light gray Honda Accord and drove off. Foster dropped Laura off at work, Vincent at a Metro subway station, and Foster arrived at his White House second-floor West Wing office at about 9:00 A.M. After a routine staff meeting, Foster attended a Rose Garden ceremony to announce the nomination of Judge Louis Freeh as director of the FBI, replacing William Sessions, whom Clinton had fired the day before.

The Freeh ceremony was a coup for the White House counsel's office and Foster, who had played a major role in Freeh's selection—a choice that was being widely applauded by Congress and the press. Sessions had come under criticism during the Bush administration following allegations that he had misused his travel office arrangements. His defenders argued point by point that the charges were baseless and were a smoke screen for those at the White House, at the Justice department, and within the FBI who wanted the bureau to steer a more political course.

By the time Clinton was sworn in, Sessions was mired in controversy, and Clinton promised to give Sessions a fair hearing.

That hearing never materialized, and in the days just before Foster's death, Clinton decided to fire the embattled director. Despite the controversial firing, it appeared on July 20 that the administration had orchestrated a smooth transition from Sessions to Freeh. In point of fact, the White House ceremony that took place that Tuesday was held solely to announce Freeh's appointment. Six full weeks passed before Freeh was actually sworn in.

After the ceremony, Foster returned to his office. Bernard Nussbaum, White House counsel, had been watching the televised coverage of the Freeh ceremony and was now watching the Senate confirmation hearings for Supreme Court nominee Ruth Bader Ginsburg. Nussbaum recalled that he told Foster, "We hit two home runs today," and that Foster "looked at me with a slight smile . . . [and] just said yes, yes, yes."

The Fiske report relates that at about noon Foster asked Linda Tripp, executive assistant to Nussbaum, to pick up lunch for him in the White House Mess. She brought a cheeseburger, french fries, and a Coke to his office, and, she noted, as he opened a newspaper while seated on his couch he removed the onions as he always did.

"At about 1:00 P.M.," according to the Fiske report, Foster "came out of his office holding his suit jacket, without a briefcase. He told Tripp that there were still some M&M's on the tray if she wanted them. He said 'I'll be back,' and then left."

That was the last time Foster spoke with anyone, according to official reports. His body was found some five hours later in Fort Marcy Park.

"We have been unable to determine where Foster went following his departure from the counsel's office at about 1:00 P.M.," Fiske concluded. The last person to see Foster leave was Secret Service uniformed officer John Skyles at security post E–4, the first-floor entrance to the West Wing, which housed the Oval Office and various presidential aides' offices.

The Fiske report noted that at about 4:30 P.M. a motorist, Patrick Knowlton, spotted Foster's Honda in the lot of Fort Marcy Park. Knowlton remembered it as having Arkansas plates. Just over an hour later, another motorist, identified only as Confidential Witness, or "CW," in the Fiske report, drove his white utility van into Fort Marcy Park in order to relieve himself in the woods. Fort Marcy has no public facilities. CW's official statement to the Fiske inquiry related that he parked his van and then walked some 770 feet into the park. He started to climb down the side of a steep embankment, or berm, to relieve himself when he spotted what he first took to be a bag of garbage several yards to his left. On second glance, he saw it was a body.

After he saw the body, CW quickly left the park, fearing possible harm from whoever might have committed what he figured was a murder. He drove about two miles up the adjoining George Washington Memorial Parkway to a parkway maintenance facility at Turkey Run, where he spotted two park service workers drinking beer. He told them there was a dead body in Fort Marcy Park and to call the Park Police. He then drove off without giving his name or any other information.

One of the maintenance workers, Francis Swann, dialed 911 and was connected with the Fairfax County, Virginia, emergency response facility. He reported the body, then hung up and dialed the Park Police to make a similar report.

By 6:10 P.M. Fairfax Fire and Rescue had arrived in the park, followed shortly by the Park Police. Foster's body was found directly in front of the barrel of the old cannon deep in the back of the park, one of the two cannons that still remained in the former Civil War fort.

Later that night the Park Police found Foster's wallet containing his White House identification. The wallet was found in his suit jacket, which was lying on the front seat of his car. They called the White House to notify them of Foster's death. The White House then dispatched Craig Livingstone and William Kennedy to the morgue to positively identify the body. However, according to the official version, the White House never requested that agents from the FBI or the Secret Service be dispatched to assist the Park Police that night.

The facts are clear. Fiske concluded that Foster, depressed, angry, and alone, had left the White House and driven around for some hours before arriving at Fort Marcy Park. He then parked his car in the parking lot and walked through the park, leaving his jacket and tie in the car on an extremely hot and humid day. He came to the Civil War cannon and climbed down a pathway that the cannon overlooked. Foster sat down in the line of fire of the relic cannon, took the 1913 Colt revolver, placed the barrel deep against the back of his mouth, and squeezed the trigger, dying instantly.

Those are the "facts" as they have become known: that Vince Foster was a good and decent man who couldn't take the glare of the spotlight and who ended his life in a park overlooking the Potomac River. To most of the American public and certainly almost all of the media, that is the Vince Foster story. Tragic, fascinating, and complete.

The problem is that these "facts" do not hold up under even superficial scrutiny. At almost every turn—from when and where Vince Foster died, to when the White House learned of his death and how they responded, to how the various authorities investigated his death—matters are not as we have been told. The discrepancies are not minor and trivial ones. They are the kind of discrepancies that become apparent from even the most cursory inquiry. The deeper one digs, the less the official story adds up.

TWO YEARS after Vince Foster's death, speculation over the cause of his demise and questions about the various investigations into the events of July 1993 had become so intense that one of America's most respected television news shows, ABC's *Nightline*, decided to focus an evening on the case.

Despite three official government reports on the death—one from the Park Police, another by special counsel Robert Fiske, and another from the Senate Banking Committee—doubts and speculation persisted. Some of the ideas swirling around the country, courtesy of the Internet, dove into the deep end of the bizarre: Foster was actually a Mossad agent killed by the CIA; Foster was assassinated by an Austrian hit squad; Foster was about to blow the whistle on a government piracy of an intelligence gathering software; and so on.

In the summer of 1995, much of the American public had become uncertain about this high-profile case. The Associated Press reported that, even after the passing of two years, 20 percent of the American public believed Foster had been murdered, and another 45 percent believed there had been a cover-up and did not believe the suicide verdict. In short, two-thirds of the nation had not accepted what the media said was a closed case of suicide.[1]

The mainstream media was still catching up to the power of talk radio and the Internet, which had endlessly worried over the Foster case for two years. The networks and big newspapers had spent much of the past two years repeating the standard story line of July 20, 1993; hence, the slightly churlish nature of *Nightline*'s opening segment that evening, narrated by correspondent Chris Bury. It was a formulaic review of the facts as they had become known, with a dash of incredulity aimed at those who still believed there were problems with the case.

Nightline's guest was Reed Irvine, head of the conservative watchdog group Accuracy in Media. Irvine, an aggressive critic of Washington's media establishment, was greeted by a blunt question from host Ted Koppel.

"I've known you to be stubborn, infuriating, sometimes bullheaded, off-the-wall, but not dishonest," Koppel told Irvine. "So I'm going to ask you flat out: Do you believe that Vince Foster committed suicide, or that he was killed?"

To much of the establishment press, that seemed to be the totality of the argument against the "official" version. Koppel's logic suggested that anyone who questioned the facts in the case really believed Foster was murdered. But Irvine refused to speculate on how Foster died. He did not profess to know. What he forcefully maintained is that the facts of the "official version" do not add up and that the death investigations were less than thorough, if not an outright sham.

Koppel continued the joust: "Reed . . . let's assume for the sake of argument that it were true [that Foster was murdered]. One would then have to also conclude that everyone who subsequently has investigated the case . . . I'm talking about the FBI; I'm talking about the Senate

Banking Committee; I'm talking about the Park Service itself—all those who have investigated came to that conclusion [of suicide]."

Koppel's argument seemed compelling. How could so many people have signed off on falsified conclusions? Since this was all but impossible, the official case had to be correct.

Koppel seemed to have forgotten that Kenneth Starr's independent counsel investigation into the Foster affair was still open. As for the official verdict of suicide, there were many, many pieces of evidence that were simply passed over—pieces that did not fit into the official version and that were simply dismissed. And numerous officials involved in the investigations—from emergency medical workers and Park Police at the scene, to FBI officers, to staff of the two special prosecutors—were uneasy about the conclusions reached, in the face of evidence they believed was ignored as inconvenient to the official verdict.

Critics of the skeptics claimed that Congress had put the stamp of approval on their chain of events. But here again, there was dissent. Speaker of the House Newt Gingrich and Senate Whitewater Committee Chairman Alfonse D'Amato voiced strong doubts about the government's ruling almost a year after the Senate had signed off on the conclusions of the Fiske report.

It was also later revealed that the investigators and experts working for the Senate committee were far from unanimous in agreeing with the Fiske conclusions. For example, a prominent pathologist, Dr. Cyril Wecht, who was asked by D'Amato's minority staff on the Senate Whitewater Committee in 1994 to review the original autopsy and Park Police report, strongly advised a second autopsy. Wecht called the initial report "incomplete and insufficiently detailed" and the police handling of the case shoddy.[2] His recommendation of a second autopsy was based on "practical and significant reasons," Wecht told the *Pittsburgh Tribune-Review.* Wecht said he was "extremely unhappy and amazed" at the U.S. Park Police handling of Foster's case, describing it as "horribly botched" and "bungled." Other factors made a compelling case for a second autopsy, such as missing evidence: the skull X-rays that were either missing or never taken, the bullet that was never found, and the strange multicolored carpet fibers found on Foster's clothing.

Wecht's opinion was not easily dismissed as right-wing conspiracy mongering. When questions first arose about the Foster case with a report in the *New York Post* in January 1994, the Clinton White House was referring press inquiries to Dr. Wecht, a prominent Pennsylvania Democrat.[3]

In the end, Vince Foster's death is important not because it may have been a homicide, or even because it is an interesting, unsolved, and mysterious death—as serious as these matters might be. The Foster case matters critically because of the reluctance or unwillingness of the official investigators to treat the case properly.

Imagine the Foster case as a multilevel building, with the first level— the foundation—consisting of the physical, forensic, and circumstantial evidence, which helps tell us whether the death was a suicide or murder. As in any death investigation, the inquiry begins with the crime scene. The physical evidence that presents itself to the first police investigators is a key indicator of whether a death can be classified as natural, accidental, suicide, or murder.

Police are trained to look for consistencies among the circumstances of the case and the apparent manner of death. In a suicide, detectives review the physical evidence by asking: Was the body's position consistent with the manner of death? Is the body's condition consistent with the known facts? Are the blood and markings on the body typical for a death of this type? Is the instrument of death consistent with the wound and the way the weapon is normally used in such circumstances?

So important is the initial review of the physical evidence that police take great care to preserve the crime scene. Medics and emergency personnel are trained not to disturb the scene or body. Police typically take pictures of the scene as soon as they can before investigators trample through, and they quickly put up yellow crime-scene tape to keep noninvestigative officials and gawkers out. These are the basic tasks completed by uniformed police even before detectives show up.

Investigators are keenly aware of the physical evidence: photographing it, searching for it, cataloging it. Since a dead body has to be promptly removed from the scene, investigators place great importance on pinpointing its location and position by taking numerous photographs from various angles showing its "relationship" to various landmarks, and by skillfully drawing a scene diagram. Incredibly, in the Foster case, no such "relationship" photos exist, the original scene diagram is shoddy and inaccurate, and several other pieces of evidence have placed the location of the body in serious doubt.[4]

A second level to the Foster case is the original police investigation, handled by the U.S. Park Police with the help of other law enforcement agencies. Even if this *was* an open-and-shut case of suicide, fair questions can be asked about the police handling of this high official's death investigation. Why was the case treated as a suicide almost from the beginning, contradicting police procedure of treating any violent death as a homicide? Where has key evidence, such as the crime-scene photos, gone? Why did the Park Police allow the White House and others to dictate how critical evidence should be handled, as well as the timing of important aspects of the investigation? These questions and others raise the specter of political pressure and interference in a death investigation.

Another important component of the police case is the autopsy. While police do not conduct the autopsy, they play an integral role in helping the medical examiner. Typically, police observe the autopsy and assist the medical examiner by offering first-hand accounts of the death scene, helping the examiner to make a judgment as to the consistency of the body with the apparent circumstances of death. Police also ensure the taking of blood, hair, and fingerprint samples and the preservation of other physical evidence such as the deceased's clothing. In this case the Park Police and coroner made significant errors or blunders at critical points of the autopsy procedure.

Compounding these problems with the original police inquiry and autopsy was the strange role played by the FBI during the initial stages of the investigation. Confusion exists about agents' presence during the events of July 20, 1993, and the nature of the bureau's assistance thereafter. Although the FBI left the details of the investigation exclusively to the less well equipped Park Police, they were quick to sign off on the Park Police's conclusions.

Another level of the Foster investigation is one that often makes a prominent appearance in crime novels but is rarely acknowledged in real life: politics. From mediating between rival gangs intent on carving up a precinct, to coping with pressure from a mayor's office for fast results in a high-profile criminal case, the police face a variety of challenges that have little to do with the strict exercise of their duties. In Washington, D.C., it was interference from the White House that tainted the Foster probe, from the scheduling of the autopsy to control of key evidence both at the scene in Fort Marcy Park and in Foster's office. On the night of his death, senior aides to the president entered, searched, and allegedly removed documents from Foster's office without the approval or even knowledge of the Park Police, who had directed that the room be sealed.

Evidence suggests that the White House knew of Foster's death far earlier than they have claimed and that the president was aware of the dubious activities in Foster's office much earlier than has previously been acknowledged.

Another level, unusual in most of the country but becoming commonplace in post-Watergate Washington, is the work of special counsels who have also investigated Foster's death. In January 1994, Special Counsel Robert Fiske began what he called an in-depth probe of the Foster case. But his handling of the matter has arguably raised more questions than it has provided answers.

In the summer of 1994, Fiske was removed from the case, and former Solicitor General Kenneth Starr was appointed as his replacement. Starr reopened the investigation into Foster's death, an inquiry Starr's office maintains is "active and ongoing" nearly four years after the event.* As

---

*Numerous news stories have reported that Starr was on the verge of issuing a report concluding Foster's death a suicide. These reports first appeared in January 1995, on the day grand jury proceedings that were to look into the death began, and have continued until July 1997.

the months have passed, questions have mounted about the handling of the case by Starr, the FBI, and the team of prosecutors under his control.

This book will explore the death of Vince Foster, not as Ted Koppel framed it—suicide or murder—but systematically, examining the significant layers, each with its own inherent problems that are worthy of public scrutiny.

A review of the questions associated with Vince Foster's death is much more than the outline to a simple murder mystery. If much that is detailed herein can be ascribed to incompetence, sloppiness, laziness, amateurishness, faulty memory, and just stupidity—and doubtless all these factors played a role—then readers are justified in drawing this conclusion for themselves. But if what is described here calls forth the question of whether witting influence tainted an investigation that should have remained inviolate, then those responsible for this abuse of power and public trust should be held accountable.

2

Formed in 1791, the U.S. Park Police is one of the oldest police forces in the nation. The officers were originally called the "night watchmen" because of their charge to guard the nation's monuments. Today, their jurisdiction is much broader. The Park Police describe themselves as an urban police force. Most of their six hundred members serve in the Washington area. Smaller numbers are in New York City at the Gateway National Recreation Area, and Golden Gate Park in San Francisco. In addition to federal parks, the U.S. Park Police patrol a web of highways, called parkways, which encircle the nation's capital. Despite their "Smokey the Bear" name, the force attracts many former military personnel, particularly ones who have hopes of joining the FBI or ATF (Alcohol, Tobacco and Firearms). Their numbers also include some who were rejected by other federal agencies.

On August 10, 1993, Park Police Chief Robert Langston, joined by other officials at the Justice Department, announced the results of the Park Police inquiry:

The condition of the scene, the medical examiner's findings, and the information gathered clearly indicate that Mr. Foster committed suicide. Without an eyewitness, the conclusion is deduced after a review of the injury, the presence of the weapon, the existence of some indicators of a reason, and the elimination of murder. Our investigation has found no evidence of foul play. The information gathered from associates, relatives, and friends provides us with enough evidence to conclude that Mr. Foster's—that Mr. Foster was anxious about his work and he was distressed to the degree that he took his own life.[1]

That summer, the facts of the case appeared indisputable to most Americans. Through six months in Washington serving the new Clinton administration, Foster had become severely depressed. After having lunch in his office on July 20, 1993, he left the White House at about 1:00 P.M. He climbed into his Honda Accord and drove to nearby Fort Marcy Park. He parked his car, walked almost eight hundred feet to a secluded corner of the wooded park, and encountered a Civil War cannon relic, one of only two then in the park. He passed next to the cannon, climbed down the slope, or earthen berm, the cannon overlooked, and sat down. He held an old .38 caliber Colt revolver in his hand. He pressed the barrel deep against the back of his mouth, just above his throat, and fired using his thumb to depress the trigger. Shortly after 6:00 P.M., following two 911 calls, Foster's corpse was found in that spot by Park Police.

In combination with President Bill Clinton's statement the next day that "we will never know" why Vince Foster killed himself, this version of Vincent Foster's death was publicized in the weeks after the death. It was ratified by Special Counsel Robert Fiske, in a report he issued on June 30, 1994.

Washington was a busy place in the summer and fall of 1993. President Clinton's tax increase package passed by one vote. The president and his team rolled out a national health care plan. They waged a hard and ultimately successful effort to ratify the North American Free Trade Agreement. And America suffered a tragic blow in Somalia with the death of eighteen marines in an ambush that led to the withdrawal of American forces from that country. Vince Foster's death faded into the background of media attention. The public had pretty much accepted Foster's death as the unfortunate suicide of a harried official who could not cope with the fast-track Washington routine.

But a review of the case in late 1993 suggested the first of many problems surrounding the official version of events.

It was December 1993, and for several months I had been an investigative reporter with the *New York Post*, the brash tabloid that had recently been reacquired by media tycoon Rupert Murdoch. Out of the blue, a journalist friend from Washington called me and related an interesting lunch conversation he had had that day. He had learned that a coroner had commented on the fact that the gun had been found firmly in Foster's hand after he was said to have fired it. Most unusual, the coroner had pointed out: A gun's recoil, together with the body's own reflexes, usually casts the gun away from the body in a suicide, sometimes fifteen feet or more.

Curiosity got the better of me, and I decided to read up on the case. The press clippings relating to Foster's death appeared to contain little information about Foster's activities on his last day, the precise location of his body in Fort Marcy Park, or any details of the crime scene at the park: the condition of the body, blood, eyewitnesses, the gun, and a host of other details that often accompany a review of a suicide's last hours and moments.

As the various articles seemed inconsistent about the site of Foster's death, it seemed a visit to Fort Marcy Park was in order.

One parkway under Park Police jurisdiction is the historic George Washington Memorial Parkway, which originally ran northwest along the Potomac River from Mount Vernon to Washington, D.C. Over time, it was expanded to a four-lane highway and extended north to 495, the Capital Beltway. About two-thirds of the way up the highway, nestled into the side of a hill, a little sign announces Fort Marcy Park.

The tiny park is less than a quarter mile wide. Residential homes abut the park's other two sides. The wooded terrain of the park rises to form a roughly squarish plateau measuring a few hundred feet in length and width—this was the area of the original fort, where cannons were once perched overlooking the steep embankments, or berms.

Fort Marcy was one of several relatively small encampments in the Washington area that President Lincoln had authorized early in the Civil War. Named after Union Brigadier General Randolph B. Marcy, it was also known as one of "Lincoln's circle forts." These garrisons, made of nothing more than earthen ramparts, encircled the capital at strategic locations to guard against Confederate attack. With its seventeen cannons, Fort Marcy's main purpose was to defend the old Chain Bridge, which linked Virginia to Washington.

It was apparent, after visiting the park, that few other reporters covering the story had bothered to do so. For example: Although *Newsweek* reported, like others, that Foster "ended up . . . on a bluff overlooking the Potomac River," had the magazine's writers actually visited the park, they would have realized that Fort Marcy does not overlook the Potomac. A road and a housing division separate it from the riverbank. Further, the two old cannons in the park do not face the Potomac River, but rather Virginia proper—another point that was incorrect in most press accounts.

Press sloppiness is nothing new, and the case had already been wrapped up by the August 10, 1993, Park Police report. Upon later review of that report, and interviews with the participants of the events of that night, confusing differences began to emerge.

TWO 911 calls were placed on July 20, 1993, and upon some investigation, two different stories about the discovery of Vince Foster's body that evening emerge as well.

In January 1994, I spoke with Sergeant George Gonzalez, lead paramedic from Fairfax County's Fire and Rescue Station No. 1, who was among the first to arrive at the scene. Gonzalez, a thirteen-year veteran of the department, recounted the details of that sweltering July day when the station received the ominous report of "a possible dead body at Fort Marcy Park." Gonzalez recalled that a 911 call had been made from a pay phone "because there was no callback number" on the dispatch.

Gonzalez was somewhat familiar with the park. Though he had never been there on duty, he had once gone on a picnic there, he said.

Once Gonzalez's paramedic truck arrived in Fort Marcy's parking lot, he saw two cars: a gray Honda to his immediate left and a white compact car, possibly of Japanese make, toward the rear of the lot. Both cars were unoccupied.

Gonzalez remembered seeing no visitors in and around the lot that afternoon. His emergency vehicle pulled in a few spaces from the Honda on the left side of the lot. (The small lot has only twenty-three spaces; the Honda was in the third spot from the entrance.) Gonzalez and the fire department rescuers were joined by a Park Police officer later identified as Kevin Fornshill. According to Fornshill's statements to Senate investigators, he was guarding the rear entrance of the Central Intelligence Agency headquarters two miles up the George Washington Parkway. He had volunteered to take the call when he learned that the Park Police officer usually on the beat, Franz Ferstl, was tied up handling a car accident.[2]

There were now seven rescuers on the scene: Gonzalez and two other EMS workers, Todd Hall and Richard Arthur; three firefighters; and Fornshill. Since the 911 call lacked specifics as to the location of the body, the group split up and began their search. Fornshill accompanied Gonzalez and Hall up the park's main trail to the northwest; the three firefighters, Lieutenant James Iacone, Ralph Pisani, and Jennifer Wacha, took a trail descending from the east side of the lot. They were joined by Arthur, an emergency medical technician who had ridden in the paramedic truck with Gonzalez.

Gonzalez recalled that he had entered the main clearing of the park, the area that constituted the original fort, through a pass in the eastern berm. He then moved quickly to the left toward the southern berm, "racing," as he put it, because he had no way of knowing the body was already lifeless. Fornshill and Hall scurried off to the right and checked the heavy brush on the northwest side of the clearing.

Gonzalez recalled running along the southern berm and passing, on his left, a cannon (sometimes referred to as the "first" cannon) overlooking the berm. It was the only cannon he knew to be in the park. He saw no body in the area of that cannon. So he moved along the berm, "at least fifteen to twenty feet," where he came upon Foster's body, his head close to the crest of the slope, lying on the side of the berm.

The body was lying faceup in a supine position, arms and legs symmetrically extended. Gonzalez recalled—and this is a critical detail—that Foster lay at the western end of the southern berm in dense brush, "knee-high." It was in the middle of what may have been a little-used, heavily overgrown trail down the side of the berm, he said.

His recollection, that the body was well away from the cannon, coincided with what a Park Police officer had told me earlier that month. Neither man was aware, when recounting this to me, that there was a second cannon deep in the park, almost one hundred yards away, on the western berm near the northwest corner. That second cannon cannot be seen from the area where they said they found the body.

This second cannon was where the Park Police would officially claim they found Foster's body, nearly a hundred yards away from where Gonzalez and the police officer said the body was found.

Upon finding the body, Gonzalez turned and yelled across the clearing to Fornshill and Hall, still within sight and earshot. Gonzalez noted that Foster was wearing a white dress shirt unbuttoned at the top with no tie, quality suit pants, and black dress shoes. He saw that a trickle of blood had come out of the right side of Foster's mouth.

Flies were swarming around the body's mouth and crotch. Foster had, as is common, urinated upon death. Without touching the corpse, Gonzalez checked for vital signs, specifically by examining the fingers where he saw blood pooling. He said the near transparent skin of the fingers showed they were cyanotic, the observable purplish color that skin takes immediately after death due to oxygen deprivation.

A radio message was sent to the team of four who had initially headed off in the other direction. They responded that they had found nothing and that the only people they had seen in the woods were a couple, whose white Nissan was in the lot. They were the only witnesses said to have been in the park at the time police found Foster's body.

The other team came over and looked at the body. At this point, no one had any idea of the prominence of the man whose body they were viewing. They soon returned to their vehicles, except Fornshill, who stayed at the death scene for several minutes until relieved by Officer Ferstl, who had handled the traffic accident.

According to FBI witness statements, at least four rescuers, upon returning to the lot, noted that the Honda, which had Arkansas plates, had a suit jacket on the front passenger seat that seemed to match the pants on the body. Jokes were made about the Arkansas plates. Someone said the dead man was probably a friend of the president's who had come to Washington for a job but had been turned down.

Based on the official logs, records show Gonzalez's departure from the park, along with other fire personnel, was at 6:40 P.M.[3]

CONFUSION BEGAN AT the very beginning, because this rendering of events was contradicted by the Park Police report and officer Kevin Fornshill, who has stated that he was the first to find Foster's body on July 20, 1993. According to his testimony, it was lying on the steep slope of the western berm directly in front of the park's "second" cannon, at the far northwest section of the park. When he saw the body, he said, he did not climb down the slope to view it; rather, he stayed at the crest and called for the paramedics in the other search team. This directly contradicts Gonzalez's account that it was he who found the body and called to Fornshill.

According to Fornshill, paramedic Todd Hall climbed down the slope to check Foster's carotid artery. Hall determined that Foster was dead and called Fornshill's attention to a revolver in the deceased's right hand. According to his FBI statement and congressional testimony, Fornshill could not see the gun from where he was on the crest, so he moved to his right along the berm but still could not see it. He speculated to investigators that it was hidden by foliage.

Even though Fornshill never bothered to get close enough to observe the gun, according to his FBI statement and Senate deposition, he nevertheless picked up his radio and transmitted a report to Park Police communications. In his Senate deposition in 1994 Fornshill stated: " . . . I believe the paramedic, when he showed the gun, or tried to show me the gun, saying there's a gun there, I advised communications that it appeared to be a suicide, and then there was dead air for a while until I was relieved." Fornshill made that transmission without ever having observed the gun himself.[4]

Fornshill added that he had observed no trampled vegetation or other signs of a struggle that might indicate something other than suicide. He estimated that he stayed at the scene for five to seven minutes; he was then relieved by Officer Ferstl and his immediate supervisor, Sergeant Bob Edwards.

Fornshill was impressed by the neatness of Foster's body and the overall scene. He told the FBI on April 29, 1994, and the *Washington Post* shortly after Foster's death that Foster's hair was "neatly in place," his white shirt "clean and apparently starched," and his trousers "extremely neat" with sharp creases.[5]

THE OFFICIAL spot of Foster's death, according to both the Park Police and the Fiske reports, was directly on a dirt path in front of the second cannon. As with many of the facts of the official case, it is difficult to pinpoint the location with accuracy, though the various reports seem to agree that the body was found on the side of the steep embankment overlooked by the park's second cannon. Foster's head was said to be near the crest of the slope. The reports also concur that Foster's body was lying on a dirt path etched by root stems, leading to the bottom of the slope.

One portion of the Park Police report states the body was "just north of the second cannon." Several pages later the same report states the body was "approximately twenty feet west of the canons [*sic*] axle. . . . " The most recent official statement designating the body's location—the third so far—is the one noted in the Fiske report, which places Foster's head approximately ten feet in front of the second cannon's barrel.

Why so much confusion on such an elementary detail? One reason might be that Foster's body was never found in front of that second cannon, and officials have been trying to make the circumstances of this wrong site "fit" the testimony of witnesses.

A Park Police officer who was on the scene the night of the death told me—incorrectly—in January 1994, on the condition of anonymity, that there was only one cannon in the park. He was emphatic that Foster's body was nowhere near the one cannon he believed Fort Marcy had. The officer told me that the body was lying on a ridge the cannon over-looked, but well past the cannon. The body's feet, he said, were pointed toward the George Washington Memorial Parkway, which could be seen from where the body lay.

At the time I was given that information, the Park Police report, with a description of the body's physical location, had yet to be released. I realized immediately that this description of the body's loca-tion was at odds with many of the press reports after the death, which placed the body immediately adjacent to a Civil War cannon in the park.

When the Fiske report was released with the accompanying FBI state-ments, it placed Foster's body on a dirt path directly in front of the sec-ond cannon, which neither Sergeant Gonzalez nor the Park Police knew existed.

Although Gonzalez corroborated to the FBI and Senate investigators essentially everything that I had reported about his account, in the Fiske report he had changed his story on where the body was found, claiming that it was lying right in front of the second cannon.

Another Fairfax County rescuer, Richard Arthur, had concerns about the body's position. Arthur was the third paramedic at the scene. In his deposition to Senate investigators, he made comments that perhaps shed light on the difference between what Gonzalez had told me and what he'd told the FBI. "George [Gonzalez]," Arthur said in his deposi-tion, "is the type of person, in my opinion, he can get pressured into doing a lot of things."

Evidence continued to mount that Park Police had misrepresented the location of the death site in their official reports. In other words, the police found the body in one place, on the berm past the first cannon, but the police report noted a different spot, an "official" location, for the press and public, in front of the second cannon.

Fairfax emergency medical technician Corey Ashford, who had placed Foster's body in a body bag that night, originally told me he could not remember a cannon near the body. This is totally consistent with the original Gonzalez site, but hard to believe if Ashford had actually been to the site where statements claim the cannon was almost perched right over the body.

Strangely, of the officials at the death scene who were later interviewed by Fiske's FBI agents, only statements from the Park Police made mention of this second cannon location. (The FBI agents were apparently concerned enough about this that they had several Fairfax workers later draw maps, which curiously located the body directly in front of a cannon's barrel.) The FBI statement of the Park Police officer who filed the initial incident report makes no mention of where he found the body.*

Of course, there should be no doubt as to where the body was found because police investigators typically have numerous "relationship" crime-scene photos—wide-area photos showing the body's relationship to its surroundings. According to records and reports, Park Police investigator John Rolla and beat officer Franz Ferstl both took Polaroids of the body and the death scene. In all, some thirty Polaroid shots were taken, including a few by Sergeant Bob Edwards, the senior police officer who remained at the death scene.

Park Police officer and crime-scene identification technician Peter Simonello, a ten-year veteran of the crime-scene unit, also took shots,

---

*In a seven-page report, Hugh Turley, a suburban Washington small-business owner who has taken an active interest in the Foster case, carefully examined FBI documents, witness statements, and the notes made by FBI agents while conducting their interviews. Turley discovered that none of the Fairfax emergency and fire personnel originally told the FBI that Foster's body was found near the second cannon. FBI interview notes show that five Park Police officers were explicit in stating the body was directly in front of the second cannon. Turley also discovered that in the few instances when Fairfax officials are cited in FBI statements as saying the body was found directly in front of a cannon, a review of the FBI agents' interview notes shows that the witnesses never mentioned the cannon. The description was later inserted into the witnesses' statements when they were prepared in the office.

but with 35mm film, which produces photos more suitable for enhancement and analysis. He claims to have taken only one roll of pictures.

Developing such film takes time, so police typically augment their evidence with instant Polaroid shots. That way they can know immediately what they have—or what is conspicuously missing. A videotape of the death scene was not made, although the Park Police usually do so in cases involving a death.

But the police file counts only thirteen Polaroids (ten are of the body), all of which are close-up shots. One Polaroid showed Foster's right hand holding a revolver. That photo was leaked to ABC News in 1994 by either the Park Police or Special Counsel Fiske's office in an apparent effort to marginalize my *New York Post* report that questioned the suicide. The hand and gun are surrounded by thick foliage just as Gonzalez had described where the body was lying in dense brush. But the image is *not* consistent with the area in front of the second cannon, which is a dirt path with little surrounding vegetation.

This troubling inconsistency was reinforced by *USA Today* reporter John Hanchette. He, along with a colleague, was among the few reporters who actually went to the park, arriving on the day after the death at about 1:00 P.M. Not knowing the precise death site, they roamed the park until they came upon some white plastic gloves of the type used at crime scenes. These were strewn around the second cannon area. On the path in front of the cannon they came upon what appeared to be a blood spot that Hanchette described as being about the size of a small melon (whereas Park Police claimed the body had left a "large" pool). Evidently whatever liquid was on the ground had been absorbed. If in fact it was a large pool of blood, then a large stain should have been evident. Hanchette's recollection of a "melon-sized" stain doesn't support that.

Hanchette wrote in his *USA Today* report published on July 23, 1993, that the body had been found on "the dirt path" directly in front of the cannon, evidenced by "a splotch of blood-stained dirt" found there. Hanchette stated in 1994 that he believes the Polaroid shot leaked to ABC News is "fishy."

Asked if the photo matched the area he examined, he said, "No, it does not." The landscape depicted by the Polaroid was "too verdant" to correspond to the site he and his colleague had visited. Hanchette agreed that there is foliage alongside the pathway, but not the thick quantities this Polaroid depicted. Other photos show Foster lying on heavy, dense vegetation as well.

Two former New York police homicide experts who visited the park found the berm in the vicinity of the first cannon—where Gonzalez, the police officer, and others said the body was found—densely vegetated and consistent with the ABC Polaroid.[6]

If Foster's body was actually found on the berm by the first cannon, how the apparent blood splotch and crime scene gloves came to be by the second cannon site, as Hanchette found them, is anyone's guess.

DR. DONALD HAUT, medical examiner for Fairfax County, Virginia, arrived at the site on the night of the death and declared Foster dead. In a recorded interview in January 1995, he described an area totally consistent with the berm where the first cannon was located: As he entered the open grove area of the park, he said, he noticed a cannon off to the left. The body lay on the berm that the cannon overlooked— some fifteen to twenty yards away from the cannon—at a right angle, and definitely not in front of it. There was absolutely no cannon in the immediate area of the body, said Haut. He was completely unaware of the second cannon in a far corner of the park, where the Park Police and Fiske claim the body was found. Further corroborating his recollection was Dr. Haut's statement to the FBI in 1994. Buried deep in his FBI record statement was his recollection that the cannon he saw was "located ten to twenty yards" from where Foster was found. Fiske stated that the cannon was just ten feet behind the body.[7]

Still other accounts place the body on the berm by the first cannon. No one knows Fort Marcy Park better than Robert Reeves, a retired army soldier who has taken a proprietary interest in Fort Marcy Park (the park service employees refer to him as the Mayor of Fort Marcy), having visited there several times a week for three decades. Reeves, a tall African American, likes to hike in the park and said he began looking after it when he returned from Vietnam and found that some kids had left a mess after partying on the Fourth of July.

Reeves was convalescing from an operation on the day of Foster's death. Yet he lent some valuable insight into the matter of where Foster's body was found. Returning to the park following his surgery, about a week after Foster's death, Reeves talked with Tyrone Brown, the park maintenance supervisor whose area covers Fort Marcy Park. Reeves recalled Brown telling him that "Mr. Foster died by the area of the first cannon." Brown told him that most of the mess and subsequent cleanup occurred near the first cannon, by the main clearing in the park.

Reeves said the matter was discussed again with Brown following Reeves's encounter with a television crew. Upon seeing the crew filming by the second cannon deep in the back of the park, the park's unofficial guardian helpfully pointed out that they had the wrong site.

The crew then showed him a map prepared for them by the Park Police indicating the body was directly in front of the second cannon. Reeves then asked Brown about the discrepancy and was assured the body had lain near the first cannon, on a berm off the open grove area of the park.

In December 1994, Brown told me the same thing he had told Reeves. "The area I believed he died at used to have a cannon . . . the first cannon," he said.

The first cannon had been removed by the park service shortly after July 1994—following my reports that raised questions about the location of Foster's body. A spokesman for the park service stated that the cannon had been taken to Theodore Roosevelt Island on the Potomac for a ceremony. While there it was said to have been set upon by vandals. Over two years later, in the fall of 1996, the first cannon was restored to the spot it occupied on the night of Foster's death.

Amazingly, this discrepancy over the body's location was never pursued vigorously by Ken Starr's investigators when he replaced Robert

Fiske as special counsel in mid-1994. Starr's staff never took the first cannon site seriously for several reasons. As far as the officials were concerned, all the witnesses seemed to be in agreement on the site. Starr's investigators also had no idea where the first cannon site had been, since the cannon had been removed. In any event the matter would have been difficult to pursue in the grand jury, because the FBI refused to draw a map of the park for use during the grand jury proceedings.*

POLICE WERE able to quickly track down who had called in the initial report of the body in Fort Marcy Park. Francis Swann, a park maintenance worker, notified authorities of a body in the park after he had been told of it by an unidentified man driving a white van. According to Swann, he made two calls—the first to Fairfax County's 911 emergency service. After providing the operator with the basic details, he hung up and immediately notified the Park Police. In neither instance did he give his name. His first call was made at 5:59 P.M. The following is an excerpt from the Fairfax County 911 transcript.[8]

> Swann: There's ah, have ah, ah this is, is a body, this guy told me was a body laying up there by the last cannon.
>
> 911: Last what?
>
> Swann: There's, there's a man laying up there by the last cannon gun.
>
> 911: Cannon.
>
> Swann: Yes, they have cannons up there. Those big guns.

This transcript corresponds with the Park Police's account of finding Foster's body right in front of the second, or "last," cannon encountered on the walk from the park's lot. When I asked Swann about his state-

---

*As I later learned from prosecutors in Starr's office, Starr's lead prosecutor in the case of the Foster death, Miquel Rodriguez, understood that having a map would be elemental to the proceedings of any grand jury inquiry. He requested that FBI agents assigned to Starr's office have one prepared. The lead agent told Rodriguez that as far as the FBI was concerned the case was closed, and his agents were not going to prepare a map of the park.

ments in that transcript, he vehemently denied ever using the term "last cannon." Indeed, he insisted he did not even know of more than one cannon.

The van driver "said a cannon," Swann recalled in a taped interview with me in January 1995. "There's nothing but one cannon up there. Just one."

Interestingly, a second transcript, this one of Swann's call at 6:03 P.M. directly to the Park Police, shows him identifying only one cannon in Fort Marcy Park. The 911 Park Police transcript reads:[9]

He [the van driver] said [the body] was back there by the cannon.

Nowhere in this transcript is there any mention of multiple cannons in the park. The Park Police transcript was transcribed immediately after Foster's death. The disputed Fairfax tape was transcribed later during the Fiske probe. When press questions first arose about Foster's death in early 1994, Fairfax County spokesman Warren Carmichael said that the 911 tape had been destroyed thirty days after the call was made as was their procedure. He said the Park Police had not requested a copy during their inquiry. Months later FBI agents working for Robert Fiske appeared at the 911 center to pick up a copy of the tape, according to FBI documents. The agents listened to the tape and took an audio copy and transcript. The original audio has never been released.

It is also important to emphasize that Swann—like officer Gonzalez, Dr. Haut, and others who have less than an intimate knowledge of the park—was aware of only the first cannon, in plain sight as one comes into the park's main clearing.

PERHAPS THE most conclusive information that rebuts the Park Police version of where the body was found is the forensic evidence. In late 1994, the Western Journalism Center* hired two former New York City

---

*The Western Journalism Center is a conservative nonprofit foundation formed by veteran news editor Joseph Farah in 1991. In 1994, the center made the Foster issue one of their major items for investigative reporting.

police homicide experts, Vincent Scalice and Fred Santucci, both with strong experience in crime-scene analysis, to review several aspects of the case, including this issue about the body's location. These experts, along with Dr. Richard Saferstein, a prominent forensic scientist, conducted a crime-scene reconstruction at Fort Marcy Park. Dr. Saferstein completed follow-up laboratory tests.

Scalice and Santucci concluded that the forensic evidence "does not support the police and Fiske conclusion that Foster's body was found on the path directly in front of the second cannon site." In their report for the Western Journalism Center, the detectives noted that the pathway was dirt-covered, with worn root stems etched into the soil, showing years of exposure. This was certainly not the vegetation-covered area that appeared in the crime-scene Polaroids. USA Today's Hanchette mentioned this dirt pathway in his report just days after Foster's death. Reeves claims the pathway has been dirt-covered for decades, as does Greg Howland, the national park service historian for Fort Marcy.

"Had Foster's body been lying at the second cannon site, especially on a warm summer day, soil and other debris should have adhered to [Foster's] clothing and shoes," the experts concluded. But according to an FBI lab report, the FBI found not a speck of soil on either Foster's shoes or clothing. The detectives had a model of Foster's size and weight walk down the dirt path and sit down while wearing clean shoes and clothing. Laboratory tests on the outfit showed significant quantities of soil adhering to each item.

The detectives noted that had Foster's body been found on the heavily vegetated area of the first cannon, his clothing may never have come into contact with exposed soil, leaving them dirt free as the FBI found them. Another piece of forensic evidence pointed to the body's being found at the first cannon site. The experts noted a leaf of an identifiable species, Magnolia acuminata, in the Polaroid released by ABC News. The experts could not find any such leaves at the second cannon. However, it is found in abundance on the berm by the first cannon.

ACCEPTING FOR a moment that the police have misrepresented the site in their reports, why would they do such a thing?*

On one hand it could have been a simple snafu made by an officer filling out the original report. When the mistake was realized, the Park Police probably circled the wagons, rather than admitting such a buffoonish foul-up. Even if it began as a silly mistake, four years later it has been compounded into a serious problem because some officials have given sworn testimony supporting the police report.

The change of site could also have represented something other than incompetence on the part of the Park Police: Homicide expert Scalice has suggested two other possibilities. The first is that Park Police intended to shield the crime scene from members of the press and others whose snooping could have hampered a further police search of the area. The Park Police may have been concerned about someone finding the fired projectile. After all, the police returned to the park two days after the death to conduct this search. Still another reason, Scalice suggests, is the possibility that there was a police cover-up initiated early on. If the actual location of the body could not be found, it would then be difficult to re-create the scene or figure out what really happened.

THE COUPLE first stumbled upon by rescuers during their search for Foster's body told police they had not heard a gunshot. They were on the other side of the park several hundred feet from where the body was said to be found. Perhaps they arrived after the shot; perhaps there were distracting noise or atmospheric conditions not favorable to carrying the sound.

The police were less than successful in locating other potential witnesses. What had happened to the driver in the white van who had stopped at the park maintenance facility to notify park service workers

---

*Several congressional investigators have claimed that my reports suggest that the Park Police moved Foster's body from one location in the park to another. This is false. My reports suggest that sometime after Foster's body was removed to the morgue, the Park Police decided to change in their official reports the location of the body's discovery.

about a body in Fort Marcy? In a routine homicide investigation the first person to report a death is not only a critical witness but also a potential suspect. The Park Police, as it turned out, could have quickly located this mysterious man by speaking to Robert Reeves. When I first interviewed Reeves in late 1994, he said he had never been interviewed by the Park Police or any other investigators. Reeves, as mentioned earlier, was in the hospital at the time of the death, but his intimate knowledge of the park has been indispensable to my own investigation.

Reeves was not retroactively fitting his knowledge to the case: Prior to my interview with him, he had been totally unaware that the "man in the white van" was a pivotal missing witness. I asked Reeves if there was anyone who regularly came to the park driving a van. He said there were only two individuals: One drove a cream-colored van, the other a white one. He knew the company names on both vehicles and gave descriptions of both drivers. His description of the white van's driver matched the one given by Francis Swann of the man referred to in the police reports only as Confidential Witness, or CW. Because he keeps detailed tabs on all of Fort Marcy's regulars, Reeves was able to tell me not only the name of CW's construction company, located in Alexandria, Virginia, but the state in which that company had been incorporated (Maryland) and even that a branch office was on record there.

Had the Park Police taken the trouble to interview Reeves, they could have easily obtained this information. Instead, they seemed more interested in discrediting key witnesses than in getting to the truth. For example, the Park Police helped spread a rumor that the man and woman in the park were having sex, both cheating on their respective spouses.* As I discovered when I talked to investigators for Special Counsel Starr, this was not true and brings into question the investigating officers' motives.

Why were these potential witnesses being discredited? After all, they

---

*I have heard from media colleagues that they were told this by Park Police off the record. A prosecutor on Starr's staff also said that the Park Police had told this to the FBI, but grand jury testimony showed it was not true.

had seen nothing suspicious, according to the Park Police report. The later revelations of the couple's FBI statements would give some clue as to why they were victimized.

According to the couple's FBI statements, they had driven into Fort Marcy Park shortly after 5:00 P.M. on the day of Foster's death, where they saw two men—neither of whom was Foster—around and even inside Foster's car shortly before his body was found. The female witness, identified as "Judy," said she drove her Nissan into the lot with her friend "Mark" seated next to her.

Judy told the FBI that as she entered the small lot she observed a white male who had dark hair and "could have been bare-chested" seated in the car located where Foster's Honda was said to be parked (interestingly, Reeves said CW regularly walked around the park bare-chested). Since Foster's car would have been to her immediate left, she had an unobstructed view of that vehicle. She then drove to the end of the lot and backed in, giving Mark an unobstructed view of Foster's Honda to his right, which was the lone car in the small lot.[10]

Mark told the FBI that right after Judy parked, he noted that a man was standing near the Honda, whose hood was up. Mark described the white male as "mid-to-late forties, approximately six feet in height, medium build, long blond hair and beard, appear[ing] unclean and unkempt."[11] The couple consumed some alcoholic beverages in the car, then left about 6:00 P.M. for a picnic in the woods. They were encountered about fifteen minutes later by emergency workers searching for the body.[12]

The statements Mark and Judy had given to the FBI are at odds with the earlier Park Police statement. That statement had the two men in and around two different cars, not Foster's.[13] When the FBI agents under Fiske showed Judy her statement in the Park Police report, she said it was not an accurate account of what she had told them.

The Park Police conducted only two interviews in the park that night—one with Mark and one with Judy—and apparently got both wrong. This may explain why the couple apparently became the subject of a smear by the Park Police.

Since one dead body was found in the park, why was a more rigorous search of the small park not completed? This was never done. The Park Police did not even secure the park's rear entrance on Chain Bridge Road with yellow crime-scene tape (in fact the Park Police claimed during grand jury proceedings conducted under Starr that they had no idea a rear entrance even existed, according to a source close to the Starr probe).

This rear entrance, a break in a chain fence that runs alongside Chain Bridge Road, is just off the main grove area of the park and allows for community access. Although vehicles cannot enter there, there is room for several cars to park just outside the entrance on the main road's shoulder.

What about all the residents in the area just across Chain Bridge Road from the park? From the second cannon site, where police say the body was found, one can see passing traffic on Chain Bridge Road below and even homes through the trees on the other side of the road. Indeed, the official residence of the Saudi Arabian ambassador is directly across the road, with its security camera trained right on that crucial rear access point. At that time two U.S. senators also lived in the tony neighborhood around the park.

In failing to canvass the neighborhood for witnesses or other evidence, Park Police were violating not just common sense but their own specific guidelines. Their homicide manual states in the section entitled "Suicide Investigations" that "in most cases, it is appropriate to canvass the area to locate any witnesses who may have seen or heard something related to the incident." A thorough canvass would have also included talking with people known to frequent the park.

The discrepancy involving a seemingly simple matter such as the location of the body is emblematic of the dozens of other disturbing questions involving the official handling of the case. For some reason, the Park Police neglected to follow the most basic of their own procedures, even for an obvious suicide. But there was good reason for the police to have suspected that this was not a suicide at all.

3

To trained investigators, a neat crime scene for a gunshot wound to the head can mean the victim did not die by the gunshot, or that the body might have been moved. For experienced homicide detectives, a gun found in a suicide's hand is also a red flag of possible foul play. What might have been disturbing to other investigators apparently raised no red flags for Fornshill, or for his colleagues who arrived later. Indeed, it fell to the paramedics to note some of the significant anomalies with Foster's body and the surrounding scene.

In the warm humid days that followed Foster's death in July 1993, significant press attention was focused on the story. Richard Arthur, one of the Fairfax paramedics who had been present at Fort Marcy, became increasingly agitated as he closely followed the media reports. Arthur was absolutely certain that Foster did not commit suicide.[1] He voiced his concerns to his Fairfax colleagues and raised important questions that eventually led to a reexamination of the Park Police probe.

Disturbed and increasingly obsessed by his observations at the Fort

Marcy crime scene, Arthur, a five-year veteran of the department, spent his days just after the death thinking and complaining about the suicide conclusion. He spent time at the fire station computer reviewing the 911 dispatches and went to some lengths to locate the phone used by park worker Swann to make the original 911 call.[2]

As Arthur later told the FBI, he had good reason to doubt Foster had killed himself or that the death had taken place at Fort Marcy. Arthur described the neat position of Foster's body as "coffin-like," as if the body had been "placed" there. He told Senate investigators that he had "just never seen a body lying so perfectly straight after shooting a bullet in his head." The gun was also too neatly positioned in the hand next to the body, he said.[3]

Arthur was not part of the first group that found the body, but had come to the death scene as an observer. Back at the firehouse, he loudly expressed doubts about the death and chided his superior, Sgt. George Gonzalez, for not taking a stronger position in challenging the suicide verdict. Another superior admitted to the FBI he was afraid Arthur might speak to the press, and he took steps to shield Arthur from the media.

Arthur was never interviewed by the press. But Gonzalez was, months later as matters involving Foster's death took on a new life with the burgeoning Whitewater scandal. By then, Gonzalez shared many of Arthur's views. Like Arthur, Gonzalez told the *New York Post* that he thought Foster's body looked as if it was "ready for a coffin." Gonzalez was also struck by the small amount of blood he found on the body—just a trickle emanating from Foster's mouth.

After Gonzalez and Arthur left the scene, EMT worker Corey Ashford came to place Foster's body in a body bag and transport it to the hospital morgue. Ashford told the FBI working for Fiske that he noticed two surprising things about the death scene as he lifted Foster's body up from the shoulders. First, he observed no blood.[4] Second, he never saw any exit wound as he cradled Foster's head in his arms.[5]

Fiske and the autopsy report claim the bullet had created a large exit wound in the top back portion of Foster's head. Ashford got no blood on him, and he did not have to wash his hands after the task. Upon returning to the station house, Ashford classified the death as a homicide in his official report.[6]

The Park Police seemed less concerned than the paramedics by these troubling points; officers rendered a suicide verdict almost instantly. Kevin Fornshill, a six-year veteran of the Park Police who was the first officer to respond to Fort Marcy, came upon the body and noted that the area in which Foster's body lay was undisturbed and neat. To Fornshill that meant one thing—Foster had simply killed himself. Fornshill had never seen a suicide by gunshot before. If there was any doubt in his mind, it was eliminated by the second thing he learned: Paramedic Todd Hall told him a gun was in Foster's right hand.

Investigators at the main Park Police headquarters in the Anacostia section of Washington had also gotten a call about a dead body found in the park, and within twenty minutes several personnel from that office, including John Rolla and Cheryl Braun, arrived at the park. In some departments they might be called detectives, but in Park Police nomenclature Rolla was the lead criminal investigator—even though this was his first homicide case—and Cheryl Braun was a senior investigator who was training him.

Upon arriving in the parking lot, the pair was first briefed by the shift commander, Lt. Pat Gavin. Gavin left soon thereafter. Rolla and Braun then split up: The inexperienced Rolla handled the death scene while Braun—the senior investigator—remained in the parking lot to deal with secondary matters.

Braun would later tell Senate investigators that the suicide conclusion had been reached before her partner or any other detectives arrived at the scene. "It seems to me that we made that determination prior to going up and looking at the body," she said.[7]

The Park Police had, of course, broken a cardinal police rule right from the start: All such deaths are to be initially regarded as homicides. Indeed, the Park Police's own manual, *Death Investigations Guidelines*, opens with this line: "All deaths shall be considered homicides until the facts prove otherwise."[8]

Testifying before Senate investigators, Braun claimed that the case was not treated as a homicide because it was "fairly obvious that it was a suicide."[9] She explained that the gun was found in Foster's hand and that when crime-scene technician Simonello went to remove it, he found Foster's thumb had been trapped by the trigger. Colt revolvers have a little notch at the top of the trigger that becomes exposed when the trigger is pulled and in which the skin can get caught as a freak occurrence. Simonello said that in order to remove Foster's trapped thumb he first had to cautiously cock the weapon. To Braun this demonstrated that Foster had "fired the weapon himself." Skeptical Senate investigators pressed Braun on this point.

"Well," she replied, "if somebody else had put it in his hand, it would not have been stuck onto his thumb the way it was."[10] What she was saying, in effect, was that if someone had placed a gun in Foster's hand, inserting the thumb into the trigger guard, the malefactor would have been considerate enough not to catch Foster's skin in the notch.

Thus, the Park Police's determination of suicide was made based on the gun being found in Foster's hand and the absence of signs of struggle. This verdict was rendered by Officer Fornshill, who was never even close enough to see the gun in Foster's hand, and who had never seen a suicide of this type before. Detectives arriving later simply took Fornshill's assessment at face value.

BECAUSE FOSTER was found in a symmetrical position on the side of a berm, faceup and arms extended neatly at his sides, Park Police theorized he shot himself while in a sitting position. Had he lain down to shoot himself, their reasoning apparently went, the bullet would have been found in the ground under his head. It was not. Had he been standing, it is highly unlikely that his body would have fallen into the "coffin" position. By elimination, this left only the sitting position. Fiske's pathology team argued that after firing the gun from the sitting position, Foster was thrown back on the "sloped terrain" with "his arms falling to their respective sides by gravity. . . ."[11]

But the two former New York City homicide experts question this scenario. They argue that the exit wound should have created a jet stream of blood, brain matter, bone, and other tissue as the bullet emerged from the back of the skull. Had Foster shot himself on the slope (as Fiske claimed) with the exit wound at the top and back of his head (as noted in the autopsy), the blood and other matter should have been evident in the area behind him. Yet of approximately twenty officials on the scene, no one noted—as the body lay on the ground—any blood on the vegetation around the body. The Park Police report and that of the Fairfax County medical examiner on the scene, Dr. Donald Haut, specifically state that no blood was observable on the vegetation.

Scalice and Santucci also assert that in such a case the legs would not likely have extended straight out, since Foster's heels would have been caught in vegetation or on root stems that etched the ground underneath his body.

Scalice and Santucci found the neat position of the body inconsistent with suicide and conducted simulations at the "official" death site by having someone of Foster's height and weight sit on the spot. They demonstrated that both of Foster's arms would have flailed outward and come to rest more at right angles to the body than parallel to it had he in fact fired the gun in the manner claimed. Both veteran investigators stressed that freak things happen in any death, and it is not impossible for a suicide to be as tidy as Foster's was, just very, very unusual. Foul play, they argue, should have been foremost in the minds of police at the crime scene.

Even the goriest movies and TV programs understate the amount of blood from a close-range gunshot death. Experienced paramedics are much more realistic in what they expect to find. Sergeant Gonzalez had been quite emphatic when he told me that a gunshot to the head should produce a "mess" or "pork brains for breakfast." Surprisingly, he observed only a trickle of blood draining from Foster's mouth.[12]

Officer Fornshill also noted the very small amount of blood at the scene, an amount he called consistent with someone who had bitten his lip.[13] Yet, for Fornshill, the neat body arrangement and gun in hand were the signs of a suicide. To top New York City police detective Jerry Giorgio those clues could have easily been the evidence for a murder made to look like a suicide. (Giorgio was one of the first New York detectives I called when reviewing the facts of the case while reporting at the *New York Post* in 1994.)

According to Giorgio, the first thing detectives look for in a murder/suicide investigation is massive blood loss. If it exists, detectives can eliminate any idea the death was caused by other means, or that the person had been killed elsewhere and the body moved. If there is not much blood after a gunshot to the head, detectives consider the possibility the gunshot might have been a cover for a homicide by poisoning or some other method. When asked what a detective would typically expect in such a case, Giorgio said that with a .38 gunshot to the mouth/head ". . . there's tremendous amounts of blood, blood all over the place, it would be a mess."

Giorgio was not alone in his assessment. According to many pathologists, blood should have poured from both the exit wound and the entrance wound. But Fiske's report claimed that the blood emanated largely from the exit wound alone.

Dr. Richard Mason, a pathologist who specializes in gunshot trauma, and Dr. Martin Fachler, former head of the U.S. Army's Wound Ballistics Laboratory, were both asked to comment on this sort of suicide. Both explained that since the head is engorged with blood, even if the heart had stopped instantaneously blood would have flowed freely from the mouth and not trickled out from one side as appeared to be the case here.

According to Dr. Mason, the medical examiner for Santa Cruz, California, the heart works on its own independent electroimpulse system and does not stop just because the brain is disabled. This basic biology lesson is impressed on every premed student when a frog's heart is removed and placed in a glucose-oxygen solution.

"It can continue to beat almost indefinitely," said Mason of the experiment. What stops the heart is deprivation of oxygen.

Mason traces the typical chain of events after a gunshot to the brain: The bullet disables the brain, which directly controls pulmonary activity. With the lungs disabled, the bloodstream is quickly deprived of fresh oxygen. Without oxygen, the heart stops. All of this takes time, he said, and the heart can continue pumping after the shot anywhere from "thirty seconds to two minutes."

Fiske, in his 1994 report, readily admits that "relatively little blood was visible" to observers at the Foster death scene for this type of wound, but he offers another explanation. The Fiske report states that since Foster "was positioned on a steep slope, with his head near the top of the berm and his legs extended down the hill," cessation of the heart together with the pull of gravity "permitted the settling of blood into the lower portions of his body rather than out of the wound in his head."[14]

Like many of Fiske's explanations, this sounds plausible to the lay reader but is disputed by experts. Vernon Geberth, author of the standard police homicide manual *Practical Homicide Investigation: Tactics, Procedures, and Forensic Techniques,* points to a case in his book that is similar in some respects to the Foster case, that of Bud Dwyer, a Pennsylvania government official whose suicide was committed in front of a roomful of press and captured on videotape in 1987.[15]

After viewing that video with a homicide expert, it is easy to understand why the paramedics in the Foster case questioned the lack of blood and the neat position of the body. When Dwyer fired the .357 magnum (which, of course, is more powerful than a .38, though not so much as to inflict an entirely different sort of wound) he was thrown back against a wall, then slid to the floor in a disheveled position. For many uncomfortable seconds there was the sight and sound of blood gushing from his mouth as from a drinking fountain. Throughout the scene, Dwyer's head remains elevated above the rest of his body.

Those who first came upon Foster's body—the man driving the van, Gonzalez, Arthur, Ashford, Fornshill, and others—saw little or no blood. Nor did anyone, including the medical examiner and the lead police investigator, see blood on the vegetation in the immediate area where his head lay. And the gun itself appeared clean.

As stories playing up these inconsistencies appeared in the papers, the Park Police scrambled to respond. First, they claimed that the emergency workers had simply failed to see a large pool of blood on the ground under the body, something that became apparent only later when the body was rolled over in the presence of the police investigators and the Fairfax County medical examiner.

This story collapsed after EMT Ashford claimed that he saw no blood when he lifted the body. And Ashford wasn't alone. Lieutenant William Bianchi was serving as Ashford's supervisor that night at the park. He stated in a recorded interview that there was "not a lot" of blood when the body was lifted from the ground and placed on a gurney.

Fiske's report ignores Ashford and Bianchi. Fiske repeats the Park Police assertion that they found a "large" pool of blood on the ground under the body. On page thirty-six of his report, Fiske states: "At approximately 7:40 P.M., Dr. Donald Haut, the Fairfax County medical examiner, arrived at the scene to examine the body. At that point, Foster's body was rolled over and those present observed a large pool of blood located on the ground where Foster's head had been. Haut observed a large exit wound in the back of the skull."

But Dr. Haut's own version contradicts this. When interviewed in 1995, Haut, who was present when Foster's body was rolled over and the exit wound examined, said that there was "not a hell of a lot" of blood on the ground. In fact, he said, most of the blood had "congealed" on the back of Foster's head.

In late January 1995, the Senate Banking Committee published a two-volume set of hearing transcripts, depositions, and documents relating to the Foster hearings from the summer before, including Haut's FBI statement to Fiske's investigation.* Notable in Haut's FBI interview

---

*The second volume, 1,328 pages long, included all the documents turned over by Fiske to Congress: FBI witness statements, FBI lab reports, Park Police reports, and notes. Apparently, in the changeover from a Democrat-controlled Congress to a Republican-controlled one, somebody released materials that should never have been entered into the public domain. Incredibly, the documents included the confidential names, addresses, and phone numbers of witnesses interviewed by the Park Police. The volumes provide a wealth of information and demonstrate that the discrepancies are not just variously nuanced versions of events but out-and-out contradictions of fact, if not falsehoods. Many of these inconsistencies were later exposed by Hugh Sprunt, a Texas accountant and lawyer who compiled a detailed analysis of the Fiske documents in his *Citizen's Independent Report*.

statement are his observations about the blood at the scene. Haut never told the FBI, as Fiske stated, that he saw a large pool of blood or a large exit wound. In fact Haut told the FBI on April 12, 1994, that there was *little* blood in evidence. He saw no blood on the shirt or face, according to the statement, nor did he see any on the vegetation around the body.[16] Haut told the FBI he saw blood around the back of Foster's head, but the "volume was small" and had largely "matted" and "clotted" to the skull.[17]

As for the exit wound, Haut indicated clearly that the wound was not "large" but small, "consistent with a low-velocity weapon." He told the agents that in a recent case he handled, a .25 caliber rifle—an even smaller bore weapon than the .38 caliber revolver found in Foster's hand—"had caused a much more devastating wound."[18]

Fiske also ignored the observations of the lead Park Police investigator, John Rolla. In his sworn deposition to Senate investigators, Rolla testified, "I probed his head. There was no big blowout. I initially thought the bullet might still be in his head."

Asked directly by a Senate investigator if the "exit wound was small," Rolla responded succinctly, "Right."[19]

Even if there was a large quantity of blood under the body—though evidence to support this, such as police photos of the scene, is either contradictory or simply missing—we are left to wonder why there was so little blood from the entry wound in the mouth.

Some congressional investigators and a few influential journalists have tried to explain the small amount of blood by noting that a Polaroid shot taken at the scene showed sufficient blood on the front of Foster's body, notably on Foster's shirt. The picture in question shows blood emanating as a small stream from the right side of Foster's mouth and nose. But the Polaroid was taken some time after police arrived. The earliest police and rescue accounts, like those of Gonzalez, Arthur, and Fornshill, indicate less blood on Foster's shirt. This suggests the blood in the photograph was not a result of massive bleeding from the gunshot, but rather the product of a slow drainage of blood from the corpse. Blood obviously continued to drain from Foster's head after the police arrived.

The fact that officials who arrived at the scene later in the evening saw more blood on the shirt than those initially present would be one clue that the gunshot occurred close to the time his body was found, at around 6:00 P.M.

According to Fairfax County medical technician Richard Arthur, Foster may have suffered more than one wound. Arthur stated to FBI investigators in March 1994 that he had noticed what he believed was a "gunshot wound," or a small-size bullet hole, on Foster's neck, just below the right ear. According to transcriptions of his FBI statement, Arthur "noted what appeared to be a small caliber bullet hole in Foster's neck on the right side just under the jaw line about half way between the ear and the tip of the chin."[20] Fiske, relying on an FBI analysis of a crime-scene Polaroid shot, dismissed Arthur's testimony as a mistaken observation of a bloodstain.

In the same statement, Arthur makes another startling contention. Interviewed by FBI agents in both March and April 1994, Arthur identi-fied the gun in Foster's right hand as a semiautomatic pistol such as a .45 or 9mm. He claimed he was certain that it was not the .38 caliber revolver later identified by authorities as the weapon found with Foster. Arthur had thought this odd from the beginning, since he noted that the neck "wound was caused by a small caliber gunshot" and he was struck by his recollection "that the weapon in Foster's hand was a high caliber weapon."[21]

If Arthur is correct, the gun found in Foster's hand may have been switched sometime after the police arrived. Arthur was emphatic about this, noting the distinguishing characteristics of semiautomatics and revolvers. For one thing, the gun he observed in Foster's hand had a square or "straight barrel" and the "handle on the weapon [was] square in shape."[22] He is clearly describing a gun that is different from the old Colt revolver that appears in the crime-scene photographs.

What little photographic evidence remains of the death scene appears to show that at some point the gun was moved or switched after the Park Police arrived. When one of the Polaroids taken on July 20 was superenhanced by prosecutor Miquel Rodriguez during the Starr inquiry and compared to a 35 mm photo taken at the same time, blades of grass or other vegetation protrude from between different fingers of Foster's hand. (Although the FBI laboratory had stated that the 35 mm film that the Park Police had underexposed was useless, an outside agency used by Starr's office was able to retrieve some useful information.)

Startling, too, was the fact that the Park Police could not positively connect the gun with Foster. Foster's wife told Park Police that the only gun she was aware of was a silver revolver—not the black one found at Fort Marcy. She recalled having packed a silver revolver in Little Rock for the family's move to Washington.

Park Police spokesman Major Robert Hines had said in January 1994 that while the gun was never positively identified by the family, Foster's sister, Sharon Foster Bowman, had believed it to be a gun once owned by her father and passed on to her brother. Police never showed her the gun; rather, a family friend, on behalf of the police, showed her a photograph. According to that friend, Bowman "said it looked like a gun she had seen in her father's gun collection."[23]

This bit of speculation was widely reported and seemed to assuage many skeptics of the suicide conclusion. Yet documents obtained by the Fiske investigators show conclusively that the gun was not owned by Foster's father and had not been part of his father's gun collection. The Foster children, too, said it was not a gun owned by their father.[24] And Foster's nephew, Lee Foster Bowman, Sharon's son, who was intimately familiar with his grandfather's collection, told the FBI that the old black Colt did not match any of his grandfather's guns.[25]

Despite this evidence and testimony some have argued that Foster shot himself with the silver revolver, the same one that Mrs. Foster packed in her home in Little Rock. Author James B. Stewart, in his book *Blood Sport,* makes this claim. But the ABC News Polaroid and all of the official documents show conclusively that the revolver in Foster's hand was black. No less an authority than Lisa Foster herself told the Park Police the gun found in his hand was not the silver revolver she had packed, according to Park Police notes of their interview with her shortly after his death.

The Park Police found one high-velocity Remington-Peters .38 bullet unspent in the gun's cylinder; in the chamber next to it was a spent cartridge, the one that held the bullet said to have killed Foster. The remaining four chambers were empty. The Foster family could not find any matching ammunition in either of their homes.

If a suicide is found with a gun he does not own clutched in his hand, investigators should be more interested in identifying "links" between the suicide and the supposed suicide weapon. Not the Park Police. They had promptly tested the gun for fingerprints and detected none—even though the gun was found in Foster's hand. There was no apparent blood or blow-back on the gun. The gun sight, which projected substantially above the tip of the barrel, caused no damage to Foster's teeth or lips—which it should have—as the gun was blown out of his mouth by the recoil.

The weapon, an old Colt revolver made from the pieces of at least two guns, had two serial numbers on it dating back to 1913. The Colt company refers inquiries about such guns to Larry Wilson, who is the foremost authority on antique Colt weapons. From my description Wilson told me it sounded like "a drop gun," an old, untraceable gun left at a crime scene to confuse investigators. Several veteran detectives offered the same analysis.

The first witness to find Vince Foster's body, the man identified as CW, claimed he saw no gun in either of Foster's hands when he discovered the body. CW has repeated this in numerous interviews and in an affidavit made to several members of Congress. On July 28, 1994, CW told Congressman Dan Burton of Indiana, "There was no gun in the hand. His—both palms were face up, thumbs out to the side. . . . I did not see a gun next to the body."[26]

Fiske theorized that Foster pressed the barrel of the gun at the oropharynx, the extreme back of the mouth just above the throat, and fired.[27] In such cases the powerful blast of flame, heat, and gases creates a vacuum at the barrel's end that sucks in blood and other tissue. Blood and tissue should have been observable on the Colt. None was. According to New York City police detective Giorgio: "Look at the gun—if it was the instrument of death, there would be blood on it. A .38 makes a powerful explosion. There's a backwash of blood and tissue."

The FBI lab, which in recent years has come under strong criticism for shoddy and even sometimes manipulative work, reported to Fiske some forensic evidence that, though inconclusive, linked Foster to the gun. Five centimeters—about two inches—from the front of the Colt barrel was swabbed for DNA evidence. The conclusion was that Foster's DNA was "a potential contributor" to the DNA substance on the gun. The lab could not determine if the DNA residue was from blood or saliva.[28] Approximately 6 to 8 percent of the population has the same DNA characteristics as Foster.

In the absence of other evidence, the finding of blood and DNA traces is often challenged in cases that suggest a police cover-up—as in the O. J. Simpson case—since existing blood samples can be used to tamper with evidence. When the FBI laboratory can link a suspect's DNA to a smear of dried saliva on the back of a postage stamp as in the Unabomber case, why could this more explosive contact with Foster's tissues not give an equally conclusive match?

Whether the gun was switched or not, to homicide experts the simple finding of a gun in the hand of a supposed suicide is grounds for immediate suspicion. As Vernon Geberth, author of *Practical Homicide Investigation*, stated in January 1994, "Under ordinary circumstances, after the firing, the gun is away from the person," sometimes landing many feet from the body due to the force of the gunshot and the reflexive actions of the victim. A gun still in the hand is "rare," according to Geberth.[29]

When my *New York Post* article appeared pointing this out, the White House referred press inquiries on the matter to Dr. Cyril Wecht, a former Pittsburgh, Pennsylvania, medical examiner. In an Associated Press report, Wecht was quoted as saying that the finding of the gun in Foster's hand could be explained by a phenomenon known as cadaveric spasm, a rare occurrence in which rigor mortis sets in instantly. "You can get, in many of these instances, an instantaneous, spasmodic reflex which is entirely voluntary, and the hand will clutch an object, in this case a gun," said Wecht.[30]

But that could not have been the case here because the officer who removed the gun from Foster's grip said the hand was still pliable. Rigor mortis had not even begun to set in.

Stretching the probabilities of such a "freak" event, the gun could have remained in his hand due to Foster's right thumb being trapped in a notch at the top of the trigger as the trigger rebounded. This is what the Park Police have claimed in FBI interviews, Senate depositions, and press statements.

The gun was not only still in Foster's hand—unusual under any circumstances—but near to his hip, with the gun barrel tucked under his right leg. Fiske's investigators chalked that up to "gravity" (just as they did the neat arrangement of the body). Yet the New York homicide detectives noted in their report that in their "combined experience of fifty years of investigating homicides, [we have] never seen a . . . gun positioned in a suicide's hand in such an orderly position."[31] Even if the thumb somehow got caught in the trigger guard, they noted, the force should have sent the arms and gun flailing outward. If Foster was sitting down and not standing, as Fiske concluded, how did the weapon end up under the victim's leg?

Perhaps most disturbing of all is the Park Police's failure to account for crucial crime-scene photos of the whole body and its surroundings, especially the so-called relationship photos of the body.

Vernon Geberth, who has written the authoritative text on homicide investigations, is also a former lieutenant commander with the New York Police Department who once headed the Bronx Homicide Task Force and has been involved in over five thousand death investigations. Geberth asserts that such photos are "imperative" because they "show the body's position and other patterns that can never be recreated." Without them, you may never know what really happened. "It's a basic requirement" to have such photos, he said.[32]

Surely the Park Police knew that, too. Why, then, did they not have these routine and required photographs? Their absence makes it difficult, if not impossible, to determine that the body was where they said it was. Had they taken these simple pictures of the surroundings, no doubts could be raised about the body's location.

On March 7, 1994, I revealed in the *New York Post* the absence of key crime-scene photos. Days later, without mentioning my reports specifically, ABC's *World News Tonight* aired a story aimed at quelling the "speculation" and "rumors" surrounding Foster's death—"for instance," ABC reported, "the rumor that there are no photographs of the scene. There are. ABC News has seen a complete set." The story was accompanied by a photograph, a Polaroid of a close-up shot of Foster's hip area with the gun in his hand. That such a Polaroid was not, for essential police purposes, a crime-scene photo—certainly not one of the whole scene—as explained in my article, was never mentioned on the segment by correspondent Jim Wooten.

Nor did ABC's disclosure explain the missing relationship photos. The Polaroid shown by Wooten could have been taken in front of the second cannon (as claimed) or down the way from the first cannon (where evidence suggests the body was actually found) or even somewhere in the vicinity of the restroom facilities at nearby parkway headquarters.

The result of ABC's report was a general impression that the complaints about "missing photos" were so much crackpot mutterings. Had we not seen with our own eyes that graphic photo of Foster with the suicide weapon in his hand?

Months later, my *New York Post* report was confirmed with the release of the Fiske documents. The Park Police claimed in the report that all the key photos—the police said they were taken on 35 mm film—had been "underexposed" in the Park Police labs. Only a handful of close-up shots like the ABC News Polaroid remained.[33] ABC's claim of having seen a "complete set" seems irresponsible considering later revelations that almost two-thirds of the Polaroids taken by Park Police also mysteriously disappeared.

Equally disturbing was the fact that the Polaroids that vanished from the case file had a direct bearing on certain disputed matters. For example, the earliest Polaroids taken of the gun in Foster's hand—the gun EMT worker Richard Arthur claimed was a semiautomatic—are missing. Those photos, taken by the second officer on the scene, Franz Ferstl, have disappeared. Ferstl has never contradicted official claims that the gun in Foster's hand was a revolver. According to a source close to the Starr probe, Ferstl did testify before a grand jury that the original position of Foster's hand did not match the remaining Polaroids taken later in the evening by Park Police.

Another dispute that could be resolved by the missing Polaroids involved the amount of blood found on the ground after Foster's body was rolled over. Park Police investigator Rolla testified in a Senate deposition that he took Polaroids of the blood on the ground but has no idea what happened to them. ". . . I put them in a jacket, God knows how many people looked through those, and I don't know what happened," Rolla testified.[34]

There is also the nagging question of where Foster's body was actually found: directly in front of the second cannon or on the berm past the first cannon. Neither the underexposed 35 mm shots nor the surviving Polaroids contain "relationship" photos to support the official claim that the body was found by the second cannon.

Even in a case of a very apparent suicide, such photos are required. Yet this was not just a questionable death by virtue of the factors observable at the scene: the blood, the gun, the body. It was also the death of a very high government official who served the president of the United States.

4

Is there a way to tell the difference between a suicide and a murder made to look like a suicide? According to several veteran detectives, there are a number of telltale signs that can help them form an opinion. Aside from the immediate issues at the death scene, investigators look for other circumstantial evidence that offers "consistencies," facts that link the person to the act. A suicide note, for instance, is one piece of evidence they look for, but is not the only thing.

Foster, a family man, had said nothing even resembling a farewell to his wife and three children and close colleagues. As far as investigators knew at the time, he had left no suicide note and had apparently made no special financial arrangements for his survivors. He had left his wife about $1 million in insurance money, a nice sum but not enough to afford the sort of life to which the Fosters had been accustomed.

There is often a significant reason why someone will choose a particular site at which to commit suicide. No such reason can be deduced as to why Foster would choose obscure Fort Marcy Park. There was no evidence he had ever visited or even knew about the place.

Police know that usually suicides by gunshot to the head are an attempt to ensure a certain, quick death in order to avoid the possibility of surviving with an agonizing lifetime disability. On the face of it, did this antique Colt strike one as the instrument of preference for a resolute suicide? There were many other problems with the physical, forensic, and circumstantial evidence. Instead of sticking to these areas, which are usually the prime focus of a police death inquiry, Park Police were more eager to probe the psychological aspects of the case.

The Park Police verdict of suicide hinges on their finding that Foster was depressed, and the most compelling evidence of depression was a torn note found in Foster's briefcase in his office almost a week after the death. There is no indication that the Park Police consulted with mental health experts or psychiatrists in reaching their conclusion.

After the office search was completed two days after the death, the Park Police went to work on their psychological autopsy of Foster. Since there were so many problems with the physical aspects of the case, this would need to be a strong part of their report in closing the case. The psychological autopsy, according to Geberth's *Practical Homicide Investigation*, "is a collaborative procedure involving law enforcement and mental health experts who attempt to determine the state of mind of a person prior to the fatal act." According to Geberth, standard homicide procedure demands a psychological autopsy, even if there is no doubt as to whether the case was a suicide, in order to establish motive for the death. For a suicide, that state of mind should show signs of instability or other "warning signs."

Since the Park Police had no circumstantial evidence—no actual note that specifically referenced death or other indications that Foster was planning suicide, such as saying farewell to friends and family—a significant event might have precipitated the act. For example, the Park Police had gotten an anonymous tip that Foster was homosexual and had AIDS. There was no evidence of the former, and a blood test quickly confirmed he did not have AIDS.[1]

One important guide to his state of mind was the last people who saw Foster alive—his office colleagues who had worked with him since his arrival in Washington. White House counsel Bernard Nussbaum had delayed the Park Police interviews of Foster's colleagues, but finally relented and allowed Captain Hume and Detective Markland to conduct interviews—albeit with White House attorneys sitting in.

These interviews did not surface any warning signs of suicidal depression. Nussbaum himself told the police that on the day of Foster's death, Foster "had not exhibited any unusual behavior."[2]

Betsy Pond, Nussbaum's secretary, gave Hume and Markland a statement: "There was nothing unusual about his emotional state. In fact, over the last several weeks she did not notice any changes, either physically or emotionally. She noticed no weight lost. . . . I asked here [sic] would she be surprised if I found out he was seeing a psychiatrist. She said yes. She was not aware of any depression problems."[3]

Foster's personal secretary, Deborah Gorham, also told the Park Police that she did not notice any "unusual behavior" on Foster's last day at the White House. Since her statement offered no additional insight, the police report states, "the interview was about to be terminated" when White House lawyer Neuwirth asked her to step outside to speak privately. Returning and perhaps prompted by Neuwirth, Gorham told investigators that Mrs. Foster had called for Foster's pay schedule because she believed his checking account had been overdrawn. She also said that within the past two weeks she had received calls from Foster's son Vincent and his wife asking about his mood. She said they seemed "concerned."[4]

Thomas Castleton, a clerk in the office, said Foster seemed oblivious when Castleton said good-bye as Foster passed him for the last time. Castleton told the Park Police that Foster seemed " 'in his own world,' focused, disturbed."[5]

Still not a lot for the police to go on. Another report shows a Park Police investigator called the three psychiatrists whose names and numbers were found in Foster's wallet. All three said they "did not know Vincent Foster, Jr., and that he was not a patient of theirs."[6]

Up until July 26, the day a White House lawyer found the torn note, there was almost no evidence to support the depression theory.

On July 27, the Park Police interviewed Foster's brother-in-law, former congressman Beryl Anthony. For the first time, the word "depression" appears in witness testimony. Anthony and his wife said that for a month preceding the death they noted "Mr. Foster's depression had become increasingly worse. . . ." Foster had said that he was worried congressional hearings looking into the travel office might harm his reputation.[7] (It is important to note here that none of the official reports on the travel office held Foster responsible for the fiasco.)

Of course, Foster's wife should have been aware of these issues and one of the first persons the police should have turned to in their inquiry. On the night of the death, Rolla and Braun had left Foster's home explaining they would need to speak with Mrs. Foster about the case as soon as possible. But it took another nine days before the police interviewed her. On July 29, as the police investigation was winding down, Captain Hume and Detective Markland met with Lisa and her attorney, James Hamilton, at his firm's Washington offices.

Signs that may have pointed to suicide, according to Mrs. Foster, were the fact that her husband had difficulty sleeping and had told his sister Sheila (though oddly, not her) that he was suffering from high blood pressure. Further, he was bothered by public criticism of the president and even the stress of the move to Washington, so much so that he said to her, "How did I get myself into this?" Lisa said her husband usually handled stress well, but that was in Arkansas where he was "in control of situations." Ultimately, she believed that "something physical came over Vincent quickly."[8]

Lisa did remember that as she saw him off for work that Tuesday, his "mood seemed better than it had been 'in a while.'" With Mrs. Foster's statement and a statement from Foster's doctor in Little Rock that he had prescribed an antidepressant the day before his death, as far as the Park Police were concerned the psychological autopsy was closed.

Without determining a clear motive for the suicide or strong evidence of depression, the Park Police should have redoubled their efforts to examine missing gaps and inconsistencies in the circumstantial evidence. One of the most obvious problems was the large gap between the time Foster was last seen alive and the time his body was found at Fort Marcy five hours later.

Officials stated that Foster left his office around 1:00 P.M., after lunch. No one saw Foster alive from the moment he left the White House's West Wing. This failure to find any circumstantial evidence—such as someone having spotted Foster driving to the park, obtaining the weapon, or at the park itself—should have aroused some suspicion. A large block of unaccounted time like this is a serious inconsistency, I was told by experts. In the days after the death, Foster's face was splashed across television screens and in newspapers, yet no one came forward to say something like, "Yeah, he's the same guy I saw in McDonald's," or, "I remember him, he was ahead of me at the gas pump." There were not even any false sightings, of which there are usually at least a few in such cases.

This problematic gap did not go unnoticed by the Park Police. Four days after Foster's death, a *Washington Times* report quoted Major Robert Hines, the Park Police spokesman: "It is unusual that, so far, we haven't heard from one person who can tell us anything about his activities after 1 p.m."[9]

It is standard procedure to vigorously attempt to reconstruct a decedent's last hours, yet no information was ever developed about Foster's activities that afternoon by the Park Police, the Fiske probe, or the Senate Banking Committee.

Special counsel Fiske concluded that he was "unable to determine where Foster went" after leaving the White House.[10] Nor did he have any idea when Foster entered the park. Had Fiske or the Park Police taken pains to conduct the admittedly tedious but nonetheless somewhat routine police work that a case like this calls for—such as combing the several routes Foster may have taken to Fort Marcy Park for possible witnesses, interviewing neighbors around the park, asking anyone who had been at or near the park that afternoon to come forward—more information might have developed.

Park Police concluded that Foster had entered the park just before

3:00 P.M.[11] They based this on the account of a CIA employee who told them six days after Foster's death that at about that time on July 20, 1993, he had seen a Japanese-make car "turn abruptly into Fort Marcy" from the George Washington Parkway, adding that the license plate was an out-of-state one with lettering in the bottom right-hand corner.[12] Fiske later dismissed this account, citing the fact that Arkansas plates have no such lettering in that spot. Handwritten FBI notes taken during the interview of this witness, conducted by Fiske's FBI agents in April 1994, offer even stronger information: When the CIA employee was shown a photo of Foster's Honda, he stated it was "definitely not" the car he had seen. This appears to mean that the Park Police never took the basic step of showing him a photo of Foster's car, despite buying a significant claim in his testimony.[13]

Though a steady flow of cars will pull into Fort Marcy's lot on an ordinary day, including Park Police cars on routine patrol, the first reported sighting of what Fiske said was Foster's unoccupied Honda had been made by a Washington man, Patrick Knowlton, who pulled into the lot around 4:30 P.M. and spotted a male individual sitting in another car parked nearby. Knowlton gave a statement to the Park Police two days after Foster's death, followed by another in April 1994 to FBI agents working for Fiske. Knowlton said he had come to the park to relieve himself. When he got out of his car, the other man, whom he described as Hispanic-looking, got out, too, and watched him as he went to the nearby trees to quickly relieve himself. Knowlton said he felt menaced by this attention, and he quickly drove away.

A couple, whose first names were Judy and Mark, told the Park Police they entered the lot around 5:00 P.M. The couple saw several people come and go in the lot, but apparently no sign of Foster. According to the Park Police report, the couple was able to identify a car consistent with Foster's Honda, but gave no hint of seeing anyone in or near it. Yet in statements to the FBI in 1994, both Judy and Mark told investigators that they had, in fact, seen two men both in and around the Honda.

IN THE absence of any evidence whatsoever linking Foster to the gun, the police investigators should have felt it incumbent on them to locate one crucial piece of physical evidence: the fired bullet. Not until the Fiske inquiry many months later was a serious effort made to find the bullet.

Why did the Park Police not conduct an immediate and vigorous search for the bullet that killed Foster? Initially a Park Police spokesman explained that no metal-detector search was conducted because the bullet likely "was lost in the woods."[14] Some homicide experts were incredulous at this explanation; they said there was more than a good chance that the bullet would be found in the immediate vicinity of the body. According to pathologist Vincent DiMaio, one of the nation's leading experts on gunshot wounds, there was only a fifty-fifty chance of the bullet's even exiting the cranium. Even if it does break through, DiMaio said, it can still, by way of its greatly reduced velocity, "get caught under the skin."[15]

In addition to claiming that no metal-detector search had been conducted, Park Police spokesperson Major Hines was cited in a July 23, 1993, Gannett News Service story as stating that "forensic tests showed only one bullet was fired from the Colt revolver, and it was the one found in Foster." But police documents indicate that such forensic tests had not been conducted on the gun by that date. The documents also report that the fired slug exited the head—making Hines's claim that the "bullet was fired from the Colt" insupportable.

As some of these discrepancies came under press scrutiny in February 1994, the Park Police reversed course. Hines said he was mistaken about the bullet not having been searched for and that, in fact, an exhaustive search for the bullet had been conducted in the park. The Park Police search was conducted two days after Foster's death, but nothing was found, according to the Park Police. They claimed that, at the time of the initial investigation some nine months earlier, they sent a team of four investigators with metal detectors to search about a hundred square yards around the supposed site of Foster's death. They reported finding nothing—absolutely nothing—including, of course, the Foster bullet.[16]

Yet in April 1994, some nine months after Foster's death, Fiske had the FBI conduct an extensive search for the missing bullet. His team came up with twelve modern-day bullets and dozens of Civil War–era artifacts—in the very same area the Park Police claimed to have searched. The FBI found a bullet, several cartridge cases, and other metal items on the path just where police said Foster's body was found. But they retrieved no bullet that could have killed Foster.[17] Assuming a Park Police search was indeed conducted, one must conclude that either it was a very faulty one or it took place at some other location.

In an ordinary gun of the type Foster was said to have used, a gunpowder blast and the residue it leaves, sometimes called powder burns, can be emitted in two places: at the end of the barrel, of course, but also at the front cylinder gap, the small opening between the cylinder and the barrel of the gun.

According to the Foster autopsy report completed by the Virginia deputy medical examiner, powder burns were found on the index fingers of both of Foster's hands, which would suggest that both hands were on or near the barrel of the gun when it was fired.

Park Police crime-scene technician Peter Simonello told Senate investigators in 1994 that the "only thing" that could have caused the powder burns on the right hand "was a cylinder blast."[18] (He was apparently unaware that the autopsy report had found burns on the left hand as well.) Using his own service gun to illustrate, Simonello showed investigators the highly awkward grip he believed Foster would have to have used to leave such burns. Simonello placed his right thumb on the trigger and stretched his right fingers uncomfortably over the cylinder and front of the gun.[19] (Rolla, too, would later tell the investigators how unusual such a clasp would be: "It is an odd grip," he commented, "no question about it."[20])

Given such a grip, said Simonello, it was essential that the left hand be on the gun's handle to stabilize it, even if the pressure required to depress the trigger had been substantially reduced by first cocking the weapon.

"You're indicating in your answer that the left hand would have been holding the handle of the gun?" asked one of the Senate staff investigators.

"Right," said Simonello without hesitation.[21]

In fact, Foster's left hand could not have been holding the grip to sta-bilize the gun as Simonello conjectured, because the finding of powder burns on Foster's left hand meant that the left hand was wrapped around the cylinder near the front of the gun.

The finding of powder burns on both of Foster's hands, and powder residue found on his shirt, only demonstrated that a gun had been fired in Foster's hands and near to his body. The results would have been the same whether Foster fired the weapon himself or grasped the gun while trying to resist its being thrust down his mouth, or whether someone placed the gun in his hand and fired it for him.

An independent pathology team that worked for Special Counsel Fiske also took note of the powder burns. Fiske's pathology team agreed that both Foster's left and right index fingers had deposits of gunpow-der residue (burns). The FBI lab noted there was only one place from which that powder could emanate: the front cylinder gap of the gun. The pathology panel concluded that "the laboratory studies and the anatomic findings indicate that Mr. Foster's index fingers [indicating, of course, that both hands were used] were in the vicinity of the [front] cylinder gap when the weapon was fired."[22] In the final Fiske report, this finding by his pathology team was cited as powerful evidence of Foster's having fired the weapon.

According to pathologists and homicide detectives, experienced killers are well aware that one of the first things police check for in a sui-cide is powder burns on the hands. Absence of such burns would instantly send a signal, which is why no professionally staged suicide would be likely to omit them. Forensic pathologists look not only for powder marks but for indications that such marks are consistent with the way the weapon was supposedly fired.

Foster's right thumb was found on the trigger, and powder burns on the right hand demonstrated that this hand was near the front of the gun. This meant that the left hand had to have been on the grip to sta-bilize the weapon, which would also allow for rearward pressure against the trigger. But powder burns indicated that the left hand, along with the right, was wrapped alongside the gun's cylinder, with the left fingers extended over the top frame of the gun.

Such a grip would have been "an extremely unnatural and awkward grasp, totally inconsistent with what both experience and logic show us to expect of a suicidal person," according to Massad Ayoob of the Lethal Force Institute.[23] Ayoob, a leading authority on guns and body trauma, suggested that the burns were more consistent with the scene having been "faked": that is, a situation where the gun was placed in the hand, the thumb inserted into the trigger guard, and the gun then fired.[24] To substantiate this, Ayoob conducted a simulation using someone of Foster's proportions and a gun like that found in his hand.[25]

Ayoob was far from alone in his skepticism. Dr. Vincent DiMaio told me in 1995 that the alleged grip "doesn't make any sense. It would be such an awkward way, you'd have to contort yourself to do this. It is not consistent with suicide." DiMaio, medical examiner for Bexar County (San Antonio, Texas), is one of the nation's preeminent experts on gunshot trauma.[26]

Dr. Martin Fachler, former head of the U.S. Army's Wound Ballistics Laboratory, also found the powder marks curious. He concluded that even if the hammer had been cocked, it would have been very difficult for Foster to have fired the gun without at least one hand on the grip. "It's . . . counter-pressure," Dr. Fachler said. He bluntly stated: "If you ask is this an indication of foul play, I have to say, yeah, maybe it is."[27]

Robert Taubert, a gun expert who spent thirty-three years with the FBI, said he had never heard of such a case. A grip employing both hands at the front of the gun, he said, would have been "completely unnatural."[28]

As noted earlier, Park Police investigators Rolla and Simonello both noted that the powder marks on the right hand made the grip problematic. Yet the Fiske report took this highly ambiguous evidence as a strong substantiation of the suicide conclusion.

There's a puzzling footnote to the powder question: The FBI lab, in its review of the physical evidence issued on May 9, 1994, found two particles of gunpowder on Foster's clothing *dissimilar* to the powder in the spent cartridge found in the gun.[29] Could this have been a sign that another gun created the head wound, and the Colt was then placed in Foster's hand and fired?

Fiske's investigators asked the Park Police how the dissimilar gun powder got there, but this possibility apparently was never considered. In a footnote to his report Fiske explained that "although the Park Police laboratory does take precautions to avoid contamination of evidence," the clothing might have been contaminated in the laboratory itself.[30]

PERHAPS THE most incredible part of the initial investigation was that the Park Police, after citing the gun as key evidence of suicide, closed the case on August 5 without even knowing for sure that the supposed death weapon worked. Park Police told me they had sent the gun for testing to the Metropolitan Washington Police laboratories as was their usual practice. When I called this institution's ballistics unit, the head of the department told me the gun had never been tested there. A newspaper article about that on January 28, 1994, in the *New York Post* set off a hubbub that the *Washington Post* then tried to quell by reporting that the gun had in fact been tested at the Bureau of Alcohol, Tobacco and Firearms laboratories in Rockville, Maryland.

It turned out that the gun had not been sent for testing until August—a full eleven days after the case was declared closed and almost a week after the Park Police announced their findings at a press conference on August 10.[31]

But these were questions treated, if at all, in quiet stories buried on back pages or discussed on the Internet, until a report by New York City police homicide investigators was released to the public in early 1995.

Vincent Scalice and Fred Santucci had been hired by the Western Journalism Center in late 1994. The pair, together with the former head of the New Jersey state police crime laboratory, Dr. Richard Saferstein, conducted a crime-scene reconstruction at Fort Marcy Park. They also conducted an exhaustive review of the FBI laboratory documents, Park

Police and Fiske reports, as well as witness statements of officials who were present at the death scene.

On April 27, 1995, following a four-month investigation, Scalice and Santucci held a well-attended press conference in Washington to announce their conclusions: The "overwhelming evidence" suggested that Foster's body was moved to the park and that he likely did not die there. Murder, the two experts concluded, could not be ruled out.

Scalice had spent twenty years with the New York Police Department and was an expert on crime-scene examination, fingerprints, and identification. His reputation led to his being hired in the mid-1970s by the Democratic staff of the House Select Committee on Assassinations investigating the deaths of President Kennedy and Martin Luther King, Jr., as well as other major investigations. Santucci was a twenty-seven-year veteran of the New York Police Department with fifteen of those years spent as a forensic crime-scene photographer.

Both men were old-fashioned cops who combined good street sense with integrity. Scalice had a gritty, swaggering manner. He spoke in a raspy voice, no doubt a symptom of his chain smoking, and gave this reporter a first-class education in homicide work. His candor was impressive. I was surprised to learn that, although he had dedicated his life to bringing murderers to justice, he opposed the death penalty. He said that he had seen too many of the "wrong guys" convicted.

One especially strong indication of the pair's integrity was their past history of testifying against police when the facts warranted it. Their testimony on behalf of a Pennsylvania man helped acquit him of the charge of murder. Scalice alleged that the state police investigators had framed the man by using a piece of Scotch tape to transfer his fingerprint impression onto a windowpane at the crime scene.

In their nineteen-page report on Foster's death, the detectives carefully outlined the circumstantial, physical, and forensic evidence supporting their conclusions. They did not make a judgment on whether the death was suicide or murder because, as Scalice told me, "it is difficult to say how someone died, if we still don't know where the person died."

Much of what detectives like Scalice use to build a case is circumstantial evidence. It is not necessarily conclusive, but in the absence of forensic evidence proving suicide, as was the case with Foster, it takes on great importance. In addition to the missing forensic evidence, Scalice also found questionable the notion that Foster, after leaving his jacket in the car, walked the length of the park with a large revolver in his hand. If it was too hot for a jacket—not something likely to concern someone taking his final steps—he would seemingly have needed to drape his jacket over his arm to conceal the weapon, lest he be stopped or challenged.

Scalice, who is a specialist in latent fingerprints, commented that the gun had none of Foster's prints though it was found in his hand and under conditions that Scalice said were ideal for leaving prints.

Scalice and Santucci accepted the idea that in any case "freak things" can happen. They were incredulous, however, that there were so many involving the gun alone: It could not be identified by Foster's family as having been owned by Foster; it was an antique gun made from the parts of two or more weapons with no less than two serial numbers traceable to 1913; it had only two bullets in its cylinder (one spent, the other unfired), yet no matching ammunition could be found in the Foster homes; it was found, unusually, in his hand, yet with none of his fingerprints and no blood visible on the barrel; no one heard the gunshot; and the powder burns on Foster's hands challenged the idea that he even fired the weapon.

ACCORDING TO the detectives, the small amount of blood observed at the scene raised the possibility that Foster had been dead before the shot was fired. The failure to find physical evidence on the vegetation around the body (specifically on the ground above the head)—such as blood, bone, and brain tissue—was inconsistent with a suicide at that location. The detectives noted that assuming Foster sat on the berm and fired the shot, blowing an exit wound out the back of his skull, a "jet stream" of blood and other matter would have sprayed the vegetation above where the head was thrown back.

Scalice noted that in cases like this the blood sometimes flows out the exit wound like a river, forming pools. Other times it explodes in a mistlike form, falling as little droplets. In either case, the blood should have been apparent—especially to observers there while it was still daylight.

Dr. Haut, the medical examiner on the scene, told FBI investigators he did not see any blood on the vegetation. The Park Police report specifically stated "there was no blood spatter [sic] on the plants or trees surrounding the decedent's head."[32] Of statements taken from approximately twenty officials at the scene that night, none contain any mention of blood being observed on the vegetation around the body.

Dr. Haut also told the FBI that when Foster's body was rolled over, he observed that a small amount of blood had matted or congealed around the exit wound. To Scalice and Santucci this was an indication that the wound could have been covered or bandaged if and when the body was moved.

For instance, an FBI forensic analysis for the Fiske probe of blood patterns on Foster's face observable from a crime-scene Polaroid showed that Foster's head assumed several positions after death—again inconsistent with the manner of death and the position in which the body was found. A careful examination of the FBI and Fiske reports indicates that Foster's head assumed several positions after instant death:[33]

- First position: The lab report found a bloodstain on Foster's right cheek presumably from having come in contact with his blood-soaked shirt shoulder.
- Second position: The Fiske report stated Foster's head had been tilted slightly to the right, explaining the right lateral blood tracks from the nose and mouth.
- Third position: The FBI lab report noted blood from Foster's right nostril running up the face—against gravity—to the right temple area above his ear. Therefore, Fiske concluded, Foster's head had to have been tilted backward slightly as it lay on a 45-degree slope.

- Fourth position: Finally, the Polaroid shows Foster's face perfectly "straight up" as the Fiske report states.

Fiske admits the head "moved or was moved" after being in contact with the blood-soaked shoulder. He endorsed his pathology panel's opinion that the "rightward tilt of his face was changed to a forward orientation by one of the early observers before the scene photographs were taken," perhaps an emergency worker checking the carotid artery.

This all sounds plausible, except that none of the rescuers acknowledged moving the head. One claimed he checked the carotid artery on the left side of the neck. But it is hard to believe a simple check of the pulse could move Foster's head as far right as possible, placing his jaw in full contact with the bloodied shirt as the stain on the jaw indicates. Nor is it easy to believe that after moving the head, accidentally or otherwise, the rescuer repositioned the head by moving it to its final, straight-up position. Even if a rescuer had moved the head twice, that still does not account for several movements of the head or the blood track from the right nostril to the area above the ear, particularly since Foster was lying feet downward on the side of a hill.

There are two possibilities suggested by these movements: Either someone moved Foster's head several times at the site where he was found, or he suffered a gunshot elsewhere and the body was subsequently moved there. Some have suggested that at the instant of death Foster's neck may have "contorted" several times. Changes in orientation of the head appear to have taken place well after death. After all, it took some time for Foster's shirt to have become blood-soaked, enabling it to stain the right side of his face.

In his report Fiske never cited key evidence that typically can rule out the movement of a body: lividity. Lividity, as Geberth writes in his *Practical Homicide Investigation,* is caused by "the pooling and settling of blood . . . from the effect of gravity." This becomes important for detectives because it leaves a purplish color on portions of the skin on which blood settles. Thus, if one dies lying on his or her back, lividity should be observed on his or her back. If the body was turned over or moved after death, additional marks might appear on the face, legs, and front of the body.

If Foster had been moved, lividity marks may well have indicated that. The Park Police report notes only that police detectives observed signs of lividity after a detective lifted both of Foster's arms. Since Foster was fully dressed, it is unclear where these lividity marks were observed.

According to Scalice, a proper interpretation of the lividity marks would have necessitated undressing Foster and examining parts of his lower body at the death scene before the body was removed to the morgue—which could add still more lividity marks. There was no sign that the Park Police carefully probed for lividity marks at the death scene.

Fiske was obviously unwilling to consider that the body had been moved, even though there was other forensic evidence pointing to this possibility: Foster's shoes were found by the FBI lab not to have a speck of soil on them.[34] FBI lab reports made no mention of grass stains on the shoes, which typically should be apparent even without the aid of sophisticated equipment.

Fiske theorized that Foster walked almost eight hundred feet through grass and brush—more than the length of two football fields—then climbed down the side of the berm and shot himself. As for the absence of soil or grass stains on the shoes, Fiske explained that the hot, dry weather, coupled with the fact that the "foliage leading up to and around Foster's body was dense," explained the absence of soil. He did not address the issue of the grass stains.[35]

If Foster had walked to the second cannon (or the first cannon for that matter), the first foot trail he would have come upon after exiting the parking lot was a dirt one (see map). It is over a hundred feet long and leads to the park's main clearing. As he entered that clearing, he would then have had to traverse a grassy expanse and, upon coming to the northwest part of the park, would have crossed terrain that had less grass and large areas of exposed soil. Obviously, there was ample opportunity for Foster's shoes to become scuffed with both soil and grass stains if he had walked some 770 feet to the second cannon as Fiske suggests.

When conducting their crime-scene examination at Fort Marcy Park, the detectives had a man of Foster's weight and height test-walk three pairs of shoes similar to Foster's on the path he supposedly took. Two pairs were walked from the parking lot to where the body was said to have been found, at the second cannon. One pair was test-walked just in the immediate area of the body's officially designated location. When these shoes were subsequently tested in Dr. Saferstein's laboratory, significant amounts of soil were found on all of them. Detectives also pointed out that soil and grass stains should have been visible to the naked eye on the shoes' soles.

In an apparent preemptive bid to rebut this solid evidence that Foster had not walked in the park, the Fiske report stated that the FBI had found tiny sandlike mica particles on Foster's shoes and socks. Fiske contended this was evidence that he walked through the park, since the soil there is micaceous. Fiske failed to mention that the FBI also found the mica on Foster's clothing. How did he get those tiny flecks of mica—with the absence of soil—on his clothing?[36]

The former New York homicide experts discovered that Fort Marcy's soil is so very micaceous that minute mica particles are constantly blown around the park. These mica flecks even cover much of the foliage and vegetation, so much so that one can hold a leaf up to the sun and see the sparkling mica. Investigators concluded that the mica traces, rather than proving Fiske's claim that Foster walked to the site, instead indicated that Foster's body had come in contact with vegetation in the park, covered as it is with mica particles. Had Foster not walked through the park, and his body simply placed there on top of the mica-laden foliage (which the remaining Polaroids depict), the investigators concluded, mica particles would have been found on Foster's shoes, socks, and the rest of his clothing, just as the FBI laboratory did find them.

Although there were no soil or grass stains, the FBI laboratory did find some other strange evidence not found in Fiske's official report. An

FBI trace analysis of Foster's clothing found "blonde to light brown head hairs" dissimilar to Foster's. The FBI lab also found six different colors of carpet fibers: white, tan, gray, blue, red, and green. These fibers were found on almost every article of Foster's clothing, including his underwear. Pink wool fibers were found on his T-shirt, socks, and shoes. The laboratory gave no explanation as to the probable origin of these hairs and fibers and, of course, neither did Fiske in his report.

Later, when questions arose about those fibers, Fiske's investigators speculated that they came to be found on his clothing because Foster had walked across carpets at his home and office. Presumably the fibers clung to his shoes and socks. After his death, the Park Police claimed that they had mixed all of Foster's clothing in the same evidence bag. But that explanation collapsed when it was discovered that Foster's suit jacket and tie were found in his car and bagged separately. Yet they, too, had carpet fibers all over them.[37]

Scalice suggested that in the absence of any evidence that Foster was alive outside of the White House complex, the logical place for investigators to begin their probe of possible foul play would have been where the person was last seen alive. Scalice pointed out that Foster's clothing was in contact either with a single carpet with several colors, such as an oriental rug, or with more than one carpet. Fiske's team admitted failing to take the elementary step of comparing the carpet fibers to those at Foster's home and office. A professional investigation, Scalice suggested, "would involve a check not just of White House office carpets, but all carpets in the complex—including those in the residence quarters of the White House." Checking White House carpets at this late stage would be difficult. Since Foster's death, the living quarters and the State floor have undergone extensive renovations and redecoration, including several carpet changes.

On the State floor, the Blue Room was completely redone, and in February 1995 Mrs. Clinton opened it to the press. The New York Times reported, "Mrs. Clinton said that she had had a 'great deal of fun' while involved in the traditional work of replacing fading drapes and worn carpets in the oval-shaped space."[38] In spite of the changes, all rugs, because of their historical value, should have been preserved in one of several secret federal warehouses in the Washington area. As I reported in a March 7, 1994, *New York Post* article, Park Police had failed to suction Foster's clothing and car for fibers and hair, which might have established his previous whereabouts. They also failed to test his shoes for material residues like soil and grass stains.

The FBI laboratory also found semen in Foster's underwear.[39] While no explanation for this was given by Fiske, a subsequent FBI report not released to the public stated that the four-inch stain on the front, inside part of the shorts was consistent with spontaneous ejaculation at death, though they could not conclusively rule out that the stain came as the result of a sexual encounter. An apparent urine stain on the underwear went untested.

New York experts found the carpet fibers to be critical proof that Foster's clothing, if not his body, had obviously been in contact with carpeting at some recent time that day. Concerning this, Scalice's comment was simple but unassailable: Fort Marcy Park is not carpeted. Fiske's report is silent as to how these fibers came to be found on Foster's clothing.

Park Police had not tested the clothes for fibers and were apparently unaware of their existence. There were other clues among the physical evidence that showed the death site did not comport with the manner of death. The first person to find Foster's body, CW, the Confidential Witness, told the FBI of having seen trampled vegetation on the pathway below Foster's body. Park Police said that none of the vegetation was disturbed when they arrived. If CW's statement is accurate, it contradicts Park Police who say there was no sign either that a struggle took place or that other persons had been to the scene who might have helped to move the body.

Park Police readily admit they found Foster's eyeglasses some nineteen feet from his head, or thirteen feet beyond his shoes. Their position relative to the body meant the glasses had to have been propelled forward from Foster's head, down the berm, across the trough at the bottom of the berm, and several feet up the side of another, smaller revetment. Fiske concluded simply that "the glasses bounced down the hill" through dense foliage.

Forensic scientist Saferstein, former head of the New Jersey State Crime Lab who examined the death scene along with the two homicide detectives, said this scenario would have been impossible without suspending the laws of physics. The Park Police, meanwhile, have speculated that Foster, in perhaps the last act of a desperate suicide, threw his glasses away before he shot himself. However, the FBI laboratory found gunpowder on the glasses, very strong evidence that they were near to the head when the shot was fired. Park Police continue to propose this explanation despite forensic evidence that proves their theory wrong. (In October 1996 the A&E network aired a documentary on Foster's death using the baseless Park Police explanation to rebut skeptics who point to the glasses as evidence of a problem.)

If the eyeglasses did get nineteen feet away by natural means, Scalice and Santucci concluded, the crime scene must have been tampered with. Certainly after the gunshot, the glasses could have been ajar or even thrown from Foster's head, but not nineteen feet through the knee-high, dense vegetation.

Even after the release of Scalice and Santucci's report, more evidence continued to emerge that the story of Foster's final hours was much more complicated than the Park Police and others would have us believe.

The official story hangs largely on the accepted idea that Foster had lunch at his desk—cheeseburger, fries, and a Coke—and immediately left the White House at 1:00 P.M., meeting no one, and drove to his final destination at Fort Marcy.

There are problems with that scenario. For instance, the first witness to have found Foster's body told the FBI he saw what appeared to be a purple-colored wine stain on Foster's white dress shirt near the right chest area.[40] A source close to the Starr probe told me this purple-colored stain—patently not blood—was evident on Foster's shirt and had never been tested by the FBI laboratory. Yet the Park Police and Fiske's report never mention this purple stain. Where did it come from?

Why did Fiske not ask the FBI laboratory to analyze and test this evidence that was so obviously inconsistent with the publicly known facts of the case?

Another problem concerns Foster's briefcase. As probably much of America knows, an alleged suicide note was discovered days after his death, at the bottom of a briefcase he had left in his office.

However, Fiske's investigators were aware of evidence that Foster left his office with a briefcase and that a briefcase was found by the Park Police in Foster's Honda at Fort Marcy. Investigators have ignored such information while specifically asserting in official reports that Foster left his office with no briefcase. Why have the investigators done this? The official story says Foster met with no one on his last day and no briefcase was found in the car or anywhere else at the Fort Marcy crime scene.

The Fiske report states on page twenty-six that Foster left his office that afternoon "without a briefcase." When Miquel Rodriguez, the lead prosecutor for the new independent counsel, Kenneth Starr, began reviewing the Foster case, he was astounded at that conclusion. For one thing, an aide in the counsel's office, Thomas Castleton, told the FBI in 1994 that he had observed Foster carrying a briefcase when he left the office that day.[41] (Oddly, Castleton's FBI statement was missing from the files handed over to the Senate Banking Committee for its investigation, though part of Castleton's account is mentioned in the Fiske report. Fiske's omission of Castleton's statement was not an isolated occurrence. More than a half dozen FBI statements from officials who could shed light on disputed matters, and who were interviewed during the Fiske investigation, were not turned over to the Senate committee.)

Castleton's earlier statement to the Park Police, on July 22, 1993, omits any mention of a briefcase. Interestingly, in the Park Police interview with one of the counsel office secretaries, Linda Tripp, which came immediately after Castleton's on July 22, 1993, the Park Police report notes: "Ms. Tripp was absolutely certain that Mr. Foster did not carry anything in the way of a briefcase, bag, umbrella, etc. . . . out of the office."[42] Why would she volunteer such information unless prompted by the Park Police to counteract Castleton's account?

Tripp's out-of-context statement to the Park Police that she saw no briefcase, along with Castleton's statement to the FBI in 1994 that he had in fact seen one, raises the possibility that Castleton told the Park Police of this briefcase in his July 1993 interview with them—an observation that was then simply omitted from his official police statement.

Park Police had good reason to emphasize Tripp's account, especially in light of the glaring problem with the Park Police reports. Their evidence reports did not indicate any briefcase had been in Foster's Honda, even though subsequent investigators for Starr found, in the FBI statements compiled for Fiske, several accounts by witnesses who saw a briefcase on the seat of the car. (Apparently this was a different briefcase than the satchel-like case found in Foster's office.)

For example, motorist Patrick Knowlton, the first to spot what Fiske identified as Foster's car in the lot, at about 4:30 P.M., told Fiske's FBI agents that he "observed in this Honda a leather briefcase or leather folder on the passenger-side seat."[43]

Lead paramedic George Gonzalez also told the FBI that upon returning to the lot from the Foster death scene he looked in the Honda and saw "a necktie, suit coat, and a black briefcase/attache case." (Significantly, Gonzalez made this observation after the police had arrived at Fort Marcy.)[44]

During grand jury proceedings by Starr and his staff in 1995, four officials confirmed that they had sighted the briefcase after the Park Police arrived, according to a source close to the probe. The police have steadfastly denied the existence of the briefcase. A Park Police photo of Foster's Honda, when enhanced by prosecutor Rodriguez, shows a black briefcase lying on the ground, near the car. During grand jury testimony, the police said it was a crime-scene carrying case. However, Park Police carrying cases are tan or silver, not black.[45]

At times the Park Police explanation about crime-scene evidence—particularly evidence that indicates Foster did not go to the park to kill himself—appears fantastic. Take, for example, the Park Police account of how they found Foster's car keys, an account that was dissected by Hugh Sprunt, a Texas accountant and Stanford Law graduate who wrote a comprehensive white paper called the *Citizen's Independent Report*. The Fiske report implies Foster's car keys were found in his pockets at the park, but here is what really happened.

According to police, Foster's clothing was initially searched for identification and for a piece of paper, specifically a suicide note. Both Braun and Christina Hodakievic, a Park Police officer, told the FBI they had observed lead Park Police investigator Rolla carefully checking all of Foster's pockets. As Rolla testified in his Senate deposition: "I searched his pants pockets. I couldn't find a wallet or nothing in his pants pockets."[46]

The Park Police also searched Foster's Honda. No keys were found, though on the passenger seat they found personal papers, and his wallet was inside the suit jacket, which lay on the car seat.

Where were the keys, then? Curiously, that question aroused no suspicion on the part of the Park Police. This is especially strange since they assumed that Foster drove to the Park and shot himself. Did the police begin another search for car keys around the body and on the pathway to the death scene, especially after having found his eyeglasses so far from his body? No. By several accounts, Foster's car was locked. Police and EMT personnel tried to enter it because of the matching suit jacket visible inside, but could not. (This, by the way, might have been another violation of proper police procedure. The car should have been dusted for fingerprints before Park Police and others began attempting to open it, much less later when they started rummaging through it. Senior investigator Braun explained in a Senate deposition in the summer of 1994, "We didn't see any reason to do that," because of what she termed the obviousness of the suicide.[47])

At about 8:20 P.M. Fairfax County rescue personnel put the body on a gurney and wheeled it across an uneven terrain to a waiting ambulance. From there the body was to be taken to the morgue at Fairfax Hospital in Falls Church, Virginia.

Park Police explain that only after the body had left the park did they become concerned about the keys. Instead of conducting a tedious "hands and knees" search of the area in which the body was found, some police apparently began having doubts about Rolla's initial search of the clothing. So Braun and Rolla left the scene and drove to the morgue for another search of the pockets. Braun says that at the morgue she checked Foster's right-front pocket and found not just a set of car keys but two rings of keys: the car keys on one and another holding four door and cabinet keys.[48]

Park Police have given conflicting testimony as to when they arrived at the hospital. But a Fairfax Hospital nurse, speaking on condition of anonymity, said that she had dealings with all the officials present that night, and she was "certain" that two White House officials, apparently Craig Livingstone and William Kennedy, arrived before the Park Police, presumably Braun and Rolla, showed up to search Foster's pockets.[49] Livingstone, in a deposition to Senate investigators, claimed he never came into contact with Foster's body and only viewed it from behind an observation window.

Homicide expert Vincent Scalice said the entire episode sounded "fishy."

"Without [even] putting your hand in the front pocket, two sets of keys should have been bulging" on the outside, he said.

AUTHORITIES WOULD have had an easier time ruling out foul play had they been able to account for Foster's time on the last day of his life. But a considerable amount of that time—almost five hours—has been totally, and quite inexplicably, unaccounted for.

Fiske and the Park Police tried to gloss over this significant gap by suggesting Foster died anytime from 1:00 P.M., when he left his office, until shortly before his body was discovered at almost 6:00 P.M. Dr. Beyer's autopsy never established a time of death.

The autopsy does give us clues, however, based on the digestive process. One way of determining the time of death is by ascertaining the stage of digestion and comparing that to the last time the deceased had eaten.

According to the Park Police report, Dr. Beyer examined the stomach contents and informed the Park Police that Foster had "eaten . . . 2–3 hours prior to death." Beyer could still discern that Foster "had eaten a 'large' meal," which Beyer thought "might have been meat and potatoes."[50]

If we accept the White House claim that Foster consumed a cheese-burger, fries, and a Coke close to 1:00 P.M. and that this was "the large meal" that Beyer found in the stomach, Beyer's interpretation means that Foster died between 3:00 and 4:00 that afternoon. This two- to three-hour lag between the time Foster left the White House and the time of death is also problematic, since no one had observed Foster during that period.

There are indications, too, that Foster may have died later than the 3:00 to 4:00 P.M. time frame the lunch-in-the-office scenario suggests. For one thing, Foster's Honda was not reported seen in the parking lot until about 4:30 P.M. On a typical weekday a steady flow of cars moves in and out of Fort Marcy's lot, not to mention maintenance, police, and other such vehicles that routinely pass through.

Another indication that Foster may have died closer to the time officials found his body at 6:15 P.M. was that when Park Police removed the gun from his hand later that evening, they noted his hand was still flexible without evidence of rigor mortis. This stiffening of the body usually begins to set in two to four hours after death.

A review of statements by officials at the crime scene that evening shows that earlier witnesses, such as those who first came upon the body, saw less blood on Foster's clothing than did later witnesses. As the evening progressed, still more blood appeared on Foster's shirt, a sign that blood was still draining from the wounds after the police arrived at the scene. As the Park Police report itself noted, the "blood . . . appeared to still be wet." Indeed, some earlier witnesses said the blood still appeared wet near the mouth and nose.[51]

Two other issues remain unexplained. First is the whereabouts of Vince Foster's appointment schedule. Fiske accepted White House assurances that Foster kept an appointment schedule only on his office computer, and the one turned over by the White House to investigators showed sparse appointments. Foster's secretary Deborah Gorham stated in a Senate deposition that Foster had a written one, but inexplicably stopped using it just before his death, opting to use the computerized one exclusively. Later, Starr's employees found the computer calendar incompatible with Foster's busy routine. Some dates on the printout of that calendar had blanks for whole days. Why would a superlawyer like Foster, going from meeting to meeting, not have a personal appointment calendar? Obviously he could not carry his computer with him in case he had to mark a date.

Second, there is an unexplained aspect of the crime scene that both the Park Police and Fiske's team knew was completely inconsistent with the official suicide version: Visible on the front-right side of Foster's starched white shirt was a purplish, wine-colored stain that was patently not blood. According to the White House account, Foster did not have wine or anything like it for lunch. Where did the stain come from? Could it have come from a drink Foster had someplace else, with persons unknown? Could it have been a sign of a struggle?

There are no indications that Foster had lunch or met anyone in the White House personal quarters after he left his office for the last time. Had this occurred, he should have been logged in to the residence by the Secret Service at the ground floor entrance.

Noteworthy, however, is the White House "Memorandum for All Executive Residence Staff." This memo is dated, coincidentally, on the day of Foster's death and addresses the subject of "the privacy of the First Family." The memo, sent by Deputy Chief of Staff Roy Neel, reminded staff working within the residence that "discussions by staff members of the first family's personal activities of any kind, or any other matter which breaches their privacy, with anyone outside of the immediate staff is prohibited."[52] The policies outlined in the memo are long-standing ones, and such a memo, according to staff, is usually distributed at the very beginning of the administration, not six months into it as was the case here.

White House interference in the case started almost immediately. For example, Vince Foster's beeper was turned over to White House officials the very night of his death. Lost was any opportunity to test it for fingerprints or to recall the last few messages Foster received. There is contro-versy surrounding the beeper, a Motorola Bravo model. Park Police investigators said that it was found on his body in the off position, but a police officer at the scene that night told me privately in January 1994 that it was, in fact, on the seat of Foster's car. (Curiously, none of the FBI statements of paramedics at the scene mention any beeper on Foster's belt, where the police claim it was found.)

Lost, too, was the opportunity to forensically examine Foster's per-sonal papers, jottings, and wallet items, all of which were turned over to the White House the following day. There was unseemly and so far unexplained urgency in White House demands for that evidence, even to the point of prompting the Park Police to contemplate breaking into a locker for it. Rolla said he had stored the evidence in his locker at Park Police headquarters in Washington before going home early in the morn-ing following Foster's death. When other headquarters' personnel could not open that locker they were ready to break into it, until Rolla directed them, from his home, to a key he had left in his briefcase.

Confusion reigned at the White House from the very beginning. For example, a confidential Secret Service memo prepared at 10:01 P.M. on the night of Foster's death states that "on the evening of 7/20/93, unknown time, U.S. Park Police discovered the body of Vincent Foster in his car. The car was parked in the Ft. Marcy area of Va. near the G[eorge] W[ashington] Parkway. Mr. Foster apparently died of a self-inflicted gunshot wound to the head. A .38 caliber revolver was found in the car."[53]

Secret Service spokesmen explain that the memo was just a mistake. But fanning the flames of controversy is the account of Arkansas state trooper Roger Perry, who has stated in an affidavit his lawyer prepared for members of the press in 1995 that while guarding the Arkansas gov-ernor's mansion in Little Rock on the evening of Foster's death he received a call from Helen Dickey, who asked to speak with Governor Jim Guy Tucker.

Dickey, the nanny for Chelsea Clinton, informed Perry that Foster had killed himself. "She told me that Vince got off work, went out to his car in the parking lot, and shot himself in the head." Perry says he assumed Dickey meant Foster shot himself in the White House parking lot. It is easy to see how Perry may have misunderstood Dickey's statement in this way. A more conspicuous mystery is how the Secret Service got the facts so wrong on such a significant issue and, as we will see, the wide variance between the time Perry was notified and the time the White House claimed it knew of the death. Dickey has since denied Perry's account.

ANOTHER QUESTION about Foster's whereabouts on the afternoon of July 20 centers on widely circulated reports that Foster shared an apartment in the Washington area with several close friends from Arkansas. In March 1994, during the Fiske investigation, the rumor first gained notoriety when a prestigious financial newsletter, *Johnson Smick International*, claimed that Senator Daniel Patrick Moynihan's office was putting out a story that Foster had died in that apartment, or "safe house." The apartment, according to the newsletter, was a place used by Clinton's senior staff to "war game long term problems without the normal distractions of the West Wing." The White House denied the report. Still, documents from the Fiske investigation show that investigators did next to nothing to query Foster's friends and colleagues about this story, or to establish his whereabouts on the afternoon of his death, and no further information was developed on the issue.

On so many points of inquiry, the Park Police, as well as later investigators, were unwilling to conduct a by-the-book death investigation. The Park Police, having quickly and uncritically accepted the notion that the death was a suicide, never conducted a homicide inquiry as police procedure demands. The snap judgment of suicide seemed to carry over into all aspects of the inquiry, including those that usually act as a check on police judgment, such as the autopsy procedure. Indeed, every component of the official investigation seemed to be guided not by procedure, but by politics.

5

To the public and much of the press, the autopsy conducted on July 21, 1993, stands as the cornerstone of the conclusion that Vince Foster committed suicide. However, an examination of the coroner's work reveals that this significant component of the death investigation was compromised, beginning with White House involvement in its scheduling.

Lead Park Police investigator John Rolla knocked off work at about 6:30 that Wednesday morning. Before he left for home, he called the medical examiner, Dr. James Beyer, to schedule the autopsy for Thursday, the following day. This would give him, as well as others present at the scene, time to sleep and to attend the autopsy, in accordance with standing procedures. In his Senate deposition of July 1994, Rolla explained why Park Police procedures require this: "There may be questions, you like to explain the scene, and the doctor likes to hear besides reading the report and looking at the photographs. He can explain things if you have questions."[1]

Upon Rolla's departure, Sergeant Robert Rule of the Park Police assumed responsibility for following up on the autopsy and other crime-scene matters. Rule testified that the White House pulled "strings" to have the autopsy time moved up.[2] Considering that the autopsy took place at 10:00 Wednesday morning, just hours after Rolla had scheduled it for the following day, they were pulling pretty hard.

Rolla later explained to Senate investigators the type of influence the White House had over a process that should have been dictated solely by the police and their procedures: "If you are in the White House . . . , I would suspect they would say, 'no, we want it [the autopsy] done today, push everybody else back.' They want it, they would get it."[3]

Rule called Rolla at home to inform him of the change but Rolla was exhausted and decided not to go. No one else from the scene was asked to go. Rule; Park Police detective James Morrissette; and two identification technicians, Wayne Johnson and Shelly Hill, attended the autopsy. The technicians' role was to preserve evidence such as Foster's clothing.

Conducting the autopsy that morning was Dr. James Beyer, the deputy medical examiner for Northern Virginia. Since Foster's body was found in Virginia, Beyer's office had jurisdiction. When police arrived at the autopsy room, Dr. Beyer was being assisted by an unidentified male. When Sergeant Rule asked Beyer the name of his assistant, Beyer snapped at him, "You are dealing with me here, you don't need his name."

In January 1994, before any real controversy had arisen over the case, Beyer told me that a member of the FBI, a member of the Secret Service, and, of course, Park Police were all present at the autopsy.[4] The presence of FBI and Secret Service seemed understandable, considering Foster's position and the window-dressing role the bureau played in the office matter and interviews at the White House. But both the FBI and Secret Service have subsequently contradicted Beyer's claim that their agents were present. (The bureau has also said none of their agents were present at Fort Marcy on the night of the death.)

Beyer, who had just turned seventy-five in June, had been a doctor since 1946. He established the coroner's office for the Northern Virginia district in 1971 and had been there ever since. Before that, he had served in the army as a pathologist for some fourteen years. He had passed the forensic pathology exam in 1970. He is fond of saying he lost count of the autopsies he conducted after twenty thousand. A humorless man, he has been described by a Park Police officer as "all business."[5]

Beyer had also been a longtime lecturer for the FBI at their academy in Quantico, Virginia. He taught there for over a decade and consulted for the FBI on various matters. He has also served as a consultant to the Pentagon.[6] Yet despite Beyer's excellent credentials and long experience, there were problems in the conduct of the autopsy.

In addition to the absence of any police investigators who had observed the death scene, Dr. Beyer started the autopsy even before the four Park Police officers arrived at his office. Beyer had already stripped the body of its clothes, washed it, and removed Foster's tongue and tissue from his soft palate.[7]

The presence of investigators was particularly important because Beyer had not inspected the crime scene himself.[8] (Dr. Donald Haut, the Fairfax County medical examiner, did visit the death scene during the police investigation. Haut's role was merely to declare Foster dead. Haut has no standing as a forensic pathologist since his practice is internal medicine. Despite his lack of expertise and the fact that Haut offered no official conclusion of suicide, he has been cited by the Fiske inquiry as confirming the suicide verdict, as well as by respected media such as 60 Minutes.) Without the benefit of a police investigator or a trained pathologist who had examined the death scene, Beyer's knowledge of the circumstances of the death was necessarily limited. So limited, in fact, that Beyer admits he never knew the caliber of the gun found in Foster's hand, even though his autopsy report specifically asks for such information. Although Beyer has asserted that the information is not important,[9] several prominent pathologists disagreed with Beyer's assertions, including Dr. Michael Baden, the former chief medical examiner for the City of New York. Baden suggested that in a case of this sort a pathologist should inspect the scene to see if bloodstains and other patterns are consistent with the apparent cause and place of death. He also said that a pathologist would want to know the weapon's caliber to see if it is consistent with the wounds, even more so when the bullet has not been recovered.

Beyer's autopsy report was almost generic for a suicide by gunshot to the mouth. An entry wound was noted at the very back of Foster's mouth just above the oropharynx, or throat. The bullet trajectory was upward and backward, cutting through the brain and exiting three inches below the crown of the head, at the midline of the skull. The exiting bullet, Beyer noted, had created a large, jagged exit wound one inch by one and a quarter inches. As is typical with such wounds, the exiting bullet created a skull fracture, its line looping around the back of the skull. Beyer also noted heavy concentrations of gunpowder soot on Foster's right and left index fingers. Other notations indicated Foster was a healthy male, who also had a stomach full of partially digested food.

Beyer's autopsy report never states the manner of death as "suicide." Cause of death is simply identified as "perforating [meaning the bullet entered and exited the head] gunshot wound mouth-head." During our first interview, Dr. Beyer said that he did not rule the death a suicide since, according to Virginia law, that determination is made by local police, with the autopsy considered as one factor. Although he told me he believed the death "consistent with a self-inflicted gunshot wound," that statement also does not appear in his autopsy report.

During Senate hearings in 1994, Beyer was emphatic that he had in fact ruled the death a suicide. No doubt it would have been awkward to say otherwise, especially since the Park Police had been telling the press that the autopsy report had drawn this conclusion. The Park Police relied heavily on Beyer's report as did Special Counsel Fiske, in reaffirming that conclusion, even though there are several serious problems with Beyer's autopsy.

Detective Morrissette's report on the autopsy states that Dr. Beyer found no gunpowder on Foster's tongue, though residue was found on the soft palate.[10] This anomaly baffled the Park Police. Typically when a gun is fired in the mouth several things are expected: thick quantities of gunpowder around or inside the wound itself, gunpowder soot on the tongue, broken teeth, and blow-back of blood and tissue from the wound onto the gun itself. Yet there was no powder on the tongue, Foster's teeth had not been broken, and the gun appeared clean.

As these problems surfaced in early 1994, the Park Police revised its theory about exactly how Vincent Foster died. Instead of claiming he had actually placed the gun in his mouth, they conjectured that he simply opened his mouth and pointed it in.[11] But experts had difficulty with that scenario: If Foster had fired the gun with the barrel outside of his mouth, gunpowder stippling would have dotted his face, with the blast leaving burn marks and damage to his lips.

There was another alternative: Dr. DiMaio told me that powder might not get onto the tongue if the "barrel is jammed really tight against the palate."[12] In that case, the powder soot would be found largely inside the wound. (Fiske would later adopt this theory, though this explanation still did not explain the absence of teeth damage or blow-back.)

In addition, some homicide detectives posited that another—or different—gun was used, possibly a smaller caliber weapon than the .38 found in Foster's hand. However, if a .22 caliber semiautomatic pistol was used, it would have created a much smaller exit wound than the one noted on Beyer's autopsy report. Indeed, there is evidence that the exit wound *was* smaller than notated on Beyer's autopsy.

As previously noted, Corey Ashford, the Fairfax EMT worker who put Foster's body in a body bag, did not remember seeing an exit wound despite having taken Foster by his shoulders while cradling his head in his arms.

Before Ashford placed Foster's corpse in the body bag, records show that at least two other individuals examined the exit wound, after the body had been rolled over and before it left Fort Marcy. One was Dr. Haut, the medical examiner. Haut's 1994 statement to Fiske's FBI investigators, oddly, offers few details about the nature and location of the exit wound. He said "the volume of blood was small," and the blood at the back of the head "was matted and clotted." Haut did say the exit wound was "consistent with a low-velocity weapon." According to his statement, Haut "recalled a separate case in which a .25 caliber rifle caused a much more devastating wound to the victim."[13]

The other examiner of the wound, John Rolla, was asked by Senate investigators why bone fragments had not been found under the body from the exit wound blowout. He testified that "the size of the exit wound is not large and bone fragments would be tiny." He then detailed how he examined the wound: "I probed [Foster's] head and there was no big hole there. There was no big blowout. There weren't brains running all over the place. There was blood in there. There was a mushy spot." So small was the exit wound, Rolla recalled, "I initially thought the bullet might still be in his head."[14]

As noted in a previous chapter, Fiske wrongly stated in his 1994 report that when the body was rolled over, Dr. Haut and Rolla observed a "large exit wound."[15] Other testimony that could shed light on the nature of the exit wound seems to have been carefully omitted in some interview statements compiled in the Fiske and Starr probes.

For example, the last person to observe the exit wound that night, before Beyer's autopsy, was Dr. Julian Orenstein, then an attending physician in the emergency room of Fairfax Hospital when Foster's body was brought in to be officially declared dead. Orenstein made a cursory review of the front of Foster's body. The body was then moved to the hospital morgue. According to Orenstein's witness statement given to Fiske's FBI investigators in April 1994, upon learning that Foster was a White House official he decided to examine the exit wound. In the morgue, with the help of Fairfax County police officer David Tipton, Orenstein lifted Foster's body "to locate and observe the exit wound on the decedent's head." But the statement conspicuously fails to include any details as to what Orenstein saw.[16]

FBI investigators again interviewed Orenstein in 1995 in the course of the Starr reexamination of the Foster death probe conducted under Fiske. That statement has yet to be released, but I have reviewed it. Once again, it offers no details of what Orenstein saw at the back of Foster's head. Why was this critical information not found in two separate FBI statements?

Beyer had noted a wound toward the back of Foster's head—typical of a suicide of this type. Park Police, in their report, adopted the phrase "up and out" to describe the bullet trajectory. Had the exit wound been lower, say, at the lower back of the head or even lower at the neck, this would have been unusual for suicide and strong evidence that the Park Police were wrong in their original conclusion of suicide. The Park Police know that when a suicide "eats the gun" as this type of death is sometimes referred to, the suicide typically fires "up" into his brain to ensure death.

The vexing inconsistencies with the exit wound were further compounded when a longtime friend of Foster's, Joe Purvis, was interviewed in March 1994. Purvis had grown up with Foster in Hope, and like Foster became a prominent Little Rock attorney. At the time of Foster's death, Purvis publicly expressed doubts about the suicide. He now says in hindsight that Foster was depressed.

But at that time just after the death, Purvis found the suicide difficult to accept and took the time to speak with one of the morticians, a friend of Purvis's, at Little Rock's Reubel's Funeral Home. Foster's body had been waked there. Purvis said the mortician had confirmed the gunshot wounds, describing the entrance as a "neat little" hole deep in the back of the mouth. The exit wound, Purvis related, was similarly sized—he took his index finger and thumb and separated them about the width of a dime and said it was found in the "neck"—gesturing to the very base of his own skull.[17]

Purvis found this reassuring, when in fact it is alarming. The autopsy and Park Police report had not been released at this point, though the Park Police said the bullet had gone "up and out," exiting at the top, back portion of Foster's head. Though the autopsy had not yet been released, Purvis had described the entry wound just as it was. His description of the exit wound was obviously at variance with the autopsy report.

As this book was going to press, startling, confirming evidence surfaced supporting the conclusion that there was, indeed, an exit wound at the back of the neck. Just days after Kenneth Starr filed his final report on Foster's death, researcher Hugh Sprunt, at the National Archives, discovered the never released report of the medical examiner on the scene, Dr. Donald Haut. On page two of the report, dated July 20, 1993, Dr. Haut's own narrative summary clearly states that he found Foster dead of a "self-inflicted gunshot wound *mouth to neck*," meaning the bullet entered the mouth and exited the neck. The finding of the neck wound is consistent with certain testimony, including that of emergency worker Corey Ashford who saw no exit wound at the top back of the head when he cradled it in his arms. The finding of an exit wound in the back of the neck is also inconsistent with suicide, and according to experts would be significant evidence pointing to foul play. There should be no doubt as to where the exit wound was located.

The controversy could have been put to rest by a careful examination of the autopsy X-rays. In a section on the report that asks "X-rays made," Beyer checked "yes." He later told the FBI agents working for Fiske that the machine, although new, was inoperable. (Reed Irvine, chairman of Accuracy in Media, had a tape-recorded conversation with Jessie Poor of Atlantic X-Rays, the Virginia firm that maintains Beyer's machine. Poor told Irvine, after checking his company's records, that the machine was new and had been installed in June 1993. It did not need servicing until October of that year, and then only for a minor adjustment, he said.) Beyer said he could have taken X-rays but that would have meant transporting the body to another facility. He claims he checked "yes" for the X-rays before he had even begun the autopsy as a matter of habit.[18]

During Senate hearings in 1994, Beyer seemed at a loss to explain the Park Police report filed by attending Park Police detective Morrissette. The report states: "Dr. Byer [sic] stated that X-rays indicated that there was no evidence of bullet fragments in the head."[19]

Lacking X-rays, the evidence of the wounds and any other trauma to Foster's skull—any blow that, for example, might have incapacitated him before the shot was fired—largely consists of the simple notations made by Dr. Beyer on a piece of paper. If X-rays were taken and since destroyed, there are several reasons why officials might have done so. For one, the X-rays may have shown that the exit wound was small and lower on the back of the head—inconsistent with an up-and-out exit wound caused by a .38. Another possibility is that the X-rays shed light on the neck wound that paramedic Richard Arthur stated he observed on Foster's neck at Fort Marcy.

An autopsy profile photo shows metal rods sticking out of Foster's mouth and another rod said to be sticking out of an exit wound from the top of the back of the head. But experts say that this is insufficient. Dr. Donald Reay, the medical examiner for Seattle, one of a team of pathologists who reviewed the autopsy and the accompanying photos for Fiske, told London's *Telegraph* he did not remember seeing any clear, direct photograph of the exit wound.[20]

Still another vexing problem turned up by the autopsy report was the laboratory analysis of Foster's blood and urine specimens taken by Beyer during his procedure. The Virginia state lab analyzed the blood by employing several drug screens, including one to check for antidepressants. The lab report stated that on all screens, no drugs had been detected.[21]

These findings, which the Park Police clearly had when they wrote their final report, did not comport with their statement that Foster's doctor had prescribed "an anti-depressant drug and one tablet was consumed by Mr. Foster on the evening before his death."[22]

There is another problem with the blood analysis report as pointed out by several homicide experts. One piece of evidence cited by the police and Beyer was that there were no signs of a struggle on the body. The blood and urine analysis also showed, they said, that no drugs had been used to incapacitate or kill him first. That was only half true. The lab report showed Foster's blood and urine had been examined for the most generic types of narcotics—Valium, cocaine, antidepressants, and barbiturates—but not any rarer knockout type drugs. "In a case like this," homicide expert Geberth explained, "I'd want to test for all sorts of drugs that normally would not be looked for."

The other evidence showing there were no signs of a struggle was Dr. Beyer's own examination of the body. But other "suicide" cases in recent years that Beyer has ruled on have raised serious questions about Beyer's propensity to carefully notate such signs. (See Appendix IV.)

Beyer's autopsy work on Foster took about an hour.[23] The procedure ended with the taking of irretrievable evidence, such as clips of Foster's hair. Beyer also took fingerprints of the corpse, but these turned out to be unusable for comparison purposes, which later became a major problem when the government revealed it had no set of Foster's fingerprints on file.[24]

The Park Police present at the autopsy were also there to ensure the proper collection of physical evidence such as Foster's clothing. Despite having four Park Police officers present, including two technicians who were there simply to collect and preserve evidence, the police later said that they violated one of the most basic procedures by mixing all of Foster's clothing, including bloodied and nonbloodied items, into the same evidence bag.[25] This lapse allowed for cross-contamination of critical trace evidence and, as Fiske's team later suggested, explained the FBI lab's finding of carpet fibers on many of Foster's garments.[26]

This explanation became the out for both the Park Police and Fiske's team: The police had not missed any suspicious evidence, and Fiske's people did not have to be troubled to find out where the fibers came from. The FBI could later claim that fibers of six different colors came upon Foster's shoes and socks from walking across carpets and, because of the Park Police's improper handling of evidence, were soon to be found all over his outer clothing and underwear.

The "cross-contamination" explanation fell flat when other reports were scrutinized. Foster's jacket and tie, which were found in his car, were bagged separately and sent directly to the Park Police labs without going to the coroner. They were submitted to the FBI lab in a separate bag and apparently had not been cross-contaminated. The FBI found that Foster's jacket and tie also had carpet fibers of various colors on them. Further, no one could explain how not a speck of soil or grass would stick to Foster's shoes while carpet fibers did attach themselves to his shoes and socks and lower portions of his pants.

The Park Police have also made much of a detail so trifling that it was never mentioned in the autopsy or the Park Police report itself: an impression or indentation that was found on Foster's right thumb. This, the police said, was an "artifact" left on his body, proving conclusively that Foster had depressed the Colt's trigger with his thumb. This "evidence" was so significant that numerous press accounts have mentioned it and was important enough to be detailed during a 60 Minutes segment on the case. Correspondent Mike Wallace stated that the "forensic evidence showed . . . Foster's thumb had pulled the trigger." Wallace quoted Republican Congressman William Clinger: "The most critical picture again for me is the indentation on his thumb because this particular weapon recoils in a way that puts an indentation on your thumb."

Leading pathologists have told me they were surprised that such an indentation would be represented as key evidence. "I would not call it on that," Dr. DiMaio explained. He said it is "virtually impossible" to find an indentation on the thumb from a single depression of the trigger. In fact, DiMaio had never heard of such a case.[27] Other leading pathologists agreed. "Try it yourself," Dr. Charles Petty, former chief medical examiner of Dallas, suggested. He explained the skin's resilience would make any indentation from a single moment on the trigger impossible to see, even at the moment of death.

"You are no more likely to see it than you would find an imprint of the steering wheel on the hand of someone who died in a car accident," Petty said.[28]

Even if the gun had been placed in Foster's hand and fired by someone else, it is improbable that such an indentation would remain, says Dr. Richard Mason. "You might get a bruise from the recoil, but not an imprint," Mason said.[29] So how did the indentation get there?

One explanation is that the heavy Colt—about two pounds—was lying in contact with Foster's hand and thumb for some hours before it was removed by police. DiMaio said that acids from the corpse "sweat" or "rust the skin," particularly on a hot day like Foster's last. "The acids can actually dissolve metal, which can impregnate themselves in the hand," DiMaio continued.[30] The ABC News Polaroid taken at the scene shows Foster's right hand around the gun, with his thumb inserted in the trigger guard.

It seems the autopsy itself did not prove that Foster killed himself. Indeed, it raised more questions than it answered. This critical procedure was compromised first by White House interference in its scheduling, by the fact that no scene officials were present, and by the fact that Dr. Beyer began his postmortem without waiting for the police so that they might testify to the integrity of the process from start to finish.

The procedure was unbelievably slipshod and incomplete. No attempt was made to determine even a proximate time of death. Critical X-rays are missing. Despite having four Park Police present to help preserve physical evidence, the police claim they violated basic procedure by mixing Foster's clothing in the same evidence bag, cross-contaminating the garments. Even the irretrievable fingerprints were not taken properly. The toxicology test—a key component of the overall autopsy— never tested for exotic drugs. On the screens it did conduct, no drugs were found in Foster's blood, though the police asserted that Foster had taken an antidepressant before his death.

Perhaps the major fault of the autopsy procedure was its apparent haste. Records state that the autopsy commenced at about 10:00 that morning and lasted about one hour—until 11:00. As Dr. Michael Baden writes in his book *Unnatural Death*, "It takes about two hours to do an uncomplicated autopsy on a person who died of a stroke or heart attack. Bullet wounds take longer."

This autopsy—the cornerstone of any death inquiry—was no cornerstone at all.

6

On the night of Foster's death, Bill Clinton was doing nothing unusual. He was in Washington at the White House and, for a critical part of the evening, under the careful scrutiny of millions of Americans. That Tuesday Bill Clinton was appearing live, by remote, from the White House Library on CNN's *Larry King Live*.

Clinton had been a frequent guest of King's during the presidential campaign, and King began his program that night explaining why Clinton was on: "Good evening. Back in Louisville, about three days before the election, President Clinton said on this program, 'I'll come on every six months.' This is the six-month anniversary. The timing is perfect. Tonight is six months in office for Clinton-Gore."[1]

Clinton went on at 9:00 P.M. EST. By that time it was almost three hours after Park Police had found Foster's body just miles from the White House. It was a half hour after the time the White House Secret Service claims it was apprised by the Park Police of Foster's death (though there was evidence they were notified earlier).

99

King, an incisive questioner, interviewed Clinton on a range of political and business issues. They discussed Clinton's faltering economic plan then before Congress, his tax policies, the controversial administration plan on gays in the military, and Clinton's decision to fire FBI director William Sessions the day before.

"Was it hard to fire Mr. Sessions?" King asked.

"It was not hard," Clinton quickly responded, then added, "but it was sad for me."

Clinton went on to praise the FBI. "I love the FBI, and I hated to be the first president ever to have to fire a director." Clinton blamed Sessions, saying he had "refused to resign." This, Clinton said, left him "no choice." But the statement was only half true.[2] Sessions had refused to resign until a replacement had been confirmed by the Senate, allowing for an orderly transfer of FBI power. Having sacked Sessions, however, the FBI would have no permanent director for another six weeks when the full Senate confirmed Louis Freeh as FBI director.

King also talked with Clinton about lighter issues, asking the president if he had seen that summer's blockbuster Clint Eastwood film, *In the Line of Fire.*

In the Line of Fire was an action-packed film about a veteran Secret Service agent played by Clint Eastwood, whose life had been about dedication and sacrifice—to the point of giving his own life—for the president of the United States. Clinton had watched the film the night before with his Arkansas friends Webster Hubbell and Bruce Lindsey. Clinton had invited Foster, but Foster said he was too busy.

"Yes, I watched it last night," Clinton said somewhat excitedly. "I think it was as realistic as it could be and still be a rip-roaring thriller."

Meanwhile, early in the show—no later than 9:15 P.M.—and apparently unbeknownst to Clinton and King, aides close to the president were being informed of Foster's death.

"Soon after the [King] show began, we were pulled from the staff room, where . . . [Chief of Staff Mack] McLarty was informed of this— that it was an unconfirmed report," Mark Gearan, White House communications director, explained to the press the day after Foster's death. Still, the president was not notified because, Gearan continued, "in the intervening fifty or so minutes, efforts were made to both confirm and to make preliminary calls. . . ."

Confirmation, Gearan said, came at 9:55 P.M., and only then was Clinton told. By then Clinton was finishing his first hour with King and had even offered to stay on for an additional half hour, when McLarty interrupted during a break to indicate there was a problem.[3]

The task of telling Clinton fell to McLarty, a childhood friend of Foster and Clinton from Hope, Arkansas. Just off the show, Clinton asked, "What is it? It's not Hillary or Chelsea." McLarty remained mum, according to Newsweek, until he had escorted Clinton to the White House elevator and up to the residence quarters. Once there, McLarty told him of Foster's death. "Oh no," the president cried out.[4]

All of this made for great drama. But did events, in fact, unfold as White House officials have claimed? There is compelling evidence suggesting that key White House aides knew hours before 10:00 P.M. that Foster was dead, and that the president himself may have known before he went on King's program.

What the White House knew, when they knew it, and what they did about it are questions still in need of definitive answers. According to conflicting accounts, the White House was notified of Foster's death at some point between 7:00 and 8:30 P.M. of the day the body was found. Why the conflict over such a simple point?

One reason, perhaps, is that White House officials were more concerned about Foster's office than even the known evidence indicates and wanted to ensure that any searches of, or changes to, his office appeared to have occurred before anyone knew that he was dead. On that point it is important to note that the Park Police never did seal Foster's office that night. And, oddly, an intruder alarm was turned off in the counsel's suite just after 7:00 P.M., several hours before anyone claimed to have first entered Foster's office.[5]

The so-called time-line problem is one of the most critical aspects of the Foster controversy. If the White House knew about the death earlier than claimed, then a concerted effort has been made to conceal that fact.

The White House said that the Secret Service was initially notified of the death by Park Police at 8:30 P.M.—just as Park Police were wrapping up their inquiry at Fort Marcy—and that key presidential aides were only told after the president went on the *Larry King Live* show at 9:00 P.M. The White House had also maintained that the president himself was not informed until about 10:00 P.M., when the show ended, some four hours after the Park Police first discovered Foster's body in Fort Marcy Park shortly after 6:00 P.M.

The Park Police have said that only late in the investigation that night did they realize Foster was a White House official. Some independent investigators found that hard to believe. Prosecutor Miquel Rodriguez, for one, was bothered by evidence—an FBI statement from a member of the SWAT team—that officers associated with the Park Police special forces, or SWAT team, were in the park within forty-five minutes of police finding the body. Neither the Park Police nor Fiske has ever accounted for the presence of these officers. As Park Police spokesman Major Hines explained, the SWAT team is "involved in sensitive duties." For instance, it works closely with White House security.[6]

Records show that the Park Police presented an innocuous but contradictory story about notification of the death to the White House. A number of these contradictions were first brought to light in the reports of Ambrose Evans-Pritchard, chief U.S. correspondent for London's *Sunday Telegraph*. Pritchard first reported that senior police investigator Cheryl Braun told the FBI that she searched Foster's Honda at about 7:00 P.M. and found his White House identification in the car, at which point she asked a Lieutenant Watson to call Lieutenant Gavin, the shift commander on duty that night. The officer apparently failed to do so. Braun's FBI statement says she called Gavin between 7:30 and 7:45 P.M.[7]

Gavin told Fiske's investigators that, upon learning of Foster's identity, he called the White House within ten minutes, making his call no later than 8:00 P.M. The Secret Service says it was notified at 8:30 P.M., leaving an unexplained gap of at least half an hour; it then took an additional forty-five minutes or longer to notify presidential aides.

There are a number of inconsistencies in Park Police accounts of the notification. For one thing, Gavin claimed that it was investigator Rolla, not Braun, who notified him of Foster's death. Rolla, for his part, gave still another account that completely contradicts Braun and Gavin. In both his FBI statement and a sworn deposition before the Senate Banking Committee in July 1994, Rolla testified that he, not Braun, searched Foster's Honda and that it was much later in the evening, closer to 8:30 P.M.—after the body had been removed to the ambulance and the death scene cleared—that he found Foster's White House identification.

Completely contradicting all of these accounts are the statements of Fairfax County emergency workers. FBI statements indicate they knew before they left the park at 6:40 P.M. that Foster worked at the White House.

Although Braun and Rolla gave conflicting accounts as to when they found Foster's White House identification in his suit jacket, both indicated they found it at 7:00 P.M. or later, well after the Fairfax paramedics and fire personnel had returned to their fire station. Yet paramedic Richard Arthur told the FBI that when he returned to the parking lot from the death scene before 6:40 P.M., he saw Park Police "gaining access to a cream-colored car with a suit jacket and tie in it, looking for identification of some sort."

By 7:00 P.M.—when Braun stated she was just entering Foster's car—the Fairfax rescuers had just returned to McLean's Station 1. Fairfax Lieutenant William Bianchi was at the station to greet them. Bianchi told the FBI agents who were working for Fiske that some of the paramedics were talking about the "strange incident" and he "also heard from the returning [Fairfax] personnel that the victim was deceased and had been employed at the White House." Bianchi, according to his statement, had this confirmed by the ranking fire department officer who had been at the scene, Lieutenant James Iacone. Bianchi's FBI statement continues, "In particular, Iacone already knew that the victim had been employed at the White House when he returned to Station 1. When Bianchi learned that the victim was a White House employee, he instructed Hall and Iacone to make their reports on the incident very detailed."[8]

Also telling were the contemporaneous handwritten notes made by investigator Rolla on the night of the death. They indicate that early in the evening, perhaps earlier than 7:00, after ascertaining Foster's Arkansas address from the Honda's license plate, Rolla called Lieutenant Danny Walters of the U.S. Secret Service at the White House and obtained Foster's Washington address.[9]

Even more stunning evidence was gathered by Fiske's investigators that never made its way into the Fiske report or was even shared with Congress.

Toward the end of the Fiske investigation in 1994, a young female makeup artist working for CNN came forward to say that she had prepared the president for his appearance on Larry King's show that night. She told the Fiske investigators that just before the air time of 9:00 P.M. she was preparing the president in the White House Map Room just across from the Library where the show was being broadcast. At that point, she said, an unidentified male, whom she presumed to be an aide, notified Clinton that a note or document had been found in Foster's office. She clearly saw the president acknowledge the remark.

Fiske could claim that this stunning information dealt with matters relating to Foster's office and that it need not be included in his report on Foster's death. Still, the Fiske report gives a detailed chronology of events before and after Foster's death, including the official account of the Park Police's notification to the White House. Fiske offered no evidence that contradicted the official version. The source close to the Starr probe that told me of the makeup artist's declaration to Fiske's investigators believed the Fiske inquiry had good reason to hide this statement—because it could blow the whole death case wide open. If the White House was not telling the truth on such a seemingly simple matter, why should they be believed about anything else? Fiske was apparently more interested in closing the case. The woman's testimony was significant on at least two counts. First, it contradicted White House claims that no aides entered Foster's office before 10:00 P.M. Second, it suggested the president knew of Foster's death an hour before he said he knew, in light of all the evidence. Third, it meant he was in fact aware of efforts to search Foster's office.[10] Fiske took the young woman's account seriously enough to have her view photographs of White House aides, but she was unable to identify the aide involved.

There were additional grounds to believe the White House knew about Foster's death much earlier than has been previously acknowledged. Arkansas state troopers Roger Perry and Larry Patterson have said in sworn statements that they knew of Foster's death well before the White House. Trooper Perry was at the governor's mansion in Arkansas when he received the call from Chelsea Clinton's nanny, Helen Dickey. Dickey has claimed that she learned of Foster's death from a White House doorman and quickly confirmed it by speaking with the president in the White House residence. She then called Arkansas's governor, Jim Guy Tucker, and his wife to notify them of Foster's death. Trooper Perry was answering the phone that evening when Dickey, whom Perry knew, called. Dickey's call came from the White House no later than 8:00 P.M. Washington time, but likely much earlier that evening. This would mean that Perry and, of course, Dickey knew of the death before the Secret Service and some of the president's closest aides.[11]

Since serious questions were raised about the credibility of the troopers following their public allegations about Governor Bill Clinton's infidelities, many journalists have dismissed their claims. Others, such as *Blood Sport* author James Stewart, have described the troopers as credible. As it relates to their learning of Foster's death, the troopers have offered some extremely provocative accounts that should have warranted further inquiry by Fiske and Starr.

If, after being questioned on these matters by the FBI or queried under oath before a grand jury, they were found to be lying or misleading, the troopers would be subject to criminal prosecution. In the course of his inquiry Fiske never questioned them about the death. Starr's investigators were concerned enough to question Perry and Patterson about Dickey's call, as I discuss in a later chapter, but the troopers claimed these investigators tried to get them to change their story to fit into the official account offered by the White House and endorsed by Fiske. The troopers were never put before a grand jury and questioned about their account, which seriously challenges the official version.

Perry stated that after receiving Dickey's call he immediately called Patterson and his attorney, Lynn Davis, both of whom have signed affidavits giving some curious testimony. Patterson avowed that he had just arrived home following his normal routine—no later than 5:00 P.M. Arkansas time, 6:00 P.M. Washington time—when his phone rang. Perry, according to Patterson's affidavit, "advised me that . . . Helen Dickey had telephonically contacted him and advised him that Vincent Foster . . . had gotten off work and had gone to his car in the parking lot and had shot himself in the head." If Patterson's memory is accurate, he learned of Vince Foster's death fifteen minutes before the body was found by police at Fort Marcy Park.[12]

Davis has given a similar account, stating that he already knew about the death sometime during the afternoon rush hour in Arkansas, which would have placed that notification well before 8:30 P.M.[13] Presidential aides Bruce Lindsey and Mack McLarty said they were not notified until after 9:00 P.M. Yet there is evidence that three White House aides—David Watkins, Bill Burton, and Craig Livingstone, the White House personnel security chief who resigned under pressure for having inappropriately requested sensitive FBI background files—knew of Foster's death before 8:30 P.M.

David Watkins was at a movie theater in Georgetown when he was paged with the news of Foster's death. The *New York Post* reported in 1996 that Watkins was paged by the White House military communications office just after 7:00 P.M.[14] Watkins had testified before the Senate Whitewater Committee in the summer of 1995 that he contacted Patsy Thomasson at 10:30 P.M. and asked her to search Foster's office. "I asked her [Thomasson] to look for a note. . . . I also knew that the Park Police had been in touch with the Secret Service for some five hours prior to making that request . . . ," placing the Secret Service contact before the time of the body's discovery.[15]

Livingstone was among the first to be notified after the Park Police called the White House, which by their own accounts meant around 8:00 P.M. Lieutenant Gavin has stated that Deputy Chief of Staff Burton called him back within five to ten minutes of Gavin's call to the White House.

WHEN PARK Police investigators Braun and Rolla found the keys in Foster's pocket at the hospital, their work for the night was far from over. The always difficult task of notifying the family fell to them as well. After retrieving the keys in the hospital's morgue shortly after 9:00 P.M., they set off for Foster's home at 3027 Cambridge Place in Georgetown.

En route they received a mobile phone call instructing them to pick up David Watkins at his home. Watkins was a presidential assistant for management and administration. They did so, and Watkins's wife trailed behind driving their own car. The White House, which by everyone's account had been consulted by this point, thought Watkins's presence would be appropriate since he had grown up with Foster in Hope.

Arriving at the Foster home, Braun, Rolla, Watkins, and his wife found Foster's sisters, Sharon and Sheila, standing outside with Webster Hubbell. They had been notified by the White House and were awaiting the arrival of Park Police. Apparently the group thought it best not to enter the house until the Park Police arrived.

Sheila Foster Anthony worked in the Department of Justice in Washington, D.C. Foster's other sister, Sharon Foster Bowman, had arrived in Washington from Arkansas that day for a planned family gathering. Foster had even made plans to take his niece, Mary Bowman, to lunch with him at the White House the following day. At the time of his death, his sister Sheila worked in the Department of Justice's Congressional Liaison Office as a political appointee. She had first been appointed to work with Secretary of Commerce Ron Brown, but the two did not get along, according to an associate of Sheila's. Sheila spoke directly with President Clinton to rectify her situation, and Clinton moved her to the Justice

Department. Sheila's husband, Beryl Anthony, a Washington lobbyist and former Arkansas congressman, was a close friend of Bill Clinton's.

The somber group moved up the steps of the Fosters' small Georgetown townhouse and Rolla rang the bell. Foster's daughter Laura let them in. As the group shuffled into the tiny foyer, Laura yelled to her mother to come to the door. Lisa was upstairs and hurried down, clad in a bathrobe. When she got to the bottom of the stairs, Rolla gave her the news directly: "Mrs. Foster, your husband, Vincent, is dead."

Senator Richard Shelby, a soft-spoken then-Democrat from Alabama, lived next door. He later told me that he heard a scream around that time and went to his window. He thought someone may have been undergoing a mugging.

Rolla recounted that Lisa "kind of collapsed on the steps and was hysterical." Mrs. Watkins came from behind the officers to comfort her. When Rolla explained that Foster had killed himself, Lisa asked, apparently referring to the gun, "Did he put it in his mouth?"[16]

Rolla told Senate investigators he thought her question was "very unusual." Lisa later told the New Yorker that she asked the question after she was reminded that her husband had recently watched the video of A Few Good Men, in which one of the characters commits suicide by placing a gun in his mouth. Lisa remembered protesting that Rolla must have been in error. "I said, 'No, no, that's my son Vincent,'" thinking her son had died in a car accident.[17]

As Rolla accompanied Mrs. Foster into the living room, he hoped to gently ask her a "basic set of questions," which might help explain the suicide. But she was too distraught.

Meanwhile, Cheryl Braun was trying to get information from one of Foster's sisters, Sheila Anthony. But Webster Hubbell intervened at that point, Rolla said. He "didn't say 'excuse me' or nothing," said Rolla, "just pushed [Braun] out of the way, and that was that."[18] Braun, a rather diminutive blonde, was no match for the hulking six-foot-five Hubbell. Hubbell, then the third-ranking member of the Justice Department, spent most of his time at the Foster home talking into his mobile phone.

Braun had tried developing a rapport with Mrs. Foster, but she would not respond. Rolla had slightly better luck, but her distraught condition and the constant flow of friends and neighbors who were now pouring in prevented any real information gathering. Turning to friends and family, Rolla asked a number of people if they noticed any signs of depression. " 'Did you see this coming?' " he recalled asking. " 'Were there any signs? Has he been taking any medication?' No. All negative answers."[19]

Within an hour or so, Secret Service entered the house. The president had arrived. He went to hug Mrs. Foster, and Rolla noted his eyes were "red and watery." Under the gaze of all present, Clinton sat down on the sofa next to Mrs. Foster and began speaking softly.

Before leaving, Braun informed Watkins that Foster's White House office needed to be secured. "He said that he would have that done," Braun testified. Rolla told Watkins he would need more information, and the police would be in contact with the family.

UNBEKNOWNST TO Braun and Rolla, and despite Watkins's assurance, Foster's office was not secured that night. Instead of seeing to this vital matter themselves, Park Police had relied on Watkins to instruct the Secret Service to protect what should have, at the time, struck all concerned as a vital potential source of information about the death. Instead, taking place at the White House were some of the most controversial events of the Whitewater scandal.

As Bernard Nussbaum tells it, he arrived at the White House sometime after 9:00 P.M. His pager had gone off while he was at Galileo's, a Washington restaurant. There, he and his wife and two friends were celebrating the "two home runs" he had hit that day: the apparent successful nominations of Louis Freeh as head of the FBI and Ruth Bader Ginsburg as justice of the Supreme Court.

After being told of Foster's death by White House communications director Mark Gearan, he abruptly left and went to the White House, where he found some of the aides weeping. Gearan told him that the president, who was still on *Larry King Live,* had yet to be informed. Since the program was not yet over, Nussbaum decided to go to the White House counsel's suite of offices located on the second floor of the West Wing.

According to reports, Nussbaum thought it wise to notify staff members by phone before they heard the news through the media; he also thought he should take a peek in Foster's office to see if there was a suicide note.

The cramped pair of offices in the counsel's suite, his and Foster's, was the center of the "little law firm" as he called it, comprised of twelve White House lawyers. The Clintons had picked Nussbaum for good reason: He was considered one of the best litigators in the country; his aggressive style earned him high respect among his peers in the New York bar.

Equally important, Nussbaum could be trusted. He had met Hillary when they both worked on the House Judiciary Committee, which was then investigating the Watergate scandal, and he had known both the Clintons for years. Given his background, many wondered about his actions on that night and the following days, which would plunge the Clintons further into scandal and lead to his own fall from grace and eventual resignation.

Nussbaum's own account is innocent enough. As he entered the counsel's suite of offices to make the calls, he noticed the door to Foster's office open and the light on, unusual for that time of night. Looking in, he saw Patsy Thomasson, then director of White House administration, sitting behind Foster's desk.

Nussbaum barely knew Thomasson, who was one of the Arkansas circle with long-standing ties to the Clintons. Thomasson, too, was looking for a suicide note, she told Nussbaum.

With Thomasson was Mrs. Clinton's chief of staff Maggie Williams. Nussbaum knew her well, since Mrs. Clinton's office was just a few doors down from his own. Williams, an African-American woman, had worked on the Clinton campaign and had been a senior staff member at the Children's Defense Fund, a private organization on whose board Mrs.

Clinton had sat for many years. At the moment, she was slumped on Foster's sofa, weeping.

Nussbaum said he joined Thomasson in a cursory search of the desktop and desk drawers, but they came up empty. In all, he said the search took less than ten minutes. However, a Park Police report of an interview with him just two days after Foster's death noted that Mr. Nussbaum stated that the office search with Patsy Thomasson lasted from 2200 to 2400 hours. Nussbaum's first account—the two-hour, not ten-minute, search—is consistent with the alarm logs for the counsel's suite. Nussbaum said the three left together, closing the office door and flipping the light switch. He then busied himself with those phone calls of notification.[20]

That harmless-sounding account stood until the Senate hearings on these events two years later, in the summer of 1995, at which time discrepancies were uncovered.

Patsy Thomasson said in Senate testimony that she and Nussbaum entered Foster's unsecured office at the same time, whereupon she commenced a quick search for a suicide note. "I sat at Vince's desk, opened the drawers to the desk. . . . I looked in the top of his briefcase." When Nussbaum entered, rather than joining her search, she remembered his pacing the office, his hands running through the puffy white hair on the sides of his head.

She recalled that after a few minutes Nussbaum left, at which point Maggie Williams came in and sat down on the sofa. According to Thomasson's testimony, Williams soon left and Nussbaum returned. "Bernie came in and said, 'We haven't found anything, so we should probably get out of there [sic],'" Thomasson recalled. "We left empty-handed."[21]

Thomasson claimed that she had gone to the office at the request of her immediate boss, David Watkins.

At the time of the summer 1995 hearings, there was speculation about Thomasson's role as a seemingly unimportant character in the Clinton administration. She was the presidential assistant in charge of certain security matters, such as overseeing White House drug testing. Despite this position, at the time of Foster's death Thomasson herself had not been issued a security clearance.

Before coming to Washington, Thomasson had been the chief operating officer of a Little Rock bond house while its owner, Dan Lasater, was serving jail time for cocaine distribution. Thomasson's name had even turned up in one Drug Enforcement Administration document detailing a passenger manifest of persons flying with Lasater from Latin America.[22]

Thomasson had enjoyed one of the choicest political appointments in the state: the all-powerful Arkansas Highway Commission, which, among other things, oversees the awarding of contracts for building and maintaining state roads. Why, of all the people who knew Foster in the White House, she was rummaging through his desk and office on the night of his death is a mystery. And why, if Thomasson and others were there for just a few minutes, do their accounts differ so dramatically on key points?

The discrepancies become even more significant with the testimony of a uniformed Secret Service officer, Henry P. O'Neill. A veteran of the uniformed division, O'Neill was detailed to the White House's West Wing on the night of Foster's death. A log showed that at 10:42 P.M. he deactivated the counsel office alarm to allow the cleaning crew to enter. Shortly afterward he entered the counsel suite, saw a light in Foster's office, and heard some noise. Later, O'Neill poked his head into Foster's office and saw a woman, apparently Thomasson, behind Foster's desk rifling through papers and files.[23] He did not question the woman, whom he didn't know, because he assumed it was Mrs. Foster looking for a suicide note.

The White House log tells us that no one was in that office from 8:04 until at least 10:42, when the alarm was turned off. This does not seem to comport with Nussbaum's account in which he stated that he left other aides and went to Foster's office because the president had still not finished on Larry King Live, which ended at 10:00 P.M.

After spotting Thomasson, O'Neill stationed himself in the hallway outside the counsel's suite. There, he testified under oath, "I saw Maggie Williams walk out of the suite and turn to the right in the direction that I was standing." He added that "she was carrying what I would describe, in her arms and hands, as folders."

Williams passed O'Neill as she walked to her own office, just two doors from the counsel's suite. Another aide passed O'Neill and mentioned to him that the woman who had just passed was Maggie Williams. O'Neill said he already knew who she was. He then observed Williams brace the folders against a cabinet with her body as she unlocked the door to her office. Seconds later, he saw her leave her office carrying nothing.[24]

In her own testimony, Williams acknowledged entering Foster's office, but only in a vain hope of somehow finding him alive. She testified, as did Nussbaum and Thomasson, that she did nothing except sit for a while on the sofa. She was emphatic: She neither touched nor removed anything from that office. "I disturbed nothing while I was there," Williams insisted under oath.[25]

O'Neill was equally emphatic that she removed those folders and insisted that he was absolutely certain it was she who carried them out. "I'm not in any doubt about it, sir," he told the Senate Banking Committee.[26]

Assuming the truth of O'Neill's testimony—and there is no apparent motive for him to lie—one can only conclude that there is serious doubt about Williams's testimony. That, in turn, would seriously undermine the testimony of the chief White House counsel and an assistant to the president as well, since it is highly improbable that Nussbaum and Thomasson would not be aware that Williams was collecting files for a purpose.

It would also strongly suggest that White House officials, despite their denials to the press and congressional investigators, were genuinely concerned about certain information in Foster's possession being revealed to the American public.

Faced with the grave appearance of high-level wrongdoing, Miss Williams volunteered to take a polygraph test about her testimony, which her lawyer claimed she passed. The White House widely disseminated those results at the time of Williams's appearance before the Senate Banking Committee. Williams took that test, according to the Senate Banking Committee Whitewater Report, after taking as many as four practice examinations with a private examiner she had hired. Williams never explained why it was necessary to take these exams prior to offering such a test with the independent counsel's office. The Senate report found that her practice examinations undermined the legitimacy of her official examination because a person who takes multiple tests increases his or her chances of fooling the polygraph machine.

Despite this glaring, unnuanced contradiction—that a veteran White House law enforcement officer unequivocally testified that he saw an official commit a certain act and that the official just as emphatically denied it—neither Fiske nor his successor, Kenneth Starr, saw fit to resolve this contradiction by seeking indictments and having the matter resolved in a court of law.

The White House later would explain that the questionable actions by aides on the night of Foster's death reflected merely the bad judgment of grieving friends looking for solace and a suicide note. But that argument makes increasingly less sense in the light of ensuing events, which seem to demonstrate that key aides and Clinton associates were making calculated decisions to protect the Clintons' interests. Their actions cannot be minimized with the argument "they did not know better" because many of the White House officials involved were highly trained attorneys who were no doubt acutely aware of the repercussions of their actions.

ON THE morning of July 21, after being apprised of the unattended death of a high-ranking government official and figuring the matter might be sensitive, Captain Charles Hume of the Park Police decided to go to the White House to search Foster's office and begin interviewing Foster's colleagues. Hume picked his best detective, Pete Markland, to head up the remaining part of the death investigation, and together they went over to the White House, just a short drive from Park Police headquarters.

Upon entering the West Wing at about 10:00 A.M., Hume was surprised to find Park Police Chief Robert Langston and Major Robert Hines already there. Though Hume had not discussed it with either of them, Langston and Hines told him they were about to meet with White House officials to brief them on the case. Furthermore, neither Hines nor Langston seemed interested in reviewing the investigation with Hume.[27]

Soon Langston and Hines went into a half-hour, closed-door meeting with David Watkins, Nussbaum, William Kennedy, Webster Hubbell, Bill Burton, George Stephanopoulos, Foster family lawyer James Hamilton, and several others. Hines, in a Senate deposition, said that during the meeting he divulged only the limited information available from the initial incident report prepared by Officer Ferstl. (Ferstl's report does not include any significant facts; it did not mention suicide, the condition of the body, or even the apparent method of death.)

Hines said he reminded all present, including Nussbaum, that the Park Police "approached all death investigations from the fact that it could be a homicide, and we needed to look closer into it and do more on-scene investigation, wait for the autopsy, and find out something about his state of mind."[28] Questions were few. Most participants were said to be in a state of shock.

Nussbaum, however, was apparently quick to take control. He told Chief Langston that the Park Police inquiry would be coordinated by the attorney general's office. Hines thought that meant the FBI would be conducting a "joint" investigation where both would participate and agree on the results.

That was not to be the case. The FBI simply reviewed some reports, spoke with investigators, and sat in on some interviews. Hines told Senate investigators that the Park Police had previously conducted joint investigations with the FBI where both agencies participated fully in the investigation, "but never like this one," where the FBI's role was that of a nonparticipating observer.[29]

Even before Nussbaum began barking commands during this conference, the White House had already started calling the shots in the Park

Police probe, beginning with the impromptu late-night entry into Foster's office.

The Park Police took this intrusion onto their turf with unusual grace. In December 1993, Park Police spokesman Major Hines told one important newspaper that he "didn't have any problem" with the entry into Foster's office because, he explained, White House officials "were in a state of shock."[30]

This "shock" among senior officials never translated into cooperation with, and deference to, police investigators in the case. Rather, White House officials were taking positive steps to hamper and control the police inquiry. For example, officials demanded that such key crime-scene evidence as Foster's beeper be turned over to the White House almost immediately. On the day after the death, White House officials were anxious to get into a Park Police evidence locker. The pattern of deliberate interference was even more apparent when, in the early morning hours on the day after the death, the White House was dictating the autopsy schedule.

Not everyone agreed with Nussbaum's strategy. Hubbell testified that during this meeting he suggested to Nussbaum that he rethink whether he should be calling the shots in the investigation. He said Nussbaum was surprised by the advice. Deputy Attorney General Heymann also testified that he warned Nussbaum some time after the meeting that it was "not acceptable" for him to be making key decisions because "a player with significant stakes in the matter cannot also be referee."

Despite the warnings and perhaps still overcome by grief, Nussbaum continued to call the shots, particularly by having the Park Police work as agents for the Justice Department. The Park Police were, and are, an agency of the Interior Department and report to the head of the National Park Service and the secretary of the interior, Bruce Babbit.

The Justice Department has its own investigative agency, the Federal Bureau of Investigation. If the Justice Department had jurisdiction to head up the inquiry, why were its investigators, the FBI, being relegated to a role as observers? As Hines stated in his deposition to Senate investigators, the FBI's strange role in this case was unprecedented.

As the Nussbaum meeting continued, and Hume and Markland waited all morning in a West Wing lounge area, another unexplained episode was taking place. The morning after the death, Secret Service officer Bruce Abbott, stationed at the West Wing's basement entrance, observed Craig Livingstone, the security aide who had identified Foster's body at the morgue the night before, walk out of an elevator after visiting the West Wing's second floor (where the counsel's office is located) carrying a briefcase. Another unidentified man with Livingstone was carrying an open box containing binders, Abbott told investigators. The Secret Service officer also told congressional investigators he remembered Livingstone passing his station four times between approximately 7:00 and 8:00 A.M. Abbott found this unusual enough to alert Park Police who later questioned Livingstone. Livingstone admitted he did carry a box of documents, but said the contents were not taken from Foster's office.[31]

Livingstone also claimed, according to a chronology he prepared for Fiske's investigators, that he arrived at the White House at 8:14 A.M. But the documents turned over to Congress in 1996 show that Livingstone arrived at the White House between 7:15 and 7:20 A.M.—consistent with Abbott's account.[32]

At around 11:00 A.M. Captain Hume of the Park Police, who was still waiting for Nussbaum, discovered Foster's office had yet to be sealed and officially requested this be done. The Park Police still had not been granted permission to enter the office.

The special briefing meeting finally broke up. As Hines and Langston left the White House, they told Hume and Markland to continue to wait until FBI agents showed up. Nussbaum then came downstairs from his offices and introduced himself, along with a woman Hume believed was Maggie Williams. Nussbaum told Hume he was waiting for officials from the Justice Department. By late morning, none had arrived. With no agents showing up, Hume himself called the FBI field office and, speaking with a supervisor, found out that none had been assigned to assist him and Markland. He was told they would be dispatched shortly.

Feeling that he and Markland did not know "what the hell is going on," they left for lunch. Since both were "brown baggers" they went back to their offices to eat and returned to the White House at about 1:00 P.M. The FBI agents also arrived, but no one seemed to be in charge, and no one knew what to do.

According to Hume's Senate deposition he telephoned Langston and said in frustration: "Chief, here we are at this point. No interviews have been conducted. We haven't gotten into the office. None of that's been done."[33]

If Nussbaum was in fact stalling the police search, why would he do so? One reason may have been that the White House wanted Foster's safe cleared first. On the morning of the death, according to a source, one of the counsel secretaries called the White House security office that safeguards all combinations.

The head of the office, Charles Easley, was out that day, leaving a female staffer to handle the matter. The counsel secretary explained to this staffer that "Bill Kennedy needed to get into Mr. Foster's safe." The aide checked Foster's file and discovered that Foster had only authorized himself to have the combination, so the aide correctly refused to give the numbers.[34] After this story was published, White House Chief of Staff Mack McLarty denied, in a lawyerly way, the very existence of a safe: "I don't think there was a safe, as I understand it. To the best of my knowledge, there was not." Meanwhile, the White House, learning the safe had several drawers, reclassified it as a "file cabinet."[35] Foster also had access to another safe in Nussbaum's office.[36]

Later that afternoon, Hume had a telephone conversation with Deputy Attorney General Philip Heymann, the number-two person at the Justice Department. Heymann said he would be handling matters as far as Justice was concerned and that he was sending two "career" Justice Department lawyers to assist Hume. He laid out to Hume how the search would be conducted and advised him to "handle this as a normal case." Hume said he testily responded, "It's not a normal case."[37]

Heymann soon found this out for himself as he and Nussbaum clashed over critical parts of the inquiry. Heymann and Nussbaum knew each other well; both were Harvard Law School graduates who had worked two decades earlier on the law review. Like Nussbaum, Heymann had also worked on the Watergate investigation. Heymann eventually resigned from the Justice Department and later made several statements questioning Reno's independence from the White House. Press reports, including one in the *Wall Street Journal,* indicated one of the serious incidents leading to his resignation dealt with Nussbaum's handling of the Foster matter.

While Hume and Markland waited, now with two FBI agents, Heymann worked out an agreement with Nussbaum. Heymann would send over two Justice Department lawyers, David Margolis and Roger C. Adams. The lawyers, with Nussbaum, would go through Foster's papers one by one, but would be allowed to review only the first page or two of each document. As Adams later said, in the absence of a suicide note it was important to investigate whether Foster killed himself because of blackmail or some other crime.[38]

Heymann did not want the Justice Department attorneys there just to make the process look kosher. Heymann, as Adams told Congress, wanted a process that was "entirely credible to us, to the investigators, and to the American public."[39] At another point he reminded Nussbaum that the case was still considered a homicide investigation. Under normal procedures it would have been, but Heymann was apparently unaware that the Park Police had already ruled that out.

MARGOLIS AND Adams arrived late that Wednesday, about 5:00 P.M. For a second time, Margolis went over details of the search procedures as Heymann and Nussbaum had agreed. They also agreed to postpone the official search for another day, until the morning of Thursday, July 22.

That Thursday morning the two lawyers, Nussbaum, the Park Police, the FBI agents, and Secret Service agents gathered in the counsel's office to begin the search. Nussbaum quickly informed Margolis that there was a "change in plans." While Nussbaum agreed to the search, he alone would examine the documents as law enforcement officers stood in the office but at a distance.

Margolis informed Nussbaum that this arrangement was unacceptable.

Associate Deputy Attorney General Margolis had been with the Justice Department since 1965 and was a seasoned hand in dealing with complex legal matters. Margolis immediately called Heymann about the change.

Heymann called Nussbaum. As Heymann recounted before the Senate Whitewater Committee: "I remember, very clearly, sitting in the deputy attorney general's conference room, picking up the phone in that very big room. I remember being very angry and very adamant and saying: 'This is a bad mistake. This is not the right way to do it. And I don't think I'm going to let Margolis and Adams stay there if you're going to do it that way, because they would have no useful function, and it would simply look like they were performing a useful function and I don't want this to happen.' "[40]

Nussbaum asked Heymann for more time before he ordered Margolis and Adams to return to Justice, saying that he first wanted to consult with others. He promised to get back to Heymann before proceeding, Heymann remembered.

Had Heymann pulled his lawyers from the White House and word of this leaked to the press, it could have proven disastrous for the White House. Nussbaum, on the other hand, clearly did not want investigators to play a meaningful role in the office search.

If what Heymann says is true, Nussbaum then played a little trick to get the best of both worlds: keeping the Justice Department lawyers, FBI agents, Secret Service, and Park Police there, but not giving them any investigative power. According to Heymann, Nussbaum did not call back and simply proceeded with the search as he wanted to undertake it.

As Heymann waited for Nussbaum's call that never came, Margolis tried once again to hold Nussbaum to the previously agreed upon arrangement. Margolis informed Nussbaum he was making "a big mistake, but it's your mistake." Margolis then added, "You know, if this were IBM . . . I would have a subpoena duces tecum returnable forthwith with these documents. . . ." He testified that Nussbaum then made a "facetious comment about 'If this were IBM rather than the White House counsel's office, a smart lawyer would have removed the documents before the subpoena ever got there.' "[41]

Adams and Margolis believed, mistakenly, that Heymann had given the green light for this unusual arrangement. Nussbaum sat down at the dead man's desk and began his search as everybody present, including Adams and Margolis, stood or sat nearby, observing.

Nussbaum alone then separated the papers into three piles: Foster's personal papers, official papers, and the Clintons' personal papers. The Park Police made no complaint, though the investigation was technically theirs. Margolis later referred to his and Adams's roles as that of "cigar store Indians." At one point, Nussbaum came upon a news clipping, but would not let investigators see it, citing executive privilege.

The Park Police and final Senate Whitewater reports noted that an FBI agent who had been sitting on the sofa for a long time got up to stretch and was scolded by one of Nussbaum's attorneys, who accused him of trying to peek at the papers.[42]

Nussbaum has testified that he had never made any agreement with Heymann or Margolis. He did admit, under questioning by Foster's former neighbor, Senator Shelby, that he had "a good long memory." Yet he could not remember his conversation with Heymann: "My memory is vague and uncertain. I have no memory of that conversation."[43] For his part, Margolis told the senators with specificity that he "was certain that day . . . that there was such an agreement and Mr. Nussbaum was aware of it."[44]

Later on the day of the search, when Heymann found out what had happened, he made another angry call to Nussbaum. "I remember saying to him, 'Bernie, are you hiding something?' And he said, 'No, Phil, I promise you we're not hiding something.' "[45]

Nussbaum has argued he did nothing wrong, that his job was to protect his client, the president. To allow law enforcement officers to review unfiltered documents would have been tantamount to waiving future rights of attorney-client and executive privilege. Nussbaum said he had never invoked any privilege because privilege is only invoked when a subpoena or court order is served.

As Nussbaum wrote, "The officers had no warrant and no basis for obtaining one." Nussbaum's actions were thus predicated on his belief that the police had no real legal right to search the decedent's office.[46]

Did Nussbaum believe a court would have denied the police a search warrant for the office in a homicide investigation of this kind? Thomas Scorza, a lecturer on legal ethics with the University of Chicago, termed Nussbaum's reasoning "nonsense." (Scorza served for ten years as a federal prosecutor with the U.S. attorney's office in Chicago, where he worked on numerous political corruption investigations. He is a Democrat and supporter of the current Chicago mayor Richard Daley.) Scorza explained that as a matter of practice in suspicious deaths, employers often allow police to search an office without a warrant. Even if one was needed, it could have easily been obtained by Park Police from a federal magistrate.[47]

No doubt Nussbaum's argument that the police had "no basis" for seeking a warrant served his client's interest. But an even more important question needed to be asked: Why were the Park Police allowing Nussbaum, a person with "significant stakes" in the matter, to dictate the terms of their investigation? Why did they not request a warrant to conduct the search themselves?

As for Nussbaum's argument that a police search would have infringed on executive privilege, Scorza said, "He should know better." Though Scorza acknowledges that the White House may have had legitimate privilege claims concerning the papers in Foster's office, this would only mean that the papers "should have been sealed, each document initialed and catalogued, and then handed over to judicial authorities for a determination."[48]

If "errors" were made during the days following Foster's death, defenders of the administration said they could be explained by the fact that White House aides were suffering from "grief" and "shock." One would think that under such circumstances, these aides would have been desirous of finding out what had happened to their friend and eager to assist the police and Justice Department investigators in any way possible. Yet they consistently seemed to make calculated decisions that stalled, stymied, or blocked a full and thorough investigation.

Nussbaum and others, including Maggie Williams and another Clinton confidante, Susan Thomases, have said that Bill and Hillary Clinton never verbalized any concern about their personal papers that were in Foster's office. Foster, as noted earlier, was working on much more than the Whitewater tax papers; he had also supervised all of their personal matters, including the creation of blind trusts for their assets.

Common sense suggests that the Clintons would be justifiably concerned about police and others rummaging through their personal papers, even if Foster's death was a suicide unrelated to his job responsibilities.

SENATE INVESTIGATORS found White House claims that the papers were of little consequence to the Clintons and their aides hard to believe. They also focused on a suspicious flurry of calls that took place early on the morning of July 22, the day Nussbaum finally agreed to the search under an agreement with Heymann but abruptly changed plans just as the search was set to start.

At 7:44 A.M. EST (6:44 Arkansas time), July 22, the day of the search, Maggie Williams called Mrs. Clinton in Little Rock at the home of her mother, Dorothy Rodham. Mrs. Clinton had been heading home on the night of Foster's death from a West Coast trip and decided to stop in Little Rock. The call lasted seven minutes.

At 7:57 EST Mrs. Clinton called Susan Thomases in Washington. The call lasted only three minutes.

Minutes later, at 8:01 A.M., Thomases paged Nussbaum. They had two conversations on the phone that morning. During the day Thomases placed nearly a dozen calls to Maggie Williams, Mrs. Clinton's White House office, the Rodham residence, and to other White House officials. Most of the calls were short—no longer than five minutes.[49]

During Senate hearings in the summer of 1995, Thomases seemed baffled by the calls. The New York superlawyer, who once ran candidate

Clinton's campaign schedule with an iron hand, was portrayed as a domineering villain in the fictional tell-all *Primary Colors*. Before the Senate committee, however, Thomases became Miss Meekness. She told senators that her calls were largely grieving ones. As for her calls to Mrs. Clinton, Thomases said the short calls were "about friends, we talked about religion, we talked about many things. Had we talked about documents I would have remembered it." Thomases said she and Mrs. Clinton "never had any conversation" dealing with Foster's papers or office.[50]

Thomases did admit that in her early morning call to Nussbaum on July 22, the subject of the office search came up. She said Nussbaum brought up the subject, mentioning the procedures he planned to employ, which she found agreeable. Nussbaum's testimony contradicted Thomases: He said *she* first raised the issue of procedures for the office search scheduled for later that morning.[51] One of Nussbaum's attorneys, Stephen Neuwirth, testified that Nussbaum told him Mrs. Clinton and Thomases were worried about investigators having "unfettered access" to Foster's office. Apparently, Nussbaum had gotten that message from Thomases.[52]

On the afternoon of the 22nd, after the police and Justice Department officials left and Nussbaum had completed his official search, a second, unofficial search of Foster's files commenced. Maggie Williams, chief of staff to the First Lady, and Nussbaum conducted a second review. Although White House lawyer Clifford Sloan testified he had little recollection of the removal of files from Foster's office that day, his own contemporaneous notes stated:

Get Maggie. Go through office. Get HRC-WJC stuff.[53]

Williams testified that on her own initiative she decided to move the Clintons' personal papers to the White House residence. Williams also stated that a series of calls with Thomases that day had nothing to do with her actions later that afternoon.[54]

Assisting Williams with the documents was Thomas Castleton, a clerk in the counsel's office. According to Castleton, "My understanding was that they contained documents of a personal and financial nature that pertained to the First Family and that they needed to be reviewed. . . . My understanding, from the conversation I had with Miss Williams, was that the First Lady would be reviewing them."[55]

Williams, with Castleton's help, brought the papers to the Clintons' quarters on the third floor of the mansion, as the White House proper is called, to be stored in a closet. The closet happened to be in the book room, which had been converted into the office of aide Carolyn Huber. Huber testified that Williams "called and said that Mrs. Clinton had asked her to call me to take her to the residence to put this box in our third floor office."[56]

During the time the papers sat in a closet in the residence, Mrs. Clinton has said that neither she nor any White House official reviewed them. On July 27, the White House said the papers were transferred to the Clintons' personal attorney Robert Barnett.

Senators seized on the fact that Thomases was logged in to the White House for six hours on July 27, the day those documents were being turned over to Barnett. The logs also showed that Thomases, Barnett, and Williams all entered and exited the living quarters within moments of each other. Thomases, for one, could not explain what she or the others were doing in the White House during those hours.[57]

ON FEBRUARY 4, 1994, the *New York Times* reported that the still-unreleased Park Police report on Foster's death detailed the investigators' belief that the suicide note was not in Foster's briefcase when originally searched. The *Times* also reported that Nussbaum had interfered in the probe by having White House attorneys sit in on Park Police interviews with aides who worked with Foster or last saw him alive. During one interview, police said Nussbaum angrily burst into the meeting demanding to know if there was any problem.

After the *Times* report, Nussbaum's own days were numbered, and he tendered his resignation in March intending to return to his lucrative New York law practice. His resignation, however, did not end the controversy.

The suspicions raised by the stymied efforts of police to search Foster's office, the contradictory and astonishingly vague recollections of aides on critical issues and conversations—Thomases had a "memory lapse" 178 times during her four days of Senate testimony—should have cast a dark shadow over the facts of Foster's death and should have raised particular interest in learning what specific materials he was working on in the days leading up to his death. The Park Police have been fairly critical about the White House handling of Foster's office, especially since questions have arisen about the police's handling of the case beginning at Fort Marcy Park. But these criticisms of White House actions never resulted in asking the logical questions. Why were the aides behaving in this way? What were they hiding? Why did Foster really die?

BY JULY 27, a full week had passed and still the police investigation had turned up no evidence of major emotional "defects" that could be a cause for suicide. Some in the White House press corps were becoming wary and even more perplexed by stories that began to surface claiming Foster was depressed and having a bad time—a complete reversal from the line Gearan and McLarty had taken at the press conference on July 21. A *Newsweek* story out that week reported that President Clinton had called Foster just before his death to cheer him up. That call had apparently slipped the president's mind: Clinton originally said he had not spoken with Foster for some time before the death.

One White House correspondent asked White House press secretary Dee Dee Myers to comment on the *Newsweek* report. The transcript that follows demonstrates that the White House initially met some real scepticism as it attempted to change its story:[58]

> *Correspondent:* Did [the President] call him to "buck him up," as *Newsweek* suggested?
>
> *Myers:* He called to talk to him, I think—a number of things. I think that he knew, as a number of people did, that Vince was having a rough time.
>
> *Correspondent:* Wait a minute. That's the first time you've said that from this platform.

Myers: No, it's not. I think what we have said in the past was that people have their ups and downs and that—

Correspondent: Well, you've acted like this was just—

Myers: No, that's not true, Brit.

Correspondent: Yes, it is true, Dee Dee.

Myers: No, it's not.

Correspondent: It is true, Dee Dee.

Another reporter: Your tone has completely changed.

Myers: Okay, I apologize. I'm sorry. It is not. Okay. Let me just try to say what I think—what I said certainly on Thursday, which was that people—there was absolutely no reason to believe that Vince was despondent, that he was in any way considering doing what happened. Nobody believed that. . . .

Another reporter: There was no indication that there was a widespread awareness at the high levels of the White House that this man was going through a particularly rough patch.

Myers: And I don't mean to change that impression.

THE PRESS effectively caught Myers in the act of changing her story. The White House was trying to do a 180-degree turn from its position that Foster was not depressed. Sarah McClendon, the White House press corps' eccentric doyenne, said the unthinkable when she remarked: "Most of the people—I bet most of the people in the United States, from what I hear—don't think it was a suicide."[59]

This change was not lost on the pundits. *New Republic* columnist Fred Barnes stated that the White House was essentially "spinning grief." Barnes found disconcerting the president's affirmations that Foster's death would remain a mystery.[60] "No one can know why things like this happen" was Clinton's first reaction to the death.[61] Speaking to reporters after Foster's funeral, Clinton said, "No one will ever know whether there was anything any of us could have done to avoid this." After news reports stated that the investigation into Foster's death would yield little results, the president stated: "I don't think we'll find out much more other than that he was deeply distressed."[62]

These presidential intuitions were somehow being imparted to the investigation itself. The week after the death, the Associated Press reported that the investigation would "not delve into why Foster apparently committed suicide," directly contravening police procedure to establish motive in a suicide. Justice Department spokesman Carl Stern told the Associated Press, "To call it an investigation conveys more than is going on here. This is not an investigation in the sense that one conducts a criminal investigation. There are no legions of FBI agents checking police blotters."[63]

At the July 27 White House press conference a reporter asked if there would be further investigation to determine motive.

Myers responded: "I think it is important to confirm, obviously, that this was a suicide and there are a number of things that would certainly—had there been a suicide note or *were one to be turned up*, something like that would confirm that [emphasis added]. . . ."[64]

Actually, the suicide note had turned up the day before this press conference. Perhaps Myers was unaware that it had "turned up," allegedly found by a White House lawyer in Foster's leather briefcase. That note, whose contents were released days later, was the peg that could complete the Park Police's psychological autopsy. Conveniently timed to squelch the growing speculation about Foster's motives, the note laid Foster's emotional disturbance largely on two matters: the travel office scandal and several *Wall Street Journal* editorials.

The circumstances in which the suicide note came to light are, to say the least, unusual. On July 26, almost a week after Foster's death and four days after the official search had been conducted by Nussbaum, junior White House lawyer Stephen Neuwirth was back in Foster's office packing the dead man's personal belongings for shipment to his family in Arkansas. He had just put two photographs in a box, he said, and decided to put the briefcase in with them. The briefcase was a soft leather satchel with two handles.

"I bent over to put it into the box," Neuwirth recounted, "and either to the left or to the right turned it so that I could fit it into the box without damaging the pictures. I don't know the exact angle at which I turned it, enough for scraps of paper to fall out as I was putting it into the box."[65]

Neuwirth collected the scraps and, noting Foster's handwriting, brought them to Nussbaum's office and laid them out on the conference table. Nussbaum quickly joined him in piecing together the twenty-seven pieces of the note, apparently torn from an 8½-by-11-inch yellow legal pad. One piece, just where a signature might have been written, was unaccountably missing.[66]

Nussbaum asked Mrs. Clinton to come into his office. She viewed the note and became distraught, leaving quickly and saying, "I can't deal with this."[67]

Nussbaum had searched the briefcase on July 22, but later stated that he did not check it too carefully.

For thirty hours the White House kept the note under wraps and did not inform the Park Police or Philip Heymann. Heymann said the White House had considered the "ridiculous" idea of not releasing the note even to the Park Police, claiming executive privilege. Finally they did release the note to the police, but not to the press.

The Park Police were apparently startled by the revelation, since they and the FBI agents present had seen Nussbaum check the briefcase. Detective Pete Markland told the Washington Post that Nussbaum had searched the briefcase not once, but twice, declaring, "It's empty." Markland told the Post that "the whole search of that office was absurd," adding that White House aides "obviously had something to hide."[68]

The Park Police turned the original note over to the FBI for fingerprint analysis and, on July 29, had a handwriting expert with the U.S. Capitol Police, Sergeant Larry Lockhart, examine the note's authenticity.

Despite their own suspicions that it had been planted in Foster's brief-case, the Park Police took a casual approach to authenticating the note. Sergeant Lockhart had never been certified as a handwriting expert, and the police used only one sample of Foster's known handwriting to make the comparison. Even Lockhart admitted that it violated his own standards, not to mention general standards, to authenticate a questioned document using only one known writing sample and to obtain such a sample—in this case, a letter written by Foster—from a family member.[69] In homicide cases, family members and other close associates are often considered suspects.

The Park Police did not seem to be bothered by other red flags. For one thing, the note suddenly surfaced just as pressure mounted for a real explanation of Foster's death. For another, it was mutilated—another technique, experts say, that forgers use to make a comparison difficult. There was no date or signature, and the missing twenty-eighth piece was just where one might have written a date or signature. Furthermore, the FBI reported that though the document had been torn into twenty-eight pieces, their lab found a smudge of a palm print, but no fingerprints, suggesting that whoever tore it up was wearing gloves.[70]

Vincent Scalice, a nationally recognized fingerprint expert who worked on the House Select Committee on Assassinations, said the FBI's findings of no fingerprints on the torn note were consistent with "someone having worn gloves." Had Foster or another person torn the note with his bare hands, there "would have been numerous latent impressions." He suggested that anyone who doubts this should try to rip a paper into twenty-eight pieces.[71]

The total lack of fingerprints is even more puzzling in light of the testimony of Philip Heymann. He stated that while at the White House initially viewing the note, "a number of pieces of the note fell down on the floor and there was a scramble to pick them up." He added that "by the time it had been reassembled, the fingerprints of everybody in the White House were on it. So if anybody wanted fingerprints, they had all the fingerprints in the world." However, as noted previously, the FBI analysis of the note reported no fingerprints were found.

During Senate hearings in 1995, Republican senators deemed the whole story suspicious and zeroed in on the fact that Nussbaum "overlooked" the torn pieces in the original search. Alaskan Republican senator Frank Murkowski tore up a note into twenty-eight pieces and placed it into the bottom of the briefcase that had been lent to him by the independent counsel's office. The demonstration made it seem implausible that all those scraps of yellow paper could simply have been overlooked when Nussbaum made his original search.

MONTHS AFTER Murkowski's demonstration, more evidence came to light undermining the White House story. In the fall of 1995, *Strategic Investment*, a widely circulated investment newsletter founded and coedited by James Dale Davidson and former *Times* of London editor Lord William Rees-Mogg, held a press conference at the Willard Hotel in Washington to announce the findings of three handwriting experts that the torn note was a forgery.

Davidson is an acquaintance of Clinton's whom, like many others, Clinton sought to cultivate. Davidson was regularly invited to inaugural balls for Clinton in Arkansas, and he donated the maximum allowable to the Clinton presidential campaign. Davidson had come to know Clinton through his participation at the New Year's Renaissance Weekend meetings in Hilton Head, South Carolina. But as allegations surfaced about Clinton after his election to the presidency, Davidson's association with Clinton quickly dissolved. More than just an investment advisory, Davidson's newsletter analyzes important political, social, and economic developments that will have a long-term impact on the economy and the nation's major institutions.

Davidson believed that Foster's death, and the apparent cover-up that took place after it, would have explosive implications. Yet he was surprised by the apathy of the American media and decided not only to publicize the issues of the case, but to examine some of the more evident problems. One such problem was the highly dubious circumstances of the discovery of the suicide note in Foster's briefcase.

In the summer of 1995, a copy of the note leaked out despite great pains to keep it from public view. Davidson asked several experts for a judgment as to its authenticity based on a photocopy of the torn note and photocopies of known writings by Foster. Such analysts prefer to base their findings on original documents, and a few declined to make a judgment. Three experts believed the copies were good enough to analyze.

"It was not just a forgery, but an obvious forgery," said one expert, Reginald Alton.[72] His credentials are impressive. For thirty years he lectured on handwriting, manuscript authentication, and forgery detection at England's Oxford University. In recent years he led a panel of experts that ruled on the challenged diaries of noted English author C. S. Lewis. His opinion has been sought by British police authorities, and he has testified in British courts about questioned documents.

Alton said the writing style did not have the characteristic ornamental "swags" found in Foster's comparison writings. The writer of the note, he said, was an "archer," someone who arches his letters. One letter in the torn note was what he called the "clincher": the letter "b" had been written with three strokes, in an artistic flourish while Foster typically wrote his "b" in one stroke.[73]

Concurring in Alton's assessment were Ronald Rice, an eighteen-year veteran of document examination who has been a consultant to the criminal unit of the Massachusetts attorney general's office, and Vincent Scalice, who, after his long tenure on the New York Police Department, spent twenty-two years as a handwriting analyst and has been hired privately by firms like Citibank and Chemical Bank to make document examinations and testify in court.

Why would someone faking such a note not mention suicide? Alton had an answer to that: Forgers often try to copy or imitate words that the person actually wrote. Alton believed the note was so disjointed because the forger had made a hodgepodge from a series of unrelated documents Foster had written.

For example, some of the first lines in the note, which could well have been taken from a legal memo Foster had written, read: "I did not knowingly violate any law or standard of conduct. No one in the White House, to my knowledge, violated any law or standard of conduct, including any action in the travel office. There was no intent to benefit any individual or specific group."

This is obviously the phrasing of a lawyer, Alton said. Later lines were more intimate, perhaps from a personal letter Foster had written: "I was not meant for the job or the spotlight of public life in Washington."

Rice agreed with this assessment, commenting that the document appeared as "an artistic forgery," wherein the author used Foster's known writings and "either drew them, used a cut-and-paste method, or used a highly sophisticated computer scanning method."

What about the fact that Lisa Foster herself said the note was authentic? Alton had an answer to that, an amusing story about a famous English poet whose wife took custody of forged papers with no doubt in her mind of their authenticity.

When I discussed these developments with Sergeant Larry Lockhart, the handwriting expert used by the Park Police, he acknowledged that the torn note was not entirely consistent with the known sample but explained that it was written by someone on medication.[74] However, Foster was not on medication at the time it was claimed he wrote the note.

The FBI's Questioned Documents Unit also validated the note in a less-than-thorough manner. Fiske originally presented the FBI with the note and, for comparison purposes, seventeen checks written by Foster, plus the sample used by the Park Police. As one of the reports shows, the unit could not make an authentication based on the checks, so it relied on the single sample previously used by the Park Police.[75]

While the FBI has no hard-and-fast rules as to how many sample documents are needed to make a comparison, the authentication was not typical of their procedures. James Lyle, former head of the FBI unit in question, told me, "If I had to come up with a minimum number of [samples] I'd want, I'd say ten."[76]

SEVERAL CONCLUSIONS seem inescapable. For one thing, the goings-on at the White House gave the appearance of hiding something that was in Foster's office. If Heymann is to be believed, Nussbaum tried to use Justice Department lawyers to give the superficial office search a stamp of approval. The presence of FBI agents, who essentially did nothing, served a similar purpose throughout the whole affair. The FBI's strange role in the original investigation explains its lack of interest in later overruling or even criticizing the Park Police during the Fiske probe.

The Park Police felt thwarted by the White House in their investigation. First they were denied immediate access to Foster's office, then denied access to his files. The White House also took the extraordinary step of insisting that White House lawyers sit in on Park Police interviews of White House personnel. The final insult was the White House's withholding the torn note for thirty hours. "I thought they should have been arrested for obstruction of justice," said one investigator familiar with the investigation.[77]

The Park Police were so alarmed by White House interference with the investigation that they appealed to their superiors in the Interior Department. Two days after the Foster note was turned over to law enforcement, Heymann received a call from the chief of staff of the secretary of the interior, Thomas Collier, stating that "the Park Police [were] very, very upset about the investigation . . . [and] that they really couldn't get the cooperation that they wanted. . . ." Heymann called the White House and "read them the riot act in unmistakable terms."[78]

The pattern of memory lapses on critical issues is also disturbing. Claims by Mrs. Clinton that she expressed no interest to aides about the personal documents in Foster's office violates common sense, especially in light of later revelations about her role in the travel office firings.

Despite the very belated Park Police criticism of the White House in the Foster office matter, the truth is that while the investigation was under way the Park Police did not assert themselves—either verbally or legally. Options open to the Park Police were numerous. They could have leaked to the press the problems they were encountering from the White House at the time. Their chief could have issued a public statement that the integrity of the police probe was threatened by White House actions. Traditional legal steps could have been taken. As legal expert Scorza noted, the police could have sought a search warrant for Foster's office, which likely would have been issued pro forma by a federal magistrate. Officials who ignored such court orders, removed and withheld documents, or otherwise interfered in the police probe could have been charged with obstruction of justice. The Park Police's conspicuous failure to take any steps on their own was just one indicator they were not really in charge of their investigation.

If pressure was used to alter normal investigative procedures by the Park Police—or, far more gravely, by the FBI—such interference with law enforcement could arguably be of much more serious concern to the public than the question of whether Foster committed suicide or was murdered.

Asked by Senate investigators whether, in an "ordinary homicide or violent-crime case," routine DNA and hair and fiber tests would have been conducted—tests that were omitted by the police in the Foster case—Peter Simonello, the veteran police officer and crime-scene technician working the case, responded tersely, "Yes."

In far more revealing testimony Simonello told Senate investigators of "general talk" among Park Police "that there was pressure, and it was usually referenced pressure from the White House, to get this thing done; let's get it wrapped up, that type of thing." Captain Charles Hume, the officer in charge of the investigation, told Simonello that he "wouldn't understand the amount of pressure that was coming down."[79]

Senate investigator: "Officer, do you believe that the White House was obstructing the course of the Park Police investigation?"

Simonello: "My opinion?"

Investigator: "Yes."

Simonello: "If it was any other investigation and what had happened, we should have had more room to investigate it, and I feel the actions that were taken there obstructed it. . . ."[80]

Critics who dismiss and even demonize those who are reluctant to accept the "official" findings in the Foster case owe it to their integrity to take this testimony seriously.

7

On January 20, 1994, Attorney General Janet Reno called a press conference to announce the selection of the "ruggedly independent" prosecutor Robert B. Fiske, Jr., to head an investigation into "whether any individuals or entities have committed a violation of any federal criminal law relating in any way to President William Jefferson Clinton's or Mrs. Hillary Rodham Clinton's relationships with (1) Madison Guaranty Savings and Loan Association, (2) Whitewater Development Corporation, or (3) Capital Management Services."[1]

Fiske's appointment was the first step in cutting through the murky layers of speculation, innuendo, and gossip to the core of the matters broadly known as "Whitewater." While Fiske did not mention Foster in his statement, it was understood that his death was one of the most profound mysteries surrounding the Clinton White House. During the press conference, he was asked point-blank about the questions connected with Foster's death and any possible link to Whitewater. Fiske replied tersely, "That will be one of the things we will be trying to find out."[2]

Fiske's appointment may be a classic example of how much influence the press can have in not only opening a criminal probe, but defining its extent. In this case, it was the conservative Washington, D.C., daily, the *Washington Times,* that drove the case.

On December 20, 1993, five months to the day after Foster's death, the *Times* reported that it had learned from Park Police sources that Whitewater documents in Foster's office had been spirited out before the Park Police could search the office.[3]* The paper also drew strong links not only between efforts by officials to prevent police from searching Foster's office and gaining access to the Whitewater papers he was said to have been working on, but also between Foster's death and improprieties conducted by a lending firm owned by former Little Rock municipal judge David Hale.

Hale, whose Capital Management Services firm provided Small Business Administration loans to companies owned by poor or disadvantaged individuals, was under federal investigation at the time of Foster's death for a series of transactions that had included a fraudulent $300,000 loan to Whitewater partner Susan McDougal. This loan was part of a bank-fraud scheme cooked up by Jim McDougal, chairman of Madison Guaranty Savings and Loan Association, involving Arkansas governor Jim Guy Tucker and McDougal's wife. Susan never paid back the loan made to her by Hale's firm, and part of her proceeds from Hale's loan were traced to the Whitewater partnership account.

Interestingly, at 1:35 P.M. on the day of Foster's death, the FBI in Little Rock obtained a warrant to raid Hale's Little Rock offices.[4] Some have speculated that the linkage between Hale, Mrs. McDougal, and the Whitewater partnership, whose tax papers Foster was working on at the time of his death, was the proximate cause of Foster's demise.

---

* On August 15, 1993, the *Washington Post* first broke the story of three aides entering Foster's office. The *Times* story of December 20, 1993, added a new facet: that Whitewater documents had been removed from the office on the night of the death.

While all of this made for intriguing speculation, there were weaknesses. For one thing, the *Washington Times*'s insinuation that the Whitewater papers in Foster's office were the primary worry of White House aides on the night of Foster's death, and after, has never been substantiated. Neither was Whitewater even mentioned in the indictment papers drawn up against Hale in September 1993 or, for that matter, in the indictment papers against the McDougals and Governor Tucker handed down by Starr's grand jury in 1995 over issues relating to bank fraud.

The all-but-forgotten Whitewater affair, first broached by the *New York Times* in 1992, might have passed forever were it not for the December 1993 coverage of the *Washington Times* and the links it was suggesting between Foster's death, the strange activities of officials in his office, and the land partnership deal. The reaction of the Clinton White House was to play dead and wait for the issue to blow over. This strategy became transparent when a letter written by James Hamilton, a Washington attorney and confidant of the president who is also the Foster family attorney, was turned over to congressional investigators nearly a year and a half later.*

Hamilton had spent many a New Year with Bill Clinton at the annual Renaissance meetings held at Hilton Head, South Carolina—a conclave of "new" Democrats and others. During the Renaissance meeting in January 1994, Clinton asked Hamilton for his counsel on the Whitewater and trooper scandals, which had just erupted. Days later, on January 5, Hamilton sent a letter of advice to Clinton.

New York Times columnist Maureen Dowd noted in late 1995 that the lessons of Watergate had not been lost on the Clinton White House. She wrote that Hamilton, who had served as counsel for the Senate committee that investigated Watergate, was telling the White House how to act "like Nixon without looking like Nixon." Watergate, she added, had

---

* On the night of Foster's death, Clinton confidant Webb Hubbell had arranged for Hamilton to represent the Foster family.[5]

provided them with a "first class, inadvertent education in the art of the cover-up."[6]

Regarding Whitewater, Hamilton advised that the scandal and investigation "must be carefully managed." He spelled out some specific points:

> The White House should say as little and produce as few documents as possible to the press.

> If politically possible, Janet Reno should stick to her guns in not appointing an independent counsel for Whitewater.

> The White House should not forget that the attorney-client privilege and executive privileges are legitimate doctrines in proper contests. . . . Bernie [Nussbaum] initially acted properly in protecting the contents of Vince's files.

> Reporters are intrigued by Vince's inexplicable death and thus continue to search for Whitewater connections.

> Because you will continue to receive reporters' questions about these matters . . . I expect that "no further comment" often will suffice.

Dowd found all of this remarkable—"Even the Nixon crowd did not stoop to asserting that questionable discussions are protected by lawyer-client privilege."[7] Many White House lawyers followed Hamilton's advice and asserted lawyer-client privilege during secret Whitewater grand jury proceedings held by Fiske and Starr. Interestingly, Dowd never mentioned Hamilton's comments on Foster's "inexplicable death," which cut right to the heart of the matter. Hamilton, who continued to represent the Foster family, was rewarded by Clinton when he was appointed to one of the prized positions on the President's Foreign Intelligence Advisory Board.[8]

Perhaps further spurred on by nagging questions about Foster's death itself, the press at this time in early 1994 seemed motivated to see some action taken to investigate the Whitewater affair. Presidential aides were unrelenting, scolding the press for harping on the matter. When Clinton's mother died early in January 1994, the administration subtly tried to use the occasion to muster public indignation against the press queries.

With a trip to eastern Europe scheduled for January 9, Clinton might reasonably have expected the spotlight to shift away from domestic squabbles. This was not to be. The very next day, January 10, 1994, a bombshell hit when New York's Democratic senator, Daniel Patrick Moynihan, called for an independent investigation of Whitewater and urged the Clintons to provide full disclosure of their involvement.

This sudden proclamation by an ally jarred White House efforts to contain the matter. By January 12, the president was thousands of miles from Washington, in Prague, but still under press siege. Even as the president insisted he had engaged in no wrongdoing, seven Democrats joined Moynihan in calling for a special counsel. On the 13th the then–Senate minority leader Robert Dole demanded the impanelment of a select committee to investigate the matter, pointing out that his Democratic colleagues had launched committee investigations eighteen times during the Reagan-Bush years.

Over the objections of his wife and Bernie Nussbaum, Clinton gave Reno the green light to appoint a special counsel. Reno then announced the formation of a three-person committee of Justice Department officials who would seek someone "ruggedly independent" to head the probe.

Following the Watergate episode, where the independence of prosecutors appointed by the Justice Department was questioned, Congress had enacted an independent counsel law allowing for a panel of impartial judges to pick the special prosecutor. The law came under congressional criticism in the early 90s because of its open-ended nature and lack of time limits, exemplified by Lawrence Walsh's Iran-contra investigation, which lasted seven years and cost taxpayers $40 million.

When the independent counsel law lapsed in December 1992, there was little interest in renewing it. Without having the law reauthorized and considering calls for immediate action, Reno took the appropriate step open to her—appointment of a special counsel.

This was the first time a special counsel would be appointed to investigate a president since Watergate, making it incumbent upon Reno to find someone like Caesar's wife, above reproach. Robert Bishop Fiske, Jr., then sixty-three, was that man—or so it seemed. One of the most prominent white-collar criminal attorneys in the nation, Fiske was a partner in the prestigious New York City firm of Davis, Polk & Wardwell. He was a seasoned federal prosecutor who had handled complex litigation. Nominated by President Ford in 1976, he served as U.S. attorney for the Southern District of New York, which included the borough of Manhattan. When Ford was defeated by Jimmy Carter in 1976, Fiske was set to resign, but New York's Senator Moynihan recommended that Carter retain this Republican prosecutor. He served almost the full four years of the Carter administration before resigning in 1980.

Fiske's Republican Party affiliation never seemed that important to him; he had no significant record of partisanship and, if anything, has been identified with the liberal wing of the Republican Party. His nominal Republicanism was, however, obviously important to the Clinton administration.

Qualifications and politics aside, Fiske was well liked. The Clinton administration must have been pleased when, just after being appointed, Fiske won praise from Senator Al D'Amato, one of the administration's sharpest critics, who said Fiske was "one of the most honorable and most skilled lawyers anywhere." The likely standard-bearer for the GOP, Senator Bob Dole, also hailed Fiske as "well qualified" and "independent."[9]

Not everyone was equally enamored, however. Shortly before Fiske's departure as U.S. attorney in March 1980, *Village Voice* reporter Wayne Barrett, in a *New York* magazine article titled "Freedom to Steal: Why Politicians Never Go to Jail," wrote that under Fiske's tenure, as well as his predecessors', the Southern District of New York had been transformed "into a red-light district for political corruption." Not one "significant corruption prosecution" was made by Fiske's office, wrote Barrett, in contrast to the numerous cases in adjoining districts made by U.S. attorneys with fewer resources than Fiske's office had available.

"Robert Fiske's professional philosophy entailed his personally prosecuting protracted, glamorous cases every couple of years . . ." Barrett wrote. An example of this, according to Barrett, was Fiske's personal handling of the prosecution of longshoreman boss Anthony Scotto, which led to Scotto's conviction.[10]

In fact, the Scotto case was developed largely by the FBI, mainly on the basis of evidence gathered by a young, ambitious FBI agent named Louis Freeh.[11] After helping Fiske put this significant feather in his cap, Freeh became one of Fiske's protégés. Despite the hoopla over Fiske's Scotto work, none of his ten public corruption prosecutors "ever made a significant corruption prosecution."

In defending his work to Barrett, Fiske said that his office had "not been flooded with people off the street who've brought us evidence against elected officials."[12] This largely passive attitude looked especially sorry, in retrospect, when one of his successors, Rudolph Giuliani, shook up New York City with a slew of anticorruption prosecutions.

This apparent reluctance to challenge the established political order led some to question whether this man had the stomach to pursue a possible case against a sitting president and his wife.

Other problems also suggested Fiske would be less than "independent." There was, for instance, Fiske's longtime association with Bernard Nussbaum, a fellow New York attorney. Nussbaum, who seemed to be in charge of White House efforts to circle the wagons in the immediate aftermath of Foster's death, had known Fiske professionally for nearly three decades. When Lawrence Walsh was putting together his Iran-contra staff, Fiske recommended Nussbaum to serve as Walsh's deputy. Anticipating the administration's need to find a replacement FBI director after Sessions's departure, one of the people Nussbaum turned to for a recommendation was Fiske. Fiske highly recommended Louis Freeh, who was nominated as the new director on the day of Foster's death.[13]

While common sense might have suggested otherwise, Fiske apparently saw no personal conflict in investigating Nussbaum and eventually gave him a clean bill of health on any matter relating to Whitewater.

Fiske's problems as a special prosecutor also included numerous potential conflicts of interest with his employer, Davis Polk. The law firm had represented International Paper Corporation, which sold 810 acres of Arkansas land to the Clinton-McDougal Whitewater partnership in 1986 for $550,000.[14] In addition, Davis Polk had a long-standing relationship with the Wall Street trading house Goldman Sachs. During Clinton's tenure as Arkansas governor, Goldman Sachs was the chief underwriter for Arkansas bonds and was a major contributor to Clinton's 1992 presidential campaign. Further, Robert Rubin, a Goldman Sachs executive, was among the first whom Clinton tapped for his new administration—first as head of the National Economic Council and later as secretary of the treasury.

The *Wall Street Journal* editorial page found all of this hard to accept. The *Journal*'s first editorial on Fiske's appointment proclaimed in a headline, TOO MUCH BAGGAGE, noting that Mr. Fiske was far from a devil's advocate who could give the Clintons a clean bill of health that would stick. The *Journal* cited that fourteen Republican senators had nixed President Bush's plans to appoint Fiske as deputy U.S. attorney general, on the grounds that Fiske had headed an American Bar Association judicial selection committee that had opposed several Reagan appointees. The *Journal* had vigorously supported Fiske for the Bush appointment, but ultimately concluded that Fiske was not right for this special counsel.

For one thing, Fiske had served as defense counsel for Clark Clifford, a prominent Democrat and head of First American Bancshares. First American had been the American subsidiary of BCCI (the Bank of Commerce and Credit International), which failed in 1990 amidst allegations of drug smuggling, money laundering, and political corruption. The *Journal* pointed out that there were "speculative but still possible connections between Whitewater and the BCCI scandal."[15]

The *Journal* had a vested interest in seeing the Foster case investigated fully and impartially because it had been heavily criticized for its editorials on Vincent Foster, which officials said helped lead to his suicide. But the *Journal* had other reasons to be suspicious. In August 1993, the Justice Department had promised to release the Park Police report within a week of their August 10 press conference, but only after news agencies had filed a pro forma Freedom of Information request. The *Journal* promptly did so, but a week passed, and the report was not forthcoming; Justice Department officials were still holding up issuance of the report, even though the case had been closed as a suicide over six months earlier.[16]

Citing my own reports in the *New York Post* that questioned police handling of the case and the fact that administration-friendly publications were already getting access to the report, Dow Jones, the paper's parent company, and the *Journal's* editor, Robert Bartley, filed suit in federal court on January 28, 1994, stating that the Justice Department had "constructively and improperly denied" their legal request.

By February 4, 1994—more than six months after Foster's death—the Justice Department indicated that Janet Reno had given authorization for an expedited release of the Park Police file, with the proviso that Special Counsel Fiske must also consent.[17] At the end of the month, the Justice Department released a letter from Fiske, stating that "the public disclosure of all or any part of the Park Police or FBI report at this time would substantially prejudice the ability of the Office of the Independent Counsel to conduct its investigation."[18] Meanwhile, other news developments were fueling renewed interest in the Foster case. In early February 1994—soon after Fiske was appointed—the *Washington Times* reported that two couriers at the Rose law firm were assigned the task of shredding any of Vincent Foster's files that the firm held in its possession. Fiske immediately said he would investigate the matter.[19]

Throughout the month of March, the *Journal* ran a series of editorial-page columns criticizing Mr. Fiske's handling of the investigation. Though the *Journal* could not offer hard evidence that Fiske was engaging in a cover-up, they were aware that special investigations and grand jury probes had been used before to shield full disclosure of information that might have been deemed embarrassing or potentially explosive.[20] In addition, when the *Journal* filed suit in January, they filed a separate request for a photocopy of the Foster note. Even though the text had been published and such a photocopy had been made available for perusal in the offices of the Department of Justice, Mr. Fiske denied the request. Nevertheless, despite the *Journal*'s suspicions that Fiske was covering something up, he still had the confidence of many Republicans in Congress.

In a letter dated February 28, 1994, Fiske responded to the *Journal*'s suit by stating that his "investigation into the events surrounding Mr. Foster's death will be thorough and complete." Fiske's court letter gave details that could only be interpreted to mean he was conducting a full-blown homicide probe—something he made no mention of at his initial press conference with Reno in January. In the wake of the *New York Post* reports on the unusual circumstances of Foster's death, Fiske apparently believed he needed to address the issue.

Fiske outlined the steps he had taken prior to that date: He had hired a former New York homicide prosecutor to head the death investigation. His office planned to hire "forensic experts and pathologists." His staff had already begun interviewing witnesses. Meanwhile, the existing evidence in the case was to be "reviewed and analyzed" by another homicide prosecutor from Texas.[21] In short, Fiske had a plan of action in what appeared to be a legitimate quest for the truth.

Fiske took a leave of absence from his lucrative position at Davis Polk and moved quickly to set up offices.

Since his inquiry dealt with two areas, separated by time and geography—activities in Washington since Clinton was president, and prior dealings of the Clintons in Arkansas—Fiske properly set up two offices. In Little Rock, space was available in the same modern building that housed the local FBI. In Washington, the Justice Department provided space at 1001 Pennsylvania Avenue, just across the street from its main building.

Few in the press seemed bothered by Fiske's use of the title "Office of Independent Counsel," even though he had not been appointed under the law and had no legal right to the office or title. A few papers, like the *New York Post*, referred to Fiske correctly as "the Special Counsel," but many media outlets continually and erroneously identified him as "Independent Counsel." This was no mere issue of semantics—especially since the title would give weight to Fiske's conclusions. The independent counsel law was promulgated precisely because a prosecutor hired by those he was meant to investigate could never be truly independent. The same sentiment was later expressed by a panel of judges who, by not selecting Fiske when the law was reauthorized, underscored the fact that he had no legal right to the title.

Congress reauthorized the independent counsel law in June 1994. Fiske, at that point, also suspended his grand jury activities, fearing the court might throw out any charges brought from proceedings before the official appointment of the independent counsel.[22] This was just one clue that Fiske knew his enterprise was distinct from one authorized under the reinstated statute.

But that was yet to come. Now it was still February 1994, and Fiske's staff was quickly taking shape. To head up the Washington probe, including Foster's death, the controversy over his office search, and matters relating to obstruction issues with the RTC (Resolution Trust Corporation) referrals about Madison Guaranty, Fiske selected Roderick C. Lankler. Like Fiske, Lankler was a Rockefeller Republican. His extra value in this case came by way of the eight years he had spent in the Manhattan district attorney's office prosecuting homicide cases. After several years as head of the Trial Bureau for the district attorney's office, Lankler was appointed first as a deputy and eventually as head of the Office of Special State Prosecutor for Official Corruption by the then–New York governor, Hugh Carey, a Democrat.

Lankler joined that office shortly after the original special state prosecutor, Maurice Nadjari, was fired from the post after he became a controversial figure. The Office of Special State Prosecutor was created in the wake of the Knapp Commission and charges of widespread police corruption. Nadjari's job was to prosecute such abuses, but he saw his scope as being much wider and began investigating judges and other top political figures in New York City. At the time of his dismissal, Nadjari's office had indicted about two hundred officials and was investigating two hundred more. Nadjari claimed that his successors, including Lankler, were simply "caretakers" appointed to close down his wide-ranging corruption probe.[23]

Lankler's time at the Office of Special State Prosecutor overlapped with Fiske's term as U.S. attorney in the latter part of the 1970s. The two were like peas from the same pod: Both had an aversion to taking on high-profile political corruption cases, both worked for Democratic administrations, and both avoided the media spotlight.

Fiske's staff was heavily dominated by New York attorneys, such as Mark J. Stein, a federal prosecutor who would become Fiske's lead prosecutor, working under Lankler on Foster-related matters. Of the eight lawyers Fiske hired, four had worked with Fiske at Davis, Polk & Wardwell. Several outsiders were also brought in: William S. Duffey from Atlanta's King & Spaulding, former attorney general Griffin Bell's firm; Carl Stich, Jr., from the Cincinnati firm of Dinsmore & Stohl; and Russell Hardin of Houston's Hardin, Beers, Hasstette and Davidson.[24]

Using his grand jury, Fiske started issuing subpoenas for White House and other documents. By all appearances, this case was going to be a textbook one—until the pages started falling out.

FISKE'S STAFF soon began leaking details of the investigation to the press, particularly related to his Washington probe into Foster's death. Leaks are commonplace in Washington, but these leaks indicated that Fiske's inquiry into Foster's death was essentially concluded before it began. The first major leak was to Mike McAlary, whose front-page story in the New York *Daily News* on March 14, 1994, reported that the "heads-up" Park Police conclusion of suicide had been "accepted by special Whitewater prosecutor Robert Fiske." Lankler had concluded the same, McAlary reported.[25]* More such leaks occurred, and they were not dismissed by Lankler or anyone else on Fiske's staff. Yet the release of case documents less than a year later demonstrated that the leaks announcing Fiske's conclusions were made before any real investigation had taken place.

---

* Lankler quickly told the *New York Post* that this was nonsense: No conclusion had been made, and the probe was continuing.

On April 4, 1994, the *Wall Street Journal* published a story headlined FISKE IS SEEN VERIFYING FOSTER KILLED HIMSELF, by *Journal* staff writer Ellen Joan Pollock. Quoting lawyers familiar with the case, the *Journal* reported that Fiske's staff was "expected to release a report this month declaring the death of White House aide Vincent Foster a suicide." Giving that statement credibility was Fiske's deputy counsel Lankler, who was quoted as saying that "he hoped to release the report in mid-April."[26] In mid-April, *USA Today* announced the Foster report might be released "as early as this week."[27] Fiske's report on Foster's death, in fact, was not released for two more months.

Documents and witness statements detailing the investigation, released months after Fiske concluded his probe, showed that no real investigation had taken place prior to the date Pollock's *Wall Street Journal* article was published.

The documents are clear: By the end of March, Fiske's FBI investigators had only conducted interviews with Fairfax County emergency workers who were present at Fort Marcy on the night of the death. Their testimony was minimal and far from conclusive evidence of suicide, since some statements actually suggested foul play, including those of paramedic Gonzalez and EMT workers Ashford and Arthur.

Despite the fact that the Foster investigation was at its most rudimentary stage with over 80 percent of their interviews not yet completed, the leaks from Fiske's office continued. On May 4, 1994, Reuters Information Services carried a wire story headlined: WHITEWATER COUNSEL TO REPORT FOSTER KILLED HIMSELF. The story noted that "Fiske has told associates his report accepting the official police version that Foster committed suicide last year because he was depressed may be released by the middle of May."[28] Within days the Reuters story had received wide confirmation, with corroborating reports in the *Washington Post* and the *Boston Globe*.

When the Fiske report was released on June 30, 1994, it relied heavily on Fiske's theory that Foster was severely depressed and that the forensic evidence, as well as an independent pathology review, supported the suicide verdict. But the chronological development of the Fiske investigation, laid out in the documents later released, showed that the critical aspects of his probe, such as the key forensic reports and the autopsy review, were all conducted in May and June, after the leaks had appeared in the press.

Here is how the chronology compares with the timing of press reports:

April 4: On the same day Pollock's story ran in the *Wall Street Journal* announcing Fiske's conclusion, an FBI team working for Fiske began the rudimentary task of searching for a bullet at Fort Marcy—almost one year after the death. The bullet was not found.[29]

April 6: The FBI report of the Fiske-appointed pathologist's interview of Dr. Beyer is written. No conclusions were drawn.[30]

April 12: Fiske's FBI agents interviewed Dr. Donald Haut, the medical examiner on the scene at Fort Marcy.[31]

April 20: Fiske's investigators were still covering initial bases as they interviewed the Secret Service officer who last saw Foster alive.[32]

April 27: For the first time, Fiske's investigators interviewed John Rolla, the lead investigator at Fort Marcy. Over the next five days another five officers present at the scene were interviewed.[33]

May 9: Five days after the Reuters report, Fiske's agents interviewed Foster's wife, Lisa. Documents show that only during this month did Fiske gather evidence addressing Foster's state of mind.[34]

Other dated documents make it hard to explain the confident press stories. Critical FBI lab reports are first dated May 9, a month after the *Journal* report.[35] Fiske's team of forensic pathologists reviewed the autopsy and FBI reports in June, issuing their report then—though it is undated.[36]

One highly unlikely explanation of all this is that several major media organizations simply invented the story that Fiske had reached a suicide conclusion out of whole cloth. The other is that Fiske's team leaked their conclusions before they had the results of their investigation.

Either way, the effect was to inhibit further press coverage. Pollock's *Wall Street Journal* article virtually ensured that there would be no future stories by major media questioning Foster's death.

The leaks may also have had another significant effect. By announcing the results early on, witnesses who perhaps were considering whether or not to come forward with important information may have been discouraged from doing so. What signal did the leaks send to investigators and experts who were part of the Fiske team but had not reached any conclusions about the case in their own minds?

The leaks may also have been intended as a trial balloon: Fiske's office may have been testing the degree of public interest in the case, especially from Congress and the media.

REGARDLESS OF the April *Wall Street Journal* report, the truth was that Fiske's investigators were having problems concluding the case and would need three months to do so. Records show that chief among the vexing contradictions they encountered were the inexplicable blood flows found on Foster's face as explained in an FBI analysis of one of the scene Polaroids.[37] An analysis of the photo indicated Foster's head moved several times after death and specifically revealed one important inconsistency: blood on the right side of his face, emanating from his right nostril and the right side of his mouth, as if the head had been tilted to the right. Foster's head had been found facing straight up. Fiske later admitted the head position was "inconsistent" with the bloodstains on the face.[38]

How did the blood drain to the right? On April 14, Fiske's agents were interviewing Dr. Haut and raised the issue of the blood tracks. Haut "could not provide any insight regarding the lateral blood flow as depicted in the photographs of Foster's face."[39]

Another vexing problem was the path of the blood draining from Foster's nose and mouth. Foster was found on a forty-five-degree berm with his feet facing down the slope. The Polaroids, however, show the blood from his mouth flowing up toward his right ear, and from his nose toward his temple. This would require that the blood flow uphill, counter to gravity. The FBI attempted to explain this away by stating that Foster's head was tilted slightly back.[40] The few scene photos do not show Foster's head tilted back. Even if it was "slightly tilted," the blood of a body found feet down on a forty-five-degree slope would most likely not have traveled up the face from the nose toward the temple.

Then lightning struck: A key witness suddenly emerged who claimed to have been the first person to find Foster's body. Nationally syndicated talk show host G. Gordon Liddy announced on an April day that he had found the man who first discovered Foster's body. The mysterious man in the white van was no mystery after all, Liddy said. He was a construction worker who had chanced upon Foster's body that hot July day as he prepared to urinate in Fort Marcy Park.

Upon finding the body, the man left the park and drove his van to nearby parkway headquarters. There he spotted two park service employees—later identified as Francis Swann and Chuck Stough. He informed them of a dead body in Fort Marcy Park. The man then drove off, not leaving his name. The witness was in fear for his life, according to Liddy, and had not come forward because he believed Foster had been murdered. Or, as the witness put it, "I don't want to end up like that guy I found."[41]

The most sensational part of his testimony, prepared in FBI statement form by Liddy—a former agent and FBI supervisor himself—was that when he came upon Foster's body, he saw no gun in either hand.*

The witness told Liddy he had come forward to him because he knew Liddy would not "give him up."[42] Liddy, of course, was one of the Watergate burglars who had never talked and served five years in federal prison. He also had a reputation from his radio show—heard locally in Washington on WJFK—of being an archenemy of the Clinton administration and a critic of the official Foster story. Liddy was well regarded by many in the various law enforcement agencies around Washington and had developed a reliable network of sources. He frequently touched on

---

* Some skeptics have cited this as proof that Foster was murdered. In fact, had Foster actually committed suicide, in all likelihood the gun would not have remained in his hand.

Foster in his commentaries and told his listeners he had little doubt that Foster did not die in Fort Marcy Park.

The media pooh-poohed both Liddy and the witness. But not so Fiske's investigators. Liddy was visited by FBI agents working for Fiske on April 12.[43] They were anxious to meet the witness, whom they later dubbed in their report "CW," for Confidential Witness. CW reluctantly consented to meet with the agents, and two days later they interviewed him at CW's home in Centreville, Virginia. He reiterated to the agents his "concern for his safety and welfare because of what he perceived as the high-profile government personalities involved. . . ."[44]

In Fiske's report CW became the main character in the unfolding case. Fiske would downplay the fact that CW did not see a gun, because CW had told the FBI that "the possibility does exist that there was a gun in or near his hand that he might not have seen." (CW later said the FBI badgered him into suggesting this.)[45]

CW helped plug the critical part for the Fiske team: "CW stated that the man's head was either straight up or slightly tilted to the right. . . ."[46] The FBI now had an explanation for the right lateral blood flow. But if Foster's head was tilted to the right, who moved it to its straight up position between the time CW found the body and the time the Polaroid was taken? Fiske's answer: one of the emergency workers, possibly checking for a pulse in Foster's carotid artery.

Although CW was useful to Fiske, there were problems with his credibility. If CW believed that Foster, a high federal official, was murdered, and feared possible government involvement, why would he speak to members of the FBI? If CW stopped at Fort Marcy because he had to urinate badly, why did he proceed to walk nearly eight hundred feet to find Foster's body? CW said he was looking for privacy, but the park affords numerous opportunities to relieve oneself—least of all the spot CW said he picked. He said he had climbed down the side of the embankment—which is not easy to do—when he noticed to his left what he thought was a bag of trash. He said he then discovered it was a body.

While Liddy thought the witness was genuine—and the witness did know many details of the park—Liddy believed he needed to be properly vetted by Fiske's team and his background checked. Yet in an amazing lapse of police procedure, Fiske's investigators never bothered to have park service worker Swann positively identify CW as the man in the white van. Swann told me that the FBI agents who interviewed him never showed him a photo or a lineup to ensure they had the right witness, even though it was Swann who placed the critical 911 call based on what the man in the white van had told him.[47]

Fiske later stated in his report that he accepted CW's bona fides because "CW provided details that have never become public, and that could only have been known by the person who discovered Foster's body."[48] Fiske apparently never considered any other ways someone might have known the details of the scene, such as the possibility that Foster had been murdered, that the body had been moved to the park by persons unknown, or even that the Park Police had engaged in a cover-up.

Swann also said he believed his coworker Chuck Stough had identified CW. Stough refused to comment, stating, "I was informed by the FBI I can't disclose information."[49] In Stough's FBI witness statement, prepared during Fiske's probe, he states only that CW, who was presented to him in the flesh, "could have been him."[50] Stough's FBI witness statement is dated June 22, 1994—meaning Stough was asked to identify CW just a week before Fiske released his final report—and, incredibly, over two months after Fiske and his team began relying on his testimony.

Homicide expert Geberth was baffled that the agents had only one of the workers—the one who did not make the 911 call—make the identification. "It's only common sense, you don't interview just one when two were present," he said. "You want the witness, the person who called 911 and said there was a dead body, to ID the man. It's basic police work. It's important to take each point [in a death investigation] to its ultimate conclusion. Apparently it wasn't done here."[51]

CW's FBI statement also mentions a purple wine-colored stain that one of the investigators told me was clearly visible on Foster's shirt and was obviously not blood. CW said he saw "light purple wine stains and what appeared to be traces of vomit on his shirt on the right upper shoulder and chest." He also noticed, just two and a half feet from the body, a wine cooler bottle still containing some wine that was "purplish in color."[52] According to the statements of officials at the scene, no one other than CW saw this bottle.

Fiske never explained what happened to the wine bottle. More important, in his report Fiske makes mention of CW's description of the wine stain, but gives no further details of his own investigation into this anomaly. FBI laboratory reports attached to the Fiske report are silent on this aspect of the physical evidence. A source close to the Starr probe who examined the shirt agreed with CW that a stain consistent with a wine color was on the shirt. The source said that Fiske had made no attempt to analyze the stain.

In other words, Fiske accepted CW's credibility, but ignored key aspects of his testimony that were inconsistent with the official version. CW also told Liddy he observed trampled vegetation on the pathway below Foster's body.[53] CW's statement on that count contradicted that of the Park Police who maintained that they saw no signs of a struggle, such as trampled vegetation.

With CW ending the mystery about the man in the white van as well as having plugged some other holes, such as helping explain the right lateral blood flow and confirming the site where Foster's body was found, Fiske was in striking distance of closing the Foster probe and issuing his report.

To help nail the case closed, Fiske had assembled a panel of four independent forensic pathologists to review the evidence. Dr. James Luke, who led the panel, was employed by the FBI; Dr. Charles Stahl was the armed forces medical examiner. The other two pathologists were Dr. Charles Hirsch, chief medical examiner for the city of New York, and Dr. Donald Reay, medical examiner for King County (Seattle), Washington.[54]

In June, the forensic panel, Fiske's team of six FBI agents, several of his prosecutors including Hardin and other experts—in all over twenty people—convened in Washington to discuss their findings. The FBI agents laid out the evidence as they interpreted it; the forensic panel reviewed matters relating to the autopsy and the handful of remaining Polaroids. By the end of the meeting, the conclusions were announced, and it was asked whether anyone had any objections to the conclusions or believed any matter warranted further investigation. There were no objections; no one called for further investigation. The case was closed.

On June 30, 1994, Fiske issued his long awaited "Report of the Independent Counsel In Re: Vincent W. Foster, Jr." There was little fanfare and no press conference by Fiske or his team. A four-page statement, signed by Fiske, accompanied each report and described two investigations Fiske was closing. The first was the Foster death probe. The second was his investigation of whether any laws had been broken "arising out of a series of meetings and other contacts between White House and Treasury Department officials from September 1993 through March 1994"—in an illegal effort to obstruct the RTC's criminal referrals relating to Madison Guaranty. On that count Fiske concluded no laws had been violated. Since the investigation into the RTC referrals had been conducted by a grand jury, Fiske offered no report on his conclusions— much of the evidence was shrouded by secrecy rules. A third investigation, to determine whether officials acted illegally in the handling of Foster's White House papers, was in "its final stages and should be completed shortly."

Fiske's report on Foster's death was definitive: Foster committed suicide at the spot where he was discovered in Fort Marcy Park. There was "no" evidence to the contrary, and Fiske found "no evidence that any issues related to Whitewater, Madison Guaranty or CMS played any part in his suicide."[55]

Without any additional explanation, Fiske's release stated, "The investigation into Mr. Foster's death was not a grand jury investigation." That rather benign statement took on great significance in the summer weeks immediately following the issuance of the Fiske report.

Fiske did not use a grand jury to investigate Foster's death though he had been using one in Washington for other parts of his probe dealing with Whitewater and the RTC referrals. Even though Foster's death was possibly at the very heart of the Whitewater scandal, Fiske exempted

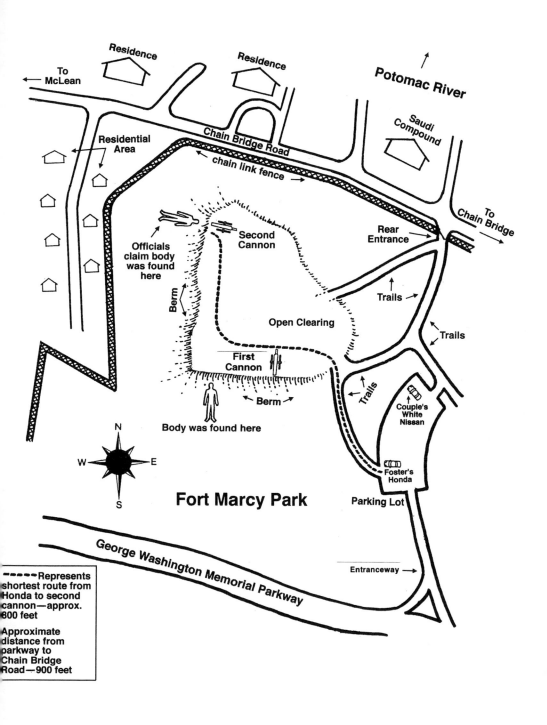

Residence

To McLean

Residence

Potomac River

Chain Bridge Road

Residential Area

chain link fence

Saudi Compound

Officials claim body was found here

Second Cannon

Rear Entrance

To Chain Bridge

Berm

Trails

Open Clearing

Trails

First Cannon

Body was found here

Berm

Trails

Couple's White Nissan

N

W E

S

Fort Marcy Park

Foster's Honda

Parking Lot

George Washington Memorial Parkway

Entranceway

- - - - - Represents shortest route from Honda to second cannon—approx. 800 feet

Approximate distance from parkway to Chain Bridge Road—900 feet

The main trail leading from Fort Marcy's parking lot to the fort's main clearing. Foster's car was located by police in one of the spaces to the immediate right of this trail. Note the wide dirt path, which park service maintenance vehicles frequently drive on. Independent experts believe a vehicle may have been used to move Foster's body to the rear of the park.

The trail from the lot leads to an open clearing or grove area of Fort Marcy. On the ridge to the left was situated the first cannon, which had been removed by the park service before this picture was taken. Several officials claimed Foster's body was found on the other side of this same ridge in the area past the picnic table depicted here. The official claim is that the body was found on a ridge directly in front of the park's second cannon. The second cannon is not visible from the clearing and is about two hundred feet into the rear portion of the park. Note the wide area of grass Foster would have traversed, yet the FBI laboratory made no mention of grass stains on his shoes.

The pathway on the berm leading up to the second cannon. Note the exposed soil and root stems. The FBI laboratory found no traces of soil on Foster's clothing, leading some experts to believe his body could not have been found here. Special Counsel Fiske and the FBI claimed they conducted an excavation that covered the entire length of the body on the pathway and carefully removed all the root stems from the pathway.

Fort Marcy's rear entrance is accessible from Chain Bridge Road. This oft-used access point was closed by federal investigators during a search for the missing Foster bullet in 1995. During Starr's grand jury proceedings the Park Police claimed they were not aware of this entrance to the park and never sought to secure it on the night of Foster's death. (SIPA photo)

First Position. Foster was found lying face up, head up on the side of a steep slope. Police found Foster's head perfectly straight up, not tilted to either side. An FBI laboratory analysis of a police Polaroid depicted blood staining on Foster's head consistent with this sketch. In addition to drainage of blood from the nose and mouth, the FBI said a bloody area on Foster's neck was a blood stain. Other eyewitnesses at the Foster death scene claimed they saw a wound or other trauma to the neck. Independent forensic experts also concluded that the blood drainage from the mouth and nose, rather than heavy bleeding, strongly suggested Foster's heart had stopped beating before the shot was fired.

Second Position. Foster was found lying on a steep incline, yet blood from the nose ran uphill—seemingly against gravity—across Foster's cheek to the area above his ear near the right temple. The FBI concluded that at some point Foster's head was tilted back slightly while on the incline, explaining the "upward" blood flow. Independent experts argued that since blood cannot flow with and against gravity at the same time, the head had to have assumed two positions after instant death. This, the experts said, was evidence the body was moved after death.

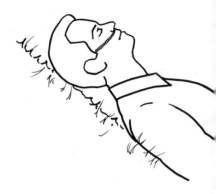

Third Position. The FBI laboratory reported that the bloody area on Foster's neck was a "contact stain" that resulted after Foster's head rolled completely to his right side, putting the jaw and neck in direct contact with a blood-stained area of Foster's shirt. Since this significant movement happened after death, officials claimed it likely happened by accident as one of the emergency workers checked Foster's carotid artery for a pulse. No police or emergency worker has stated he or she moved the head.

Fourth Position. Blood flows from the mouth and nose show that for some time Foster's head was tilted slightly to his right side. Yet, scene Polaroids depict the head in a perfectly straight-up position.

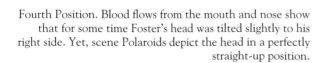

rk Police claimed to have found Foster's body a position similar to this. Foster's body was und in a neat position, arms at his sides, with e gun in his right hand. The police said the dy was lying on a dirt path down one of the old t's berms, directly in front of an old cannon.

Independent experts have challenged officials' claims about the position of Foster's body on the slope. While agreeing that the most probable scenario was that Foster fired the gun while in the sitting position, experts found the final, neat lying position of the body unnatural for one caused by violent means. Experts argued that had Foster fallen back after the gun's explosive firing, his head would likely have not fallen into a perfectly straight-up position, nor would his arms and hands have fallen close to his sides. Instead, experts theorize a much more disorganized but natural position as depicted here. If Foster's hands were on the gun when it was fired in his mouth, the explosive recoil, as well as gravity, should have sent Foster's arms and hands flailing outward—even if the gun remained in one of the hands.

The root-stem-etched dirt path directly in front of Fort Marcy's second cannon. This stake was placed by the FBI during the third search for the bullet in September 1995 and marks the spot where Special Counsel Fiske claimed Foster's head fell to repose. While the various investigative agencies have claimed that Foster's body was found in front of the second cannon, they have given varying locations for the body at this cannon site. The Park Police reported that Foster's head was found eighteen feet in front of the cannon's barrel. Fiske arbitrarily changed that location, moving the reported location of Foster's body closer to the cannon by some eight feet.

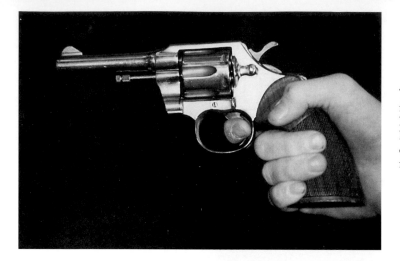

The conventional way of firing a .38 Colt revolver. Note the strong grasp of the hand on the gun's grip necessary to allow the index finger to pull the trigger.

Typically suicides have at least one hand on the gun's grip. If Foster placed the barrel of the gun deep into his mouth, his right hand should have grasped the gun's grip, allowing for rearward pressure on the trigger as depicted here. If he employed only his right thumb to pull the trigger, he could have used his left hand to grasp the grip and stabilize the gun. Since the autopsy noted powder burns on both of Foster's hands, experts say neither Foster's left or right hand held the grip as would have been typical.

A Park Police Polaroid taken at the Foster death scene. The Polaroid depicts a .38 Colt Army service revolver hooked on Foster's thumb. Independent experts found the gun position near the hip and in the hand after the explosive recoil unusual. The gun is usually not found in the hand of a suicide. Other evidence indicated Foster did not own this gun, no blood or blowback was visible on the gun, no one heard the fired shot, no fingerprints were found on the weapon, and the fired bullet was never located. Also note the heavy foliage around the body, inconsistent with the dirt pathway in front of the second cannon where the police claim the body was found. (Reuters/ABC/Archive Photos)

According to the autopsy report, gunpowder burns (heavy powder deposits) were found on the inside area of Foster's left and right index fingers as depicted here. For the powder burns to have been found there, an independent pathology report compiled by Special Counsel Fiske concluded, both of Foster's index fingers, hence his hands, were in close proximity to the gun's front cylinder gap when the gun was fired.

Forensic experts say that based on the location of these powder burns, Foster's hands were wrapped around the gun in a highly unusual and awkward grasp, as depicted here. Massad Ayoob of the Lethal Force Institute stated that such a grip is not consistent with the actions of a suicidal person. He also stated that the grip would have interfered with the cylinder action of the gun and would have made it difficult for the person to have depressed the trigger.

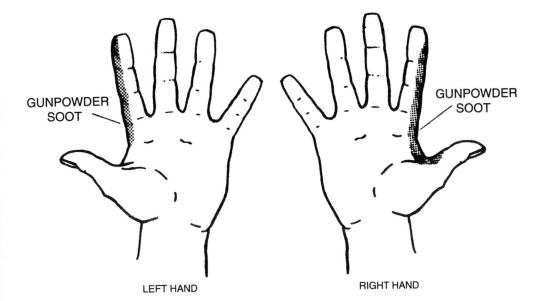

GUNPOWDER SOOT

GUNPOWDER SOOT

LEFT HAND

RIGHT HAND

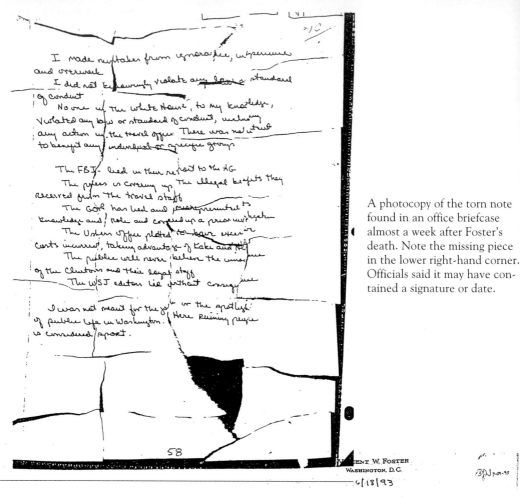

I made mistakes from ignorance, inexperience and overwork

I did not knowingly violate any law or standard of conduct

No one in the White House, to my knowledge, violated any law or standard of conduct, including any action in the travel office. There was no intent to benefit any individual or specific group

The FBI lied in their report to the AG

The press is covering up the illegal benefits they received from the travel staff

The GOP has lied and misrepresented its knowledge and role and covered up a prior investigation

The Usher's Office plotted to have excessive costs incurred, taking advantage of Kaki and HRC

The public will never believe the innocence of the Clintons and their loyal staff

The WSJ editors lie without consequence

I was not meant for the job or the spotlight of public life in Washington. Here ruining people is considered sport.

58

VINCENT W. FOSTER
WASHINGTON, D.C.

6/18/93

A photocopy of the torn note found in an office briefcase almost a week after Foster's death. Note the missing piece in the lower right-hand corner. Officials said it may have contained a signature or date.

The exemplar. A photocopy of a note Foster wrote a month before his death, which was used by the Park Police to certify the torn note as authentic.

car Exploration Co —

I am returning your check no. 0482 0598. interests it represents were owned by our father. As reflected by the enclosed the order these interests were distributed my mother. As reflected by the enclosed telamended she assigned the interests to.

Please revise your records

Sincerely

Vincent W Foster

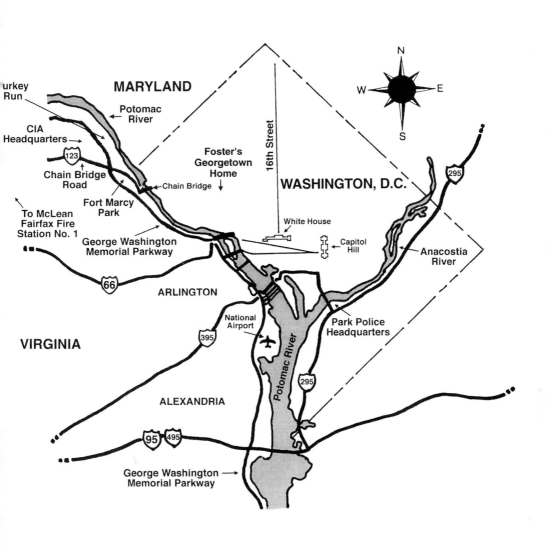

Park Police investigators Cheryl Braun and John Rolla (center), along with police spokesman Major Robert Hines (right), testify before the Senate Banking Committee in the summer of 1994. The Senate spent only one day of public hearings looking into the death.

Special Counsel Robert B. Fiske, Jr., meets the press after briefing congressional leaders in May 1996. Fiske had been appointed to his post by Attorney General Janet Reno in January 1994. Joining Fiske was his deputy, Roderick Lankler, who headed up the Washington end of the Whitewater probe, including matters relating to Foster's death. Fiske and Lankler concluded that Foster committed suicide in a report issued on June 30, 1994. *(AP Worldwide)*

A sign along the scenic George Washington Memorial Parkway announces Fort Marcy Park. The small roadside park is one of many that are found around Washington.
(AP Worldwide)

Fort Marcy's open clearing where the main fort was once situated. This area is just off the park's parking lot. The park's first cannon is off to the left as one enters the clearing. Several witnesses indicated Foster's body was found on the ridge this cannon overlooks, but many yards well past the cannon. Police claim the body was found in front of a second cannon in the rear of the park, which cannot be seen from the main clearing.

A police artist's sketch of a still unidentified man who was observed by witness Patrick Knowlton in Fort Marcy Park on the day of Foster's death. Knowlton's FBI statement claimed that he could not identify the man he saw. Knowlton later called that claim a "lie" manufactured by the FBI and helped London's *Sunday Telegraph* publish this composite.

Former White House counsel Bernard Nussbaum was unapologetic during congressional hearings into White House actions after Foster's death.

Congressional investigators focused on Susan Thomases's activities after Foster's death and believed she played a pivotal role in limiting investigators' access to Foster's office.

Hillary Clinton's chief of staff, Maggie Williams became a central figure in the case. A Secret Service officer accused her of removing papers from Foster's office on the night of the death.

Craig Livingstone, former nightclub bouncer and White House personnel security chief, became the point man in White House's handling of Foster's death. Livingstone identified Foster's body at the morgue, and the morning after the death a Secret Service officer observed him suspiciously carrying papers from the area of Foster's office.

fter pleading guilty to fraud charges, Webster ubbell reneged on his plea agreement to cooperate th Kenneth Starr's office. Hubbell was close to oster and gave investigators conflicting accounts out Foster's last days.

Key Whitewater witness David Hale. Special Counsel Fiske didn't bother to find out Foster's connection to Hale and his illegal financial dealings.

Mark H. Tuohey III serve as Starr's Washington deputy handling the most sensitive aspects of the probe, including Foster's death. In September 1995 Tuohey resigned to join the law firm that represented the Rose Law Firm before Starr's office and investigating congressiona committees.

Independent Counsel Kenneth W. Starr and his Little Rock deputy, W. Hickman Ewing, hold a press conference in Little Rock. Ewing, a former Reagan-appointed U.S. attorney from Memphis, became Starr's chief prosecutor in Little Rock, but he also played a pivotal role in Washington to help bring the Foster case to closure after the resignation of Miquel Rodriguez, Starr's lead Foster prosecutor.

Dr. Henry Lee, the head of th Connecticut State Crime Laboratory, testified in 1995 a key defense expert for O. J. Simpson at his murder trial. To Lee's left, Simpson attorney Johnnie Cochran. Lee's controversial "something wrong" analysis came under withering criticism from FBI experts. While working on th Simpson case, Independent Counsel Ken Starr's office hired Lee to help bolster government claims Foster killed himself at Fort Marcy.
(AP Worldwide)

Assistant United States Attorney Miquel Rodriguez in Sacramento, California. Rodriguez had served as associate independent counsel and had been the lead prosecutor investigating Foster's death. His resignation in March 1995 from Starr's staff has raised serious questions about Starr's integrity.

July 19, 1993: FBI director William S. Sessions takes questions from the press after being fired by President Clinton. Sessions's ouster left the bureau without a permanent FBI director for six weeks. On July 20, the day after the firing, Foster was found dead. Months later Sessions charged his firing by Clinton had politicized the bureau and compromised the FBI's role in the Foster death case. *(AP Worldwide)*

Deputy White House Counsel Vincent W. Foster, Jr. Foster was involved in the Clinton administration's most controversial actions, such as the failed nominations of Zoe Baird and Kimba Wood for attorney general, the Waco standoff, the health care proposal, and the travel office affair. At the same time, Foster was also serving as the personal attorney for Bill and Hillary Rodham Clinton. His work for the Clintons and the actions of White House aides to clear his office in the days after his death fueled speculation as to why and how he really died. *(AP)*

Foster's death investigation from the rest of the proceedings. No one was put under oath. The evidence was not examined by an independent citizen's committee known as a grand jury.

In a footnote to a section of the report dealing with the FBI interviews, Fiske noted that if the interviewees had given false answers to the FBI staff, they "would be prosecutable under Title 18, United States Code, Section 1001."[56] But experts say that the statute is rarely used and therefore carries almost no practical weight. It "is very, very, very, very seldom used," noted William F. Roemer, Jr., the FBI's highest-decorated former agent. "I have never heard it applied. We never observed it."[57]*

Former federal prosecutor Thomas Scorza also thought it "real odd" that Fiske had not used the grand jury in that part of the probe. "You don't have a grand jury on just one aspect of the Whitewater case," he said. "It should be taking evidence on every aspect." A grand jury greatly reduces the chances of a cover-up, he said, because the threat of perjury charges militates against witnesses "spinning and fibbing and not telling the whole truth."[58]

Homicide expert Vernon Geberth believes there was insufficient skepticism on the part of the investigating team. If Fiske's staff had been routinely suspicious, he commented, they would have "put everyone— medical examiner, emergency medical workers, police, witnesses— under subpoena to get sworn testimony under oath. What doesn't jibe with official reports, you charge those [giving wrongful information] with either issuing false reports or perjury." By failing to do so, Geberth concluded, Fiske effectively "accepted the fact it was a suicide from the beginning."[59]

Neither Fiske nor his deputy Roderick Lankler would comment on this matter. According to Mike Wallace of 60 Minutes, Fiske told mutual associates that he did not use a grand jury because "it would take him

---

* Roemer, who, as previously noted, was the lead agent for the FBI's Organized Crime Strike Force in Chicago, was quoted in my special report. "If Fiske had the power [of subpoena] and he didn't use it, something could be inferred from that. I would certainly use the hammer," he said, using law-enforcement jargon for sworn testimony, because it is "a powerful lever—to put witnesses before a grand jury with the threat of perjury charges hanging over them."

such a long time."[60] So superficial was Fiske's report that it failed to establish a plausible motive for Foster's suicide, something a police inquiry of this type is usually supposed to do. "It is impossible to completely understand how or why he came to the point at which he decided to take his own life," the report stated.[61]

The Fiske report on Foster was only fifty-eight typewritten pages. The bulk of the bound report—some 196 pages—had nothing to do with the investigation but rather consisted of the medical résumés of Fiske's pathology panel and a consulting psychiatrist, a total of ninety-one pages.

In lieu of strong evidence pertaining to motive, and with a weak assemblage of physical evidence supporting suicide, it is no wonder Fiske relied so heavily on the opinion and reputations of his forensic pathology panel.

During Senate hearings one of Fiske's pathologists, Dr. Charles Hirsch, exposed how shallow the panel's review had been. Pathologist Hirsch said little of substance during the hearing, but interjected at one point to give a forceful opinion in an attempt to add authoritative weight to the FBI's conclusions. "I do have an opinion about something you raised, and that concerns the place of Mr. Foster's death," he told one of the senators. "It is my unequivocal, categorical opinion that it was impossible for [Foster] to have been killed elsewhere."[62]

Hirsch, along with the three other members of Fiske's pathology team, had stated in the joint report that Foster died "where the body was found, at Fort Marcy Park."[63] Only Hirsch himself knows how embarrassed he might have felt—he gave no outward sign—when Senator Lauch Faircloth subsequently asked his simple but pregnant question: he gently asked Dr. Hirsch, "have you ever visited Fort Marcy Park?"

"No, sir," was the astonishing reply.[64] He and three others had signed off on a report that Foster died at the spot where he was found and that the bloodstains were consistent with that location, which only two of the pathologists had bothered to visit. Moreover, this judgment was "unequivocal" and "categorical." Hirsch also admitted that only one member of the pathology team had bothered to interview Dr. James Beyer, Virginia's chief medical examiner, who performed the autopsy.

Apparently only two members of Fiske's pathology team thought it important enough to travel the few miles from downtown Washington to Fort Marcy Park, and all but one could not find time to meet or even call Dr. Beyer before acquiescing in a sweeping statement about the absolute certainty of the findings.[65]

Dr. Michael Baden, former chief medical examiner for New York City, was another expert who challenged the methodology employed. "The panel of forensic pathologists looking into this I thought left a lot to be desired," he said of the Fiske team. He was especially critical of their failure to visit the death scene and surprised that only one member of the team had talked with the original pathologist. They "tended to just adopt whatever was given to them," he commented. "You can't just adopt what the person who hires you says or gives you."[66]

The large number of résumés appended to the report suggested that Fiske was more interested in the appearance of thoroughness than in thoroughness for the sake of truth. Other appended items seemed to bear that out. Appended to the report were several sections of exhibits: the FBI lab reports, the autopsy report, copies of the *Wall Street Journal* editorials mentioning Foster, and Foster's speech to the University of Arkansas Law School. Exhibit section nine, the last two pages of the voluminous document, was the "Fort Marcy Artifact Inventory," which listed dozens of Civil War artifacts unearthed at the park by the FBI during a fruitless search for the bullet. Perhaps the inclusion of this particular report (while dozens of significant FBI reports were not attached) served to show just how painstakingly diligent Fiske's inquiry had been.

The Fiske report states that an "excavation" for the fatal bullet, bone, and blood residue had been conducted in Fort Marcy Park. "On April 4, 1994, sixteen individuals from the FBI lab went to Fort Marcy Park to conduct a search in the area where Foster's body was found." Fiske's report acknowledged that no matching bullet, bone, or blood residue was located (as noted previously, dozens of Civil War artifacts and modern-day bullets were retrieved from the area), but the search served to indicate that Fiske's team was serious about getting to the bottom of the case.

According to the Fiske report, investigators searched "the area immediately beneath where Foster's body was found . . . by digging and hand sifting the soil and other debris. FBI lab personnel excavated to a depth of approximately eighteen inches, searching the soil through various screening methods. No bone fragments or bullets were found."[67] But evidence suggests that the much-heralded excavation never took place.

Active participants in this supposed search of the area in front of the second cannon were Robert Sonderman, a National Park Service senior staff archaeologist, and Dr. Doug Owsley, a forensic anthropologist with the Smithsonian Institution. In interviews, Owsley said he was there to help locate bone fragments and then determine if they were of human origin. Sonderman's role was to ensure that the historical site was protected and to help with the metal-detector search as he had done previously on many such searches. Both men were there for the entire period and were an integral part of the search team. Both denied that the focal point of the investigation, the excavation of the pathway where the body was found, ever took place.[68]

According to the contemporaneous notes found in the FBI report, which was written on the day of the search by field personnel and released by the Senate Banking Committee, numerous metal items were found at a depth of about four inches, but no deeper.[69] However, another FBI report of activities that day, one later typed in Fiske's office and turned over to Congress, made this assertion: "The entire area of the path where the body was positioned was excavated down to approximately 15–18 inches, the soil and roots removed and then meticulously hand searched by various screening methods."[70]*

Owsley said explicitly that no "excavation" or cutting of root stems took place. Owsley and Sonderman both referred to their activities as a "survey," not an excavation. Owsley said the Fiske team concentrated its

---

* I subsequently visited the area, and found that the roots were still there, right on the path.

efforts not on the pathway where the body was found, but, reasonably enough, at the bottom of the hill where fragments may have been washed by rain, and above and behind the berm's crest, where bone material may also have been propelled as the bullet exited the back of Foster's skull.[71]

According to Owsley, there was "no reason" for digging, since any such material could be found by "raking" the surface. "There was very little digging," Sonderman agreed. He had a vivid recollection of Owsley sifting surface material—"overburden" as Sonderman called it—in a wire mesh box with a quarter-inch screen. Sonderman also said no roots were cut and noted that investigators took great pains not to disturb the historic nature of the site, even where the body was found.

Asked if digging at the site at any time went to the fifteen- to eighteen-inch depth noted in the Fiske and FBI reports, Sonderman was emphatic: "No way." He said the FBI thought the bullet should be near the surface, maybe an inch or two below, but no more.

Foster was a large man, six feet four inches; had the excavation taken place of the entire length of Foster's body to the depth Fiske claimed, it would have involved the unearthing of roughly twenty-two cubic feet of soil—more than a half ton—on the pathway alone. Those present could hardly have missed such a feat.

This discrepancy over the "excavation" was "real serious," said former prosecutor Thomas Scorza, adding, "It's not a small matter. An excavation is a very specific maneuver," and the discrepancy becomes "worrisome" when considered in the light of all the other discrepancies.[72]

Considering Fiske's vulnerability on the "excavation" issue, it is perhaps no surprise that his probe never asked the Park Police why their metal detector search turned up nothing while the FBI found dozens of objects in the same search area.

A close examination of the report showed that Fiske was "ratcheting-up" facts, evidence, and his own procedures to help him make his conclusion of suicide "solid." Such, for example, was Fiske's assertion on page two of his report that "Russell Hardin, Jr., also an Associate Counsel, reviewed and analyzed the evidence compiled during this investigation."[73] In his response to the *Wall Street Journal* lawsuit mentioned previously, Fiske had used the same words, "review" and "analyze[d]," to describe Hardin's role as a "homicide prosecutor."*

Hardin himself acknowledges that although he has tried homicide cases, this is not his forte. Nor had he ever referred to himself as a "homicide prosecutor." As for his "review" and "analysis" of the case, that was confined to one day's participation at the end of the conclave convened by Fiske in Washington. To suggest that he was a significant player in an investigation that accumulated ten thousand pages of documents requires a stretch of logic.

Even before the Fiske report was released, there were indications that the investigation had not been a thorough, by-the-book homicide probe. One would have thought that the many nearby residents of Fort Marcy Park would have been carefully interviewed about any violent death that occurred near their homes, let alone a high-profile case such as this. Yet contrary to the Park Police's own "Death Investigation Guidelines" regarding suicides, these residents were not sought out. Even more disconcerting is the fact that Fiske's investigators—seasoned agents of the FBI—also failed to follow these rudimentary police procedures. A reporter from the London *Telegraph* was equally amazed when he discovered that these important potential witnesses were never contacted by authorities. (Fiske's investigators interviewed only security personnel at the nearby residence of the Saudi Arabian ambassador.)[74]

A look at a map of the Fort Marcy Park area (photo insert) will show why such a canvass should have been an integral part of any investigation. The rear entrance on Chain Bridge Road is much closer to where the body was said to have been found than is the main entrance. Neighbors, understandably, frequent the park and potentially could provide useful information about the incident.

Fiske played down the significance of the park's rear entrance in his

---

* Hardin, a former state prosecutor who in 1989 had been named "Texas State Prosecutor of the Year," had limited experience in white-collar crime. Fiske needed an experienced trial lawyer, as Hardin told me, "from any state contiguous to Arkansas," believing it would be wise to have a Southerner rather than a Yankee appearing before an Arkansas jury.

report, noting that it was "for use by pedestrians."[75] This is not quite accurate; there is a quasi "parking lot" in the form of a shoulder on Chain Bridge Road that provides space for several cars and even invites parking with a prominent sign. Indeed, Fiske's chief witness, CW, was said to have frequently parked his white van there.

Fiske also reported that a blood analysis conducted by the FBI lab found trace amounts of Trazadone, an antidepressant, and Valium, a tranquilizer, in Foster's system.[76] That finding contradicted the earlier blood and urine analysis conducted for the Virginia medical examiner, which found no drugs or alcohol in Foster's blood. As noted before, the testing of blood for drugs, particularly exotic ones, is critical in a case like this because of the possibility the deceased was first incapacitated or even slain before being shot.

The FBI blood analysis, which contradicted the original report prepared for Dr. Beyer's autopsy, should have raised concerns about the validity of Beyer's other conclusions. It did not. A detailed FBI report on Foster's blood that includes the screens employed in the testing of the samples is strikingly missing from other FBI findings exhibited in the Fiske report, as well as documents turned over to Congress by Fiske. Did the FBI conduct all the screens that homicide investigators say should be employed to rule out poisoning? Neither Fiske nor the FBI has told us.

Many important discrepancies are missing or unexplained in the report. Fiske said that the doubts of paramedics Gonzalez and Arthur about the suicide were not due to their questions about the paucity of blood or the neat arrangement of the body or gun, but "in large measure" to their observation of additional wounds on Foster's face.

Arthur told Fiske's investigators he saw a bullet hole on Foster's neck. Gonzalez said he saw a bullet hole in the forehead. Fiske summarily dismissed their testimony by stating simply, "These wounds did not exist."[77] But Fiske never asked why these important observations were never mentioned in the paramedics' official reports prepared for Fairfax County immediately following the death.

Backing up Fiske's claim that what Arthur saw was only a blood-stain on Foster's face was an FBI analysis of one key close-up Polaroid analyzed for Fiske. The FBI lab had described a bloody mark on Foster's neck, in the precise area that EMT worker Richard Arthur claimed he saw a bullet wound or trauma, as a stain. But a later review of the photographic evidence led others to believe that the FBI working for Fiske had done some finagling to cover much more than a stain. Soon after Fiske departed, Starr's prosecutor, Miquel Rodriguez, after considerable haggling, was able to gain custody of the original 35 mm film that had been underexposed through apparent negligence in the Park Police labs. Fiske and the FBI had stated the photos were useless. He also got custody of the scene Polaroids. Rodriguez and his assistant, Lucia Rambusch, then took the photos to Asman Photo, a private agency in Washington used by the Smithsonian Institution. Rambusch stood by as the photos were enhanced.

The results were nothing short of remarkable. The private lab recovered more pictures from the 35 mm photos than did the FBI lab (such as a photo indicating Foster's right hand had been moved after the police arrived); even more significant results were achieved by enhancing the Polaroids.

The enhancement of a Polaroid made by the outside agency was showing something more awful than a simple bloodstain: A large gash, with black powdery marks, was evident on the right side of Foster's neck. In addition, the enhanced photo showed that some blood from Foster's shirt may have stained his neck, but this didn't provide an explanation for the apparent damage to the neck or the black marks.

Rodriguez went back and looked at the enhanced photo used by the FBI during the Fiske probe. He noted how blurry it looked compared to the one he had had enhanced at the outside agency. He then began to review the handling of the photos by reading the notations made on the back of each set during the time they were enhanced. These markings showed that the FBI lab had not used the original Polaroids for enhancement as he did when he sent Lucia Rambusch to have them enhanced. Instead, the FBI lab had made copies of the original Park Police Polaroids with another Polaroid camera. Then the second-generation Polaroids were photographed by a 35 mm camera in the FBI lab to make enhancements for analysis. These blurred and enhanced photographs, made from copies of copies, were utilized by the FBI experts and Fiske's pathology team to make conclusions about the stains and blood patterns.

According to Fred Santucci, a former New York City detective who spent fifteen years as a forensic crime-scene photographer and analyst, the multiple generation of photos was done "because someone wanted to hide something." As Santucci noted, Polaroids are of lesser quality to begin with. There is no good reason to make a copy with another Polaroid camera, unless one wanted to further distort and blur the original.[78]

Then there is Fiske's arbitrary altering of the official crime-scene diagram.

Fiske knew there was a problem with the disputed second cannon site where the police have claimed they found Foster's body. The original Park Police report, as noted in two scene sketches, claimed that Foster's body was found lying on the side of a berm, directly in the line of fire of the cannon (which, by the way, is anchored by a concrete slab)—exactly twenty feet in front of the cannon's wheels, or about eighteen feet from the front of the barrel.

But Fiske did not accept that police version. The Park Police put Foster's head eight or more feet down from the crest of the berm. This placement contradicted almost all the eyewitnesses who claimed Foster's head was near the crest. In fact, Officer Fornshill has testified that he could see the head from the other side of the open clearing. Fiske and his team must also have realized that had Foster actually walked farther down the side of that berm, it would have been a highly awkward and risky maneuver—the slope becomes much steeper—and would have left him at the sharpest part of the incline with an uneven and unnatural place to sit down.

For his own report, Fiske asserted that Foster's body was much closer to the cannon, with his head being found about ten feet in front of the cannon's barrel, thereby shaving some eight feet off the Park Police account. Fiske could now say that Foster walked to the dirt path and sat down on some root stems, which formed a natural seat. If Foster sat there and his body fell back with the gunshot, it would have landed close to the crest of the berm and about ten feet in front of the cannon's barrel. Once again the question needs to be asked, was the body really found at the second cannon site?

Fiske's version of the body's placement also helped him explain his investigators' inability to find the bullet. Had Foster's head been eight or more feet from the crest of the berm as the initial Park Police drawing suggests, the bullet may have been found in the berm. By placing Foster closer to the top of the berm, this report allowed for a much larger area in which the projectile could have been found. The larger the possible area, the less likely the bullet is to have actually been recovered. In fact, it never was.

Consider this statement from Fiske's report: "Everyone known to have been in Fort Marcy Park on the afternoon or evening of July 20, 1993, also was questioned"[79] (patently false). Motorist Patrick Knowlton said he observed a Hispanic-looking man sitting in the lot at 4:30 P.M., possibly guarding a Honda that Fiske implied was Foster's. The couple Mark and Judy told Fiske's FBI agents that they saw two men in and around Foster's Honda, one with a beard and long blond hair who was seen near the car with the hood up shortly before the body was found. (Fiske stated blandly that the couple had not "observed anything unusual.")[80] The couple also remembered at least two other motorists who drove into the park.

The Hispanic-looking man, two men around Foster's car, two more motorists: in all, at least five people Fiske never identified, let alone interviewed. And that is not all.

Because the Park Police failed to secure the park's rear entrance, some people entered the park during the crime-scene investigation, including a jogger. The police never bothered to get their names. Fiske never mentioned these people. Nor did he mention the members of the Park Police SWAT team who also appeared in the park that night.

One of the Park Police officers told Fiske's FBI investigators that the police encountered a group of men wearing red or orange vests on a trail in Fort Marcy Park the night of the death.[81] The Park Police explained that these people were simply "volunteers" helping to maintain the park.

They never bothered to get the names of these volunteers, and Fiske never tried to track them down.

During the grand jury proceedings begun by Starr, a Park Police officer said that when the search of Foster's car took place that night, a "liaison officer" with the U.S. Secret Service was present at Fort Marcy. This person has never been identified or accounted for.[82]

In short, a dozen or more people were in Fort Marcy on the night of the death whom Fiske has never interviewed. As with several major issues in the case, Fiske was either woefully ignorant of the basic facts of the case, or he willfully obscured them.

8

"In view of the nature of this case," William F. Roemer commented in 1994, "the FBI should have been involved." At the time Roemer was the highest-decorated living former FBI agent. He once headed the bureau's Organized Crime Strike Force in Chicago. Roemer said he had heard from his network of FBI friends that Janet Reno and the White House had played too great a role early on. The bureau, he said, "allowed the tail to wag the dog. . . . The FBI would normally be finding reasons to get involved in a high profile case."[1]

Roemer spoke to me just as my own investigation began in 1994 and little was known about the problems associated with Foster's death. What was known, and irksome to people like Roemer, was that Reno's Justice Department had given exclusive jurisdiction to the Park Police, an agency of the Interior Department. One need not be an expert on such matters to realize that the Park Police had little of the political and investigative muscle needed to tackle a complex homicide case touching upon some of the most powerful people in the federal government.

Stranger, too, was the observer status bestowed on the FBI in the original Park Police investigation. The FBI had claimed that their agents were not present at the crime scene or the autopsy and had not conducted any forensic work relating to the physical evidence (save a search for fingerprints on the torn note). Even the old Colt was sent to the BATF (Bureau of Alcohol, Tobacco and Firearms) laboratory rather than the FBI's. FBI agents had sat in on Park Police interviews with White House colleagues of Foster and were even among the "cigar store Indians" who watched Nussbaum search Foster's office. Yet the FBI issued no report on the death itself and conducted no real inquiry. Peculiar then was the presence of Robert Bryant, special agent in charge for the FBI's Washington field office, at the Justice Department–Park Police press conference announcing the results of the police inquiry. Even more peculiar was the statement he made that the FBI's role in the case had been to "find out if there was a violation, if [Foster] had been harmed, you know, assaulted or assassinated or whatever. We concluded no."[2] On what basis did Bryant and the FBI make their conclusion? Nothing more than the Park Police inquiry and the autopsy report.

The FBI report of its involvement with the Foster case in the days after the death was released to Congress in 1996. The two-page report, dated August 9, 1993, contains an additional twenty-four pages of attachments, mostly FBI interviews relating to Foster's office and the finding of the so-called suicide note. The opening lines of the report describe the death inquiry as "being conducted by the U.S. Park Police" and state that FBI involvement came after the Department of Justice asked them to enter the case, but only "to focus FBI efforts on the turning over of a note found in the office of Vincent W. Foster."[3]

One line of the note supposedly written by Foster states: "The FBI lied in their report to the [attorney general]."[4] Later, some Park Police officers would cite Foster's anger over the FBI's travel office report to Attorney General Reno as one reason the FBI was not given jurisdiction over the Foster death case. It remains unclear as to why, if the FBI was somehow prejudiced against Foster, they would be given responsibility to investigate Foster's claims in the note, which specifically accused the FBI of malfeasance.

The truth was that the FBI had been kept at arm's length during the entire Park Police probe.[5] Thus, the same Clinton administration that was quick to summon the FBI over imaginary irregularities in the travel office had blocked the agency from taking any real role in matters relating to Foster's death.

ONE REASON the Foster death case may not have been given to the FBI is that it had no permanent director on the day Foster died. President Clinton had called Director William S. Sessions that Monday, July 19, ordering him to vacate his office immediately.

In a statement in January 1994, Judge Sessions, a plainspoken Texan, charged that the FBI was kept out because of "a power struggle within the FBI and the Department of Justice." According to Sessions, the Justice Department and the White House had been trying to wrest political control over the bureau, which he doggedly resisted. According to his statement, political interference by the White House and Justice Department in the running of the FBI, which ultimately resulted in his firing, led him to conclude that "the decision about the investigative role of the FBI in the Foster death was therefore compromised from the beginning."[6]

Sessions also stated that his longtime nemesis at the bureau, Floyd Clarke, was acting director on the day of Foster's death and remained so until Freeh's official confirmation, leaving Clarke in charge during the critical time of Foster's death investigation. Sessions believed Clarke had "long been involved with the Department of Justice to effect the power shift at the FBI," and he implied that this was why the Park Police were given the sole responsibility of investigating Foster's death.[7]

Sessions's stunning analysis raised new suspicions about his firing. Clinton had stated on *Larry King Live* the night of Foster's death that the idea of having to fire Sessions was anathema to him and that he did so only because Sessions had refused to resign.[8]

This was not exactly true. Sessions had offered to resign once his replacement, Judge Freeh, had been confirmed by the Senate, to allow for a proper (and nonpolitical) transfer of power. On the day of the firing, the *Wall Street Journal*'s lead editorial headlined WHAT'S THE RUSH? and began, "So the gang that pulled the great travel office caper is now hell-bent on firing the head of the FBI."[9]

Whether Sessions, had he remained director, would have forced a showdown with the White House over jurisdiction in the Foster matter is moot. What is clear is that the Park Police were essentially given exclusive jurisdiction in a matter that was beyond their capabilities.

Official investigators and congressional inquiries have glossed over the serious issues raised by Sessions, as well as questions as to why the FBI was not given lead or even secondary status to participate at each step of the Park Police probe.

Special Counsel Fiske had promised he would examine how jurisdiction fell to the Park Police, and his report has a brief section on this issue. In it, Fiske acknowledges that while Foster as a high presidential aide was covered under the presidential and presidential staff assassination statute, giving the FBI jurisdiction over such deaths, the FBI never entered the case because a "preliminary inquiry by the FBI . . . failed to indicate any criminal activity."[10] That preliminary inquiry—the above-mentioned two-page report—shows that the FBI simply adopted the preliminary Park Police ruling. Fiske gave no adequate explanation as to how the FBI could have drawn such a conclusion without taking a more active role, such as completing interviews relating to the death scene or conducting any independent laboratory work.

The FBI did enter the case in 1994 when Fiske requested and assigned a half dozen FBI agents to help his prosecutors conduct their inquiry. Though under no legal requirement to use FBI agents as his investigators, like most independent counsels Fiske opted to utilize their services.

THE SIGNIFICANT role the FBI played in Fiske's probe became apparent in the summer of 1994, after Fiske had released his report. At that time, Fiske and his prosecutors were asked to appear before the Senate

Banking Committee, which was holding hearings on Foster's death as part of the Senate's Whitewater probe. Fiske and his lawyers balked at coming before the committee to explain the report they had prepared.[11]

On July 29, 1994, at 10 A.M. the Senate hearings began in Room 106 of the Dirksen Senate Office Building, with Senator Don Riegle, a Democrat, presiding. The first panelists were FBI agents Larry Monroe and William Colombell, whom Fiske had chosen to lead his probe, and Dr. Charles Hirsch, chief medical examiner of New York City and a member of Fiske's pathology team.

Already there was something odd about the whole arrangement: Neither Fiske nor any of his prosecutors wanted to explain the report they had written. Monroe, the senior of the two agents, offered a statement that followed the outline of the Fiske report. He and Colombell then fielded questions.

It soon became apparent that the purpose of the hearings was not to probe for the truth but, rather, to reinforce the conclusions of the Fiske report by way of the powerful image of two authoritative FBI figures, special agents Larry Monroe and William Colombell, declaring that there was nothing untoward about the case.

> *Sen. Christopher Dodd:* Mr. Monroe and Mr. Colombell, how long have you been with the agency, the Bureau?
>
> *Monroe:* . . . about 29 years.
>
> *Colombell:* . . . 30 years.
>
> *Dodd:* It's fair to assume you've been involved in hundreds, if not thousands, of investigations?
>
> *Monroe:* Mr. Colombell more than myself, but those rough figures are probably in the ballpark, sir.
>
> *Dodd:* It's your conclusion, as has been stated, that Mr. Foster committed suicide. There's no doubt in any of your minds about that?
>
> *Monroe:* No doubt.
>
> *Colombell:* No doubt at all.[12]

At FBI headquarters also, some eyebrows were said to be raised when they learned of the agents' testimony. The FBI is strictly an investigative agency—gathering evidence and checking facts—and studiously avoids drawing conclusions in criminal matters. That is typically the business of prosecutors. Yet here were two high-profile agents drawing their own conclusions and implying that the FBI had officially done so as well.

Fiske and his supporters on that committee would likely have suffered no small embarrassment had anyone questioned the pair about their investigative experience with homicides. Monroe had spent the better part of the previous twenty years as a lecturer and administrator at the FBI Academy in Quantico, Virginia. He was what some field agents good-naturedly refer to as an "innkeeper." Colombell, a former supervisory agent, had spent the last five years as a unit chief at bureau headquarters dealing with Freedom of Information requests. While Colombell had considerable investigative experience, this did not make him a homicide expert. Indeed, most FBI agents have scant homicide experience since most such cases fall outside federal jurisdiction.

As with the original Park Police investigation, the FBI was playing a passive role. This was apparent when the two agents verbally signed off on the blatantly flawed Park Police report. Asked by Senator Dodd if the Park Police were competent in their investigation, Monroe responded, "We do not know of any significant irregularities."

Dodd turned to Colombell, who affirmed, "Senator, I do not know of any."[13]

Some senators had difficulty accepting this idea, given that the Park Police had turned over Foster's beeper and personal belongings to the White House and had also put his clothing into the one evidence bag, allowing cross-contamination. Monroe and Colombell explained that if the case had been a homicide, these oversights would have been problematic. But since this case was obviously a suicide, there had been no need for such special care.[14]

Yet when the agents were asked to explain why the police had jumped to a suicide conclusion, contravening established investigative procedure, they were quick to say that the police had properly treated the case as a homicide at first, which contradicted their earlier statement.

Since the FBI sometimes must investigate police corruption, it does not make a practice of getting overly familiar with the Park Police or any other law-enforcement body. But Colombell was hinting that the FBI had a special relationship with the Park Police—one that might shed light on the agents' desire not to criticize their federal law-enforcement brothers—when he noted that "the Park Police are colleagues of ours that we work with frequently. . . ."

Colombell also took a defensive tack with the Park Police's handling of the case, adding, "They didn't have 20/20 hindsight and we didn't have 20/20 hindsight and we're being subjected to quite a bit of criticism with regard to our investigation. But I think the nature of your questions, the Park Police concluded fairly quickly, I would say a matter of 20 to 24 hours, that it was clearly a suicide and had substantial evidence, I believe, to support that conclusion. And once they had reached that conclusion, I think some of the questions that you're asking now could best be directed to them . . ."[15]

THOUGH FISKE'S report found no evidence of any connection between Foster's death and Whitewater, Madison Guaranty, or David Hale's firm Capital Management Services (CMS), both Colombell and Monroe were at a loss to explain what light their investigation might have shed on it, especially given the possibility that Foster may have been alerted to the issuance of a federal warrant to search Hale's Little Rock offices on the day of Foster's death.

The committee Republicans noted that several witness statements by Little Rock individuals familiar with the issuance of the warrant were not turned over to the Senate.[16] This oversight was striking since the timing of the warrant had led to speculation about a link between Foster's death and the scandal involving Hale, the McDougals, and the Clintons. Colombell apologized for the oversight to Senator Kit Bond: "Senator, I'm sorry we don't have the information you wanted. We met with the staff of the Committee yesterday to discuss possible areas and the focus of this hearing. We did not think that was going to be one of the areas. Had we known so, we could have possibly made an effort to have that information for you, but we will have that information for you, I will assure."[17] Still more strange is that in the dozens of interviews conducted by Fiske's staff with Foster's friends and colleagues, no one was asked about Foster's knowledge of, or interest in, Hale or CMS. In the depositions taken by Fiske of Bill and Hillary Clinton, they also were not asked about such pertinent matters.

Agent Monroe offered, "What I know about [the CMS] aspect of the case, Senator, was that everyone who had knowledge of the particular issuance of that search warrant were interviewed . . . and our investigation shows that information was not given out specifically to Mr. Foster."[18] Such a carefully phrased response did not preclude the possibility that the information may have been passed to Foster via a third party.

This was not lost on Senator Bond, who stated, "The Independent Counsel's only evidence appears to be this one interview of Fletcher Jackson . . . in which he further stated that it was possible that someone could have made a telephone call."[19]

Fletcher Jackson was the assistant U.S. attorney for the eastern district of Arkansas who sought and received the CMS warrant on July 20, 1993, at 1:35 P.M. Fiske investigator Monroe stated to Senator Bond that there were indeed other interviews taken at the U.S. attorney's offices in Little Rock regarding the issuance of the warrant, but could not explain why they had not been turned over to Congress for their hearings.[20] Fletcher's FBI interview, the only one that was available to Congress at the time, is seven pages in length. Six of those pages are redacted in the public report.

Senator Bond noted that prior to the Committee's public hearings on that date, "the Chairman and the Ranking Member approved a request to conduct telephone depositions with employees of the Little Rock U.S. Attorney's Office. The Department of Justice concurred. Arrangements were made, and the Department of Justice sent a representative to Little Rock."

Bond continued: "Depositions were scheduled for Tuesday, July 26,

1994, to conduct simple telephone interviews of members of the U.S. Attorney's Office. . . . When we were notified at the last moment—after the court reporter had been sent to the office, after the representative of the Department of Justice had been sent there—that there was some problem. There was a delay. All of a sudden the depositions were beyond the scope of the Senate hearings. The depositions were not allowed to go forward and finally at 3:45 P.M., on Tuesday afternoon, Minority Counsel was informed that the depositions could not be taken."

Senator Bond was dismayed. "Mr. Chairman, this raises questions as to why the depositions were not allowed . . . because in the investigation of this matter [CMS] we continue to run into areas where all of a sudden normal investigative channels are precluded."[21]

Fiske himself had articulated his mandate regarding the Foster case in the opening paragraphs of his report: "If Foster committed suicide, was it motivated in any way by concerns Foster may have had about legal issues related to the Clintons' involvement with the Whitewater Development Company [sic], Inc. ('Whitewater'), Madison Guaranty Savings and Loan ('Madison Guaranty'), or Capital Management Services, Inc. ('CMS')?"[22]

A review of the approximately 125 FBI interviews conducted by Fiske's team shows that interviewees were indeed asked if Whitewater or Madison Guaranty was an issue of concern for Foster. They were even asked if Travelgate was an issue of concern for Foster, although that was not in Fiske's mandate.

Oddly missing, however, was questioning regarding CMS.

Interestingly, in his "Summary of Conclusions," Fiske wrote, "Moreover, in the spring and summer of 1993, Whitewater and Madison Guaranty related matters were not an issue of concern either within the White House or in the press."[23] This is true. However, the omission of CMS in that statement is glaring. In fact, the White House was well aware of the CMS issue in the spring of 1993. In May 1993, Small Business Administration (SBA) Associate Administrator Wayne Foren briefed Erskine Bowles, the new head of the SBA, about the "on-going investigation of David Hale's Capital Management Services because the case involved President Clinton." Shortly after, Foren also briefed White House Chief of Staff Mack McLarty.[24] What alerted Foren to the president's involvement in CMS in the spring of 1993, months before David Hale went public with accusations of pressure from Clinton to make the questionable loan, is not clear.

Fiske had still more alarming information that linked Foster to Hale. Two sources close to the Fiske and Starr probes have said that David Hale told Fiske's investigators that Foster, whom Hale knew, called Hale a week to ten days before his death. Hale said he was never able to make contact.

But even if Fiske did not have that information from Hale, his mandate from the Justice Department was to investigate matters relating to the Clintons and Hale's CMS. Foster was the Clintons' personal business attorney at the time of his death. Thus, Hale's CMS, a critical component of Fiske's inquiry, was glossed over in the Foster death investigation, and Senate investigators were thwarted in reviewing the warrant's role in Foster's death.

It is important to note that Hale's allegations had little to do with the Whitewater partnership, but more to do with widespread political corruption he claimed involved Bill Clinton, Arkansas governor Tucker, the McDougals, and possibly others. Bizarre, then, was the failure of Fiske, and later the Senate, to properly examine CMS's role in Foster's death and to find out whether CMS would be the pathway to unlocking the mystery of why Foster really died.

While Senate hearings helped to shed some light on the CMS problem, other key issues were never broached at the hearings: the failure to use a grand jury; the discrepancies in the Fiske report; or the allegations by the confidential witness that he had been badgered by Monroe and Colombell into changing his story about not having seen a gun in Foster's hand.

One of the few such issues to be addressed was the matter of the blond hairs and unusual carpet fibers found on Foster's clothing. "Our objective," Monroe said, "was to find out how Mr. Foster died, why did he die, and whether Whitewater at all played any role. It was our professional judgment that trying to determine [the origin of that hair] would not lead us, or advance us, in this objective. And let me go one step further, if I could, sir. The source of the hair could have been boundless."[25] As for the carpet fibers, Monroe said they were inconsequential "for the same reasons I provided in response to your first question relative to the hairs." Though the fibers had never been compared to any White House rugs, Monroe assured the committee that they "most likely came from [Foster's] residence or from his office . . ."[26]

If the hairs and fibers were of little importance, why did the FBI bother to collect and test them in the first place? Would it not also have been simple enough to establish whether the fibers came from Foster's home or office?

Contrary to Monroe's imputation, Fiske's team *had* been concerned about the carpet fibers. One FBI report shows that on June 10, just weeks before the Fiske report was issued, an agent on the Fiske team called the Park Police about the carpet fibers. He was told of the cross-contamination that occurred when—as the police claimed—all the clothing was placed in one bag at the coroner's office and sent to the police lab.[27] Yet a careful examination of the FBI reports showed all the clothes had in fact not been mixed together. The explanation that the carpet fibers came to be found on Foster's clothes through cross-contamination was faulty. Fiske, as was so often the case, accepted lame excuses from the Park Police and others to explain away evidence that pointed to foul play.

FOSTER'S STATE of mind, determined by the FBI to have been "deeply depressed," was a key component of Fiske's case that Foster killed himself. This was the first and most important contention made by Special Agent Larry Monroe: "First there can be no question that Vincent Foster committed suicide. Interviews . . . revealed that Mr. Foster was deeply depressed. . . ."[28] In addition to the official witness statements compiled by the FBI and referred to by Monroe, Fiske also cited the torn note found in Foster's briefcase and a handwritten list of three psychiatrists found in Foster's wallet. With the help of a clinical psychiatrist, Fiske concluded that Foster's "depressed state" as depicted by "interviews with Foster's family and friends" directly contributed to his suicide.

Yet a careful review of these FBI interview statements and other documents including the torn note and autopsy report paint a far more equivocal picture. Consider, for example, the statement given by Foster's personal secretary, Deborah Gorham, who worked intimately with him almost every day. Her assessment was considered significant enough for three of Fiske's top lawyers—Rod Lankler, Mark Stein, and Carl Stich— to join the FBI in interviewing her. "She viewed [Foster] as reserved, not depressed or unhappy. . . . He had a very long fuse so it was relatively rare for him to show agitation. . . . Even with hindsight, Gorham did not see anything in Foster's behavior which would indicate a distressed state of mind. . . . Foster had not ever made any statements or comments to Gorham indicating despondency and she had not noticed any physical changes in Foster from the time she started as his secretary to his death. [On the afternoon of his death] he appeared relaxed and normal."[29]

According to Fiske, Foster's Little Rock physician, Dr. Larry Watkins, had prescribed for him the antidepressant Trazodone. But a careful review of Watkins's statement shows that the drug was prescribed mainly to treat insomnia. The FBI record of that interview notes that Watkins, who presumably knew Foster well and had discussed his state of mind with him, "did not think that Foster was significantly depressed nor had Foster given the impression that he was 'in crisis.' "[30]

While Fiske states that a symptom of Foster's depression was weight loss—"It was obvious to many he had lost weight"—medical records contradict that claim; if anything, Foster had gained weight during his White House tenure.[31] Weeks before leaving Little Rock for Washington, Watkins had weighed Foster at 194 pounds.[32] Dr. Beyer's autopsy records his body as weighing 197 pounds—presumably not including the weight of lost blood.[33] Even Foster's wife told the FBI that any weight loss that might have occurred took place before her husband came to Washington.[34] (James Stewart in *Blood Sport* asserts that Foster's weight fluctuated while at the White House.[35] Nowhere in the FBI documents is there evidence to support this claim.)

Other evidence of depression cited by Fiske was Foster's stopping by the White House infirmary to have his blood pressure checked. Foster believed he had high blood pressure. It was found to be normal.[36]

FOR MANY, of course, the list of psychiatrists' names and numbers found on a scrap of paper in Foster's wallet was ample proof of serious depression. Fiske noted that Foster's telephone records showed he called one of them on the afternoon of Friday, July 16. The first call was placed at 12:41 P.M. and the second less than an hour later, at 1:24 P.M. Both calls lasted one minute or less, suggesting that Foster had simply gotten the office answering machine and hung up.[37] Perhaps Fiske's explanation was not completely honest. Two of the three psychiatrists on the list told the FBI they personally handled all appointments, and were "convinced" and "positive" that Mr. Foster had never contacted them for an appointment.[38]

Both calls were placed from the White House and, inexplicably, were put on Foster's calling card. Why would anyone make a local call from the White House on his calling card? If the call had been dialed in the normal manner, there would have been no record of it. Prosecutor Rodriguez entertained the possibility that the calls were made that way by someone other than Foster in order to create a record that would bolster a finding of suicide.[39]

Rodriguez became further suspicious when he and others in Starr's Washington office noted that the phone numbers jotted on the note did not *appear* to match the way Foster wrote his numbers.[40]

While Foster never did visit any of these psychiatrists, one of the three, Dr. Robert Hedaya of Chevy Chase, did tell Fiske's FBI investigators that on Friday, July 16, he received a call shortly after noon from Foster's sister, Sheila, who told him that her brother Vincent was in need of help and would be calling shortly. Hedaya told the FBI that he waited by the phone for Foster's call during the lunch hour, that he did not use his answering machine, and that Foster never called him.[41] Foster's sister had said that her brother "was dealing on a daily basis with Top Secret matters and that his depression was directly related to highly sensitive and confidential matters." He told the FBI that Sheila gave him the "distinct impression [Foster] was in a bind, needed desperately to talk to someone . . . his depression was a direct result of sensitive and confidential issues."[42] Hedaya's statements about waiting for the call were not included in his official FBI statement.[43]

The strongest evidence of Foster's "depression" was the torn note discovered in his briefcase almost a week after his death. None of the items it mentions appear related to "Top Secret" issues. Nor did they include some other major issues that *were* bothering Foster. For example, Mrs. Foster said her husband had been "horrified" by the FBI's raid on the Branch Davidian compound at Waco, which resulted in the deaths of 75 civilians, including 25 children.[44]

The Fiske team accepted the validity of the note, though they were well aware of the problems associated with the circumstances of its discovery. As stated in a report prepared for Fiske, the FBI's experts failed to find a conclusive match between the note and several checks written by Foster.[45]

Fiske also did not have the FBI examine the note for psycholinguistic indicators: Did the ramblings in the note match the patterns of Foster's known writings? Foster's two longtime law partners, Kennedy and Hubbell, both told the FBI that the use of the word "lie" (mentioned in the note five times) was very unusual for Foster, whose language was always more measured. " 'Lied' is not a word that Vince used," Hubbell told the FBI.[46] Likewise, Kennedy's official FBI statement says that he "was surprised to see the word 'lie' in Foster's note. . . . Kennedy was asked if Foster ever used the term in describing other matters. Kennedy said he never recalled Foster calling someone a liar."[47] Even the tearing of the note was out of character. Loraine Cline, Foster's longtime secretary at the Rose firm, told the FBI that Foster "generally did not tear things up." Typically he would "crumple" a paper and "pitch it in the waste basket."[48]

Five of the items in the note dealt with the travel office. To Fiske, this impending scandal provided sufficient motivation for Foster's having taken his own life. Fiske mentioned that Foster's friend, former Arkansas law partner Webster Hubbell, supported that contention.[49] But in Hubbell's extensive initial interview with Fiske's FBI agents, conducted on April 13, 1994, Hubbell made only one passing reference to the travel office. On that occasion Hubbell merely noted that Foster thought William Kennedy had gotten a "bum rap" in the matter, and that this bothered Foster.[50] William Kennedy's first FBI interview statement, given on May 6, 1994, makes no mention of the travel office matter, though Kennedy was a key player in that affair.

Actually Hubbell and Kennedy seemed at a loss to explain Foster's suicide. Both noted that no one could pinpoint any event that might have provoked it. Furthermore, Hubbell told the FBI that he had not "observed any noticeable behavioral or emotional changes . . . prior to his death." The best he could say was that the demanding work schedule with little time off was "wearing on us all."[51]

Fiske mentioned Foster's workload as contributing to his stress in the opening line of his section detailing Foster's state of mind: "Foster's position at the White House generally demanded that he work from between 7:30 in the morning until 9:30 or later at night, either six or seven days per week."[52] But Foster's personal secretary testified in a Senate deposition that he generally showed up for work between 8:30 and 9:00 in the morning.[53]

Hubbell also said that he had noted no changes in Foster's "personal appearance, physical ailments, headaches, loss of appetite, or any kind of stomach trouble." He also stated he was not aware that "Foster was experiencing any type of stress."[54]

By June, as Fiske was wrapping up his report, the supporting evidence for his travel office theory was minimal. In an attempt to fill that void, Fiske's investigators returned to reinterview Hubbell and Kennedy, this time zeroing in on the travel office. Again, Hubbell and Kennedy seemed to offer little support for the theory that the travel office matter had led Foster to take his own life.

"Foster was upset, but not terribly so, about the criticism," Hubbell told the investigators.[55] The statement quotes Hubbell as saying that for Foster the travel office "got worse" and that he became "very upset" that

Kennedy received a reprimand. The statement reads as though the agents were trying to draw something out of Hubbell that was not there.[56]

According to the second statement, Hubbell told the FBI he believed the "Travel Office matter couldn't be put to bed or die and be over with."[57] In the actual Fiske report, the statement sounded more ominous: Foster "further told Hubbell he thought the [travel office] matter would never end."[58]

If the travel office matter had been such an important worry of Foster's, particularly Kennedy's reprimand, why was there only a passing mention of it in Hubbell's first FBI statement and no mention of it in Kennedy's? David Watkins, the White House administrator who actually fired the travel office employees and who had known Foster since childhood in Hope, Arkansas, told the FBI he was unaware of any "internal hostility" about the agency's report on the matter, let alone from Foster. The statement continued: "Watkins never heard directly or indirectly that Foster was distressed about [the FBI's report], or about anything else for that matter."[59]

Based on such shallow testimony, Fiske asserted that the travel office matter was a significant factor in Foster's depression. Fiske has stated that Foster was so concerned about improprieties in the travel office matter that he had even sought outside legal counsel for himself.[60]

Since the issuance of the Fiske report, additional documents have been released that indicate that Foster was interested in finding legal counsel not for himself but for the Clintons. The September 1996 House Committee on Government Reform and Oversight describes Foster's last days this way: "Mr. Foster repeatedly suggested to Nussbaum that President and Mrs. Clinton needed outside counsel in the matter. These were not the rantings of a man losing touch with reality. In fact, it appears that, despite his depression, Vince Foster was one of the few White House officials who saw matters clearly."[61]

As for the committee report that Foster was suffering from "depression" as a result of the travel office imbroglio, the report itself offers no evidence. Instead, it cites the Fiske report, which claimed that the travel office, according to "those close to Foster," was "the single greatest source of [his] distress. . . ."[62]

If Foster was so depressed, as Fiske suggests, why did Hubbell, Kennedy, and Watkins not detect apparent signs of this depression?

Like many others, Hubbell would later change his story. While serving a prison sentence on mail fraud and tax evasion charges in July 1995, Hubbell completely reversed himself and told a Senate hearing about Foster's "depression." He told the senators that during Foster's last week he "talked about how tired he was, how down he was."[63] Hubbell told the committee that he was so worried that he had set up a meeting with White House chief of staff Mack McLarty upon returning from a weekend trip with Foster and his wife. Hubbell said the purpose of the meeting, never mentioned in any of his FBI statements, was "to see what we could do to help our mutual friend."[64] None of this seemingly important information was even mentioned in Hubbell's two FBI statements compiled during the Fiske probe.

"I think you know, we were all concerned," Hubbell testified. "Vince had lost weight, had seemed to be depressed," he told the senators. So depressed, Hubbell said, that Foster thought his phone was tapped.[65] This strange but possibly significant concern about security was not mentioned in other statements Hubbell gave to Fiske.

No one challenged Hubbell about the discrepancies in his testimony. His changing testimony reflects poorly on Fiske, who had failed to use a grand jury or put anyone under oath. The acceptance of Hubbell's FBI statements at face value, even to the point of referencing his statements in the final report on Foster's death, seems incongruous with the fact that Hubbell was at the same time a focus of Fiske's Arkansas probe. As one of Starr's Little Rock prosecutors pointed out to me, on the very day Fiske's Washington FBI agents were interviewing Hubbell about Foster and the travel office, Hubbell's lawyer was denying requests by Fiske's Little Rock office to turn over his credit card and financial records. Neither half of the Fiske probe knew what the other half was doing: One side was relying on his unsworn testimony as the basis for their report at the same time that he was stonewalling the other side for documents in a criminal probe.[66] Fiske, who was said to be intimately involved in the details of both sides of his investigation, should have known better.

FISKE ALSO relied heavily on Mrs. Foster's statement to support the conclusion of depression. The word "depression" appears throughout Mrs. Foster's FBI statement. For example: "Lisa Foster recalls that he [Foster] mentioned his depression to her on approximately July 16, 1993."[67] Yet this was at odds with what Mrs. Foster subsequently told Peter Boyer of *The New Yorker*. In his September 1995 article, Boyer reported that Lisa noticed no depression while he was alive and only saw it in retrospect after his death. "At the time, Lisa never considered the possibility that Vince was suffering from depression. In her world, emotional problems were not discussed, and depression in its clinical sense was an alien concept. 'I'd never had any experience with this at all—I hated it when people said he was depressed because I didn't know what depression was.' "[68] The evidence of this, as she noted in hindsight to *The New Yorker*, was that her husband "began absently wringing his hands, incessantly rubbing the thumb and forefinger of one hand into the palm of the other." Had Foster lived, she might never have remembered these signs of apparent "depression."[69]

While some might see evidence of depression in the observations found in the FBI reports, it is far from conclusive. Among the manifestations of his supposed suicidal depression were Foster's compulsive hand rubbing, insomnia, belief that he had a heavy heartbeat, and a suspicion that his phones were tapped. It is also possible that Foster may have been afraid of something. A source close to Starr's staff came to that conclusion, based on several reasons, including Foster's effort to protect his Georgetown home with an expensive alarm system.

According to Mrs. Foster's FBI statement, Foster had told his wife that he wanted to resign, and apparently the travel office scandal had been a significant factor. Rather than feeling oppressed by a sense of personal failure in the matter, evidence suggests that Foster was much more concerned about the heavy-handed White House response and Mrs. Clinton's efforts to distance herself from the scandal.

Shortly after Foster's death, *Newsweek* reported on the significance of the travel office matter: "When the scandal broke, Foster thought that he had hurt his friend [William Kennedy]. Worse, he felt compelled to drag in the First Lady. An old Washington hand advised Foster to make full disclosure: the coverup, he warned, is always worse than the crime. Foster, over the objections of other White House aides, pushed for a report showing, among other things, that Hillary Clinton had knowledge of the misbegotten purge of the Travel Office. The press seized on this fact, and Foster grimaced at another headline."[70]

Notes taken by Foster during the travel office controversy were released to *The Washington Times* in the summer of 1995. The notes indicated that Foster was particularly uncomfortable with Mrs. Clinton's role, and he questioned whether there was justification for the administration's actions in the matter. "Odds small—there will be smoking gun," Foster wrote in one note, seeming to minimize the extent of the actual threat in contrast to the extreme reactions of some in the White House.[71] He also recorded that Mrs. Clinton was unhappy with his handling of the matter and with the actions of David Watkins, a presidential assistant who managed the travel office, and Harry Thomasson, an intimate of Bill and Hillary who reportedly took an interest in the travel office because of his links to the Arkansas travel firm that hoped to take over that White House contract.

In another note, Foster wrote, "Suggest, in light of HRC inquiry previous day, DW [Watkins] might want to update [Mrs. Clinton] on audit results."[72] Those jottings, by the way, hardly comport with the official White House line that Mrs. Clinton played little or no role in the travel office takeover.

According to the *Times*, Foster listed several times that cash missing from the travel office accounts, supervised by director Billy Dale, could be explained. Indeed, contrary to assumptions that Foster was plunged into despair about the outcome, at one point he seemed rather optimistic. There "could be [a] plausible explanation" or "reasonable explanation" for the approximately $18,000 in funds that Dale had written out to cash, Foster wrote.[73] At another point Foster wondered whether "there is [he underlined "is" twice] actual wrongdoing" involving Dale. Foster wrote that Kennedy also questioned whether an investigation into the office was even "worthwhile."[74]

According to some published accounts, Foster's long-standing intimate relationship with Mrs. Clinton began to break down as the travel office matter unraveled in May 1993. Though Foster had been one of Mrs. Clinton's chief confidants in Arkansas and was now handling all of the Clintons' personal business matters, and though each had offices close to one another in the West Wing, Mrs. Clinton later admitted that she had not spoken to Foster for a full six weeks before his death. If Foster had a problem with anyone, arguably, it was with Hillary.

SINCE FISKE and his investigators did not rely solely on physical evidence and forensic analysis to make a conclusion, but on Foster's state of mind as well, the integrity of the FBI witness statements used to paint that mental picture should have been meticulously established. Yet at times, straightforward testimony contradicts official claims made in the Fiske report, and a comparison of testimony, like that of Webb Hubbell, suggests that FBI agents were less than thorough in compiling their statements. Indeed, a close examination shows that the FBI went to some lengths to remove any suggestion that Foster's death was anything but a suicide. Agents working for Fiske were clearly aware that Webster Hubbell, as well as others close to Foster, had strong initial fears that Foster's death had been the result of foul play.

Such initial doubts are not unusual. What is unusual is that no such comments can be found in the more than one hundred FBI statements compiled by Fiske's agents and released to Congress. No one mentions ever doubting for a second the official ruling of suicide.

One person who held such initial doubts was a highly reputable associate of Foster's, Phillip Carroll, a senior litigator at the Rose Law Firm. Shortly after the death, Carroll was unequivocal in telling Esquire magazine: "I keep saying no. That wasn't Vince Foster. He was my favorite. He was so competent. He was a very strong individual. I keep coming back to foul play. There had to be foul play involved."[75]

Carroll knew Foster well. Foster was his protégé. They lived in the same neighborhood. Carroll was the godfather of Foster's oldest son.

Carroll had witnessed firsthand how Foster stood up under some of the worst pressure imaginable when, during the 1992 presidential campaign, a longtime Arkansas Clinton critic, Larry Nichols, was hawking a story to supermarket tabloids about an alleged affair between Foster and Mrs. Clinton. In a small, relatively close-knit city like Little Rock, a scandal like this could be devastating.

Inevitably, Foster got wind of the rumored story. Though clearly disturbed by it, Foster had not panicked. Instead, he prudently informed Carroll and his other law partners about the possibility of such a news story and prepared his wife and children. Foster declared the allegation a fabrication.

It was such remembrances of Foster that made Carroll doubt that this man could, with no warning or clear indication, go off to a remote park and shoot himself because of an ethical conflict. As Carroll told the FBI, "Foster handled stress wonderfully."[76] No doubt that was why Carroll had little difficulty accepting the seemingly bizarre evaluation of then–associate attorney general Webb Hubbell, who was among the first to break the news of his friend's death to him.

"Webb called me at midnight the night it happened," Carroll recalled to *Esquire*. "He said, 'Don't believe a word you hear. It was not suicide. It couldn't have been.' "[77]

As Hubbell wandered around the Fosters' Georgetown home with cell phone in hand calling Foster's associates in Little Rock, his doubts would not have been unusual. And Carroll, who now believes that Foster did commit suicide, told me that many other people initially doubted the suicide ruling. As Carroll explained, "A lot of people felt that way" who knew Foster well because he was "the last person" who would commit suicide.[78]

Later, when Carroll's and Hubbell's FBI statements were released, not a word could be found about these initial doubts. In fact, as noted above, in thousands of pages released from the Park Police and Fiske investigations, including countless statements of friends, associates, and family, there is not one mention that anyone ever doubted the suicide finding.

Carroll was interviewed at length by the FBI in the spring of 1994. There is no mention of his doubts about the suicide, or even Hubbell's, though they had been well publicized in *Esquire*. Instead there is an oblique reference in Carroll's FBI statement, indicating the FBI knew of these doubts. The summary reads: "A little later that night Webb Hubbell called him and notified him. On July 21st, both Carroll and his wife flew to Washington, D.C. He discussed the death with Hubbell and Hubbell himself communicated no suspicions to him *at the time* that Foster's death was anything but a suicide" [emphasis added].[79] As Carroll told me later, Hubbell never expressed any doubts after the first night, and Carroll never claimed he did. The FBI agents working for Fiske had handled this artfully.

THE FACT that doubts about the suicide were simply omitted from official FBI statements is serious. Since the issuance of the Fiske report a significant number of allegations have been made about the handling of FBI witness statements during the Fiske investigation. These statements are compiled by FBI agents on documents known as "FD 302s," which are part of the raw material prosecutors use to judge whether a crime has taken place in a given case.

The FD 302s are prepared in a two-step process. First, the interviewing agent takes handwritten notes of the interrogation. The agent then returns to the office and dictates the notes to a secretary, who types them on an FD 302, completing the official witness statement.

Manipulation of these statements can take place at either part of this two-step process. The interviewing agent can lead the witness with questions or present him or her with possible scenarios to make a statement less certain or clear. The agent can also decide which information to record. The statement can be further manipulated in the recording of the notes, when the agent might "spin" what is dictated to the secretary.

Serious allegations have been raised about the way FBI agents working for Fiske compiled their FD 302s. The first challenge came three weeks after the release of the Fiske report, when the witness called CW called radio talk show host G. Gordon Liddy, claiming that the FBI had badgered him into changing his story. CW said the agents had asked him as many as twenty-five times if the gun could have been hidden by foliage and never showed him the scene Polaroid released by ABC News. He would later say in a recorded conversation with Reed Irvine of Accuracy in Media that FBI agents also persuaded him to change his story as to the exact location of the body.[80] As a former FBI agent, Liddy knew this was unusual. When completing witness statements, the interviewing agent is not supposed to lead the witness but to simply take down raw information—even if it appears inaccurate or contradictory.

Motorist Patrick Knowlton, the first to spot what Fiske identified as Foster's Honda in Fort Marcy Park, has subsequently claimed that FBI agents "lied" in compiling his official statement. According to Knowlton, whose account first surfaced in a report by Ambrose Evans-Prichard in London's *Sunday Telegraph*, he was shocked when he read his official FBI statement, which said that he would not have been able to identify a man he saw in the park. Knowlton insisted that he *could* identify the man and went on to help a police artist do a composite sketch for the *Telegraph*.[81]

Knowlton told the *Telegraph* that when he was interviewed by agents Larry Monroe and William Colombell, he pointedly told them that he could identify a Hispanic-looking man sitting in a car near to Foster's. He said he had a haunting memory of this man and told the agents as much. Yet his FBI statement reads: "could not further identify this individual [the Hispanic-looking man] and stated that he would be unable to recognize him in the future."[82]

Knowlton, whose friends say has a keen memory, also told the *Tele-*

graph that agents Monroe and Colombell went to extraordinary lengths to convince him that the Honda he saw in the lot was a blue one of recent vintage. Knowlton insists that the car was an older model and that it was brown.

Fiske's investigators seem to have been bothered by Knowlton's testimony about the man who observed him and his differing description of the Honda with Arkansas plates. If, as Scalice and Santucci contend, the body might have been moved to the park, the man could have been there to secure the front entrance of the park and lot, and the car could have been placed there for some other reason.

It is worth noting that the same agents who interviewed Knowlton, Monroe and Colombell, interviewed CW, who also claims that he was badgered into altering his statement. Knowlton and CW were not acquainted and are not known to have made contact with each other since Foster's death.

During proceedings led by prosecutor Miquel Rodriguez, the grand jury received testimony at odds with almost every FBI witness statement. For instance, paramedic Todd Hall, one of the first to come upon Foster's body, testified he saw a man wearing a red vest running away from the death scene on the trail at the bottom of the berm. Hall said his FBI statement misrepresented what he told them. His first statement reads that he "saw something moving in the woods. He was unable to determine if it was a person."[83] This was an important question considering the group of unidentified men wearing such vests later encountered by Park Police on a park trail.[84]

As noted previously, the Park Police simply dismissed these unidentified men wearing red/orange vests as just "volunteers" working on one of Fort Marcy's trails. Hall's observation from the area of the body of an individual wearing an orange or red vest should have raised red flags for Fiske's investigators. It didn't.

Both Fiske and Starr willingly accepted this explanation of the red-vested individuals as volunteers without further inquiry. I called park regular Reeves and asked him if he had ever heard of any such volunteers who wore orange- or red-colored vests in the park. His answer was an emphatic no. Next I contacted Fort Marcy's maintenance supervisor Tyrone Brown. Brown, too, said he knew of no volunteers who wore vests. Brown said volunteers do occasionally work on the Potomac Heritage Trail that traverses Fort Marcy, but he doubted any volunteers would be in the park that late in the evening. Usually they work on weekends and with the assistance of the park ranger, he said.

The park ranger who handles Fort Marcy, Bart Truesdale, said he was unaware of volunteers who wear red or orange vests. He said anyone who works on the parkway has to wear such a safety vest. "It's a requirement," he said. Truesdale claimed that volunteers for the park trails are organized through the Potomac Appalachian Club. Like Brown, he was somewhat surprised club members would be working on the trails that late in the evening.

Terry Cummings, public relations chairman for the Potomac Appalachian Club, said that his club does help maintain the trail in Fort Marcy. "We don't wear any kind of vests. Everyone goes to work wearing whatever they want," Cummings explained to me. He added that it "seemed very unlikely" that any volunteers would be in Fort Marcy after 6:00 P.M. on a summer weekday.

Yet based on available information, Hall saw a man wearing the vest around 6:15 P.M., and the Park Police located the volunteers at 6:30 P.M. or later. Why were volunteers working late on a summer Tuesday, and during the dinner hour, no less?

Reeves, Brown, Truesdale, and Cummings said they had never been questioned about any volunteers in Fort Marcy. Rather than fully investigate this glaring problem, Fiske's investigators simply "re-interviewed" Hall in late April 1994, showing obvious concern about Hall's observations. Hall's second statement reads that he "believed he saw something moving in the trees surrounding the location of Foster's body." He told the agents he saw a "bright orange or red color." His statement then notes that "Hall believes it is possible that he could have seen vehicular traffic on Route 123."[85]

According to a source close to the Starr probe, Hall testified to the grand jury that he told the FBI he saw a person, not an object such as a car. While he acknowledged that the possible car scenario was broached, he said it was not broached by him but, rather, by the interviewing FBI agents.[86]

Hall's was not an isolated case. Of nearly a dozen witnesses called by Rodriguez, almost every one gave testimony at variance with what Fiske's FBI investigators had recorded based on their interviews the year before.

James Stewart's *Blood Sport* also called into question the integrity of the FBI statements. Susan Thomases, a primary source for Stewart, told him of having seen Foster alone two weeks before his death at a high-priced Washington boardinghouse where she regularly stayed. There Foster confided to her that his "marriage [with Lisa] had not been what he'd hoped for, and it hadn't been for years."[87]

The FBI record of the interview conducted by Fiske's investigators presents a different account. According to that statement, completed on June 14, 1994, Thomases told the FBI she could offer no explanation for why Foster had killed himself and recalled that she last saw him alive the week before he died, at lunch with several other people.[88] Stewart had access to Thomases's FBI statement, but never questioned her about this serious discrepancy. It was serious enough that Thomases was recalled to testify in the spring of 1996 about this and other matters. Thomases told the Senate Banking Committee that the FBI agent inaccurately took down her statement.[89]

If Thomases or other witnesses interviewed during the course of the Fiske probe intentionally misled the FBI, that is a federal crime under section 1001 of the federal code. Agents, however, do not tape-record their interviews, and the possibility of miscommunication makes prosecution of witnesses relatively rare, legal experts have said. Moreover, the pattern of such inaccuracies in this case might lead one to infer that it was the investigators—not the witnesses—who were doing the misleading.

Examination of the evidence involving the second stage in the FD 302-compiling process, when the agent writes up the statement based on handwritten notes, affords an even more compelling case for this conclusion.

As a result of a lawsuit filed by myself and the Western Journalism Center in federal district court in Washington, the independent counsel agreed to release the handwritten interview notes of Fiske's FBI investigators. Several documents were missing from the batch subsequently turned over, including the one used to compile the FD 302 on Susan Thomases. Others are heavily redacted. Still others show that agents, in preparing official statements, tried to downplay any evidence that countered the official claims.

For example, in the handwritten notes of the FBI interview with Fairfax EMT worker Richard Arthur, he was emphatic—more so than his statement implies—that he saw both a wound on Foster's neck and an automatic pistol in Foster's hand, not the Colt revolver police later found. An excerpt of notes taken during the Arthur interview reads as follows:

> 100% sure automatic weapon (was in Army, looks at magazines, knows diff. between automatic and revolver). Appeared like .45 automatic. right side jaw line small caliber bullet hole (approx. between ear and tip of chin). Didn't see any other bullet holes. . . . gun bigger than hole, gun underneath leg. About approx. ½ barrel under leg. . . . Cory [Ashford] told me head was intact, didn't notice any exit wound. From the size of gun I saw would've been an exit wound.[90]

When preparing Arthur's statement on an FD 302, the agent made some subtle changes. Arthur's declaration that he was "100% sure" about the gun being an automatic, not a revolver, was written up as, "He remembers the gun as being an automatic weapon of approximately .45 caliber." As for his discussions with Cory Ashford about the exit wound, Arthur's official statement only reads: "Arthur speculated that from the size of the gun he thought he had seen, there would have been an exit wound." No mention of the serious doubts about the suicide among his colleagues, or Arthur's recollection of Ashford's comment that he did not see an exit wound.[91]

Agents were apparently concerned enough about Arthur's statements to return to interview him a second time, focusing on the gun. Again the handwritten notes show that Arthur was certain the gun in Foster's hand was not a revolver but an automatic pistol:

> Gun under right hand, tucked under right leg. A pistol not a revolver . . . based on that looked like a 9mm pistol, straight barrel, square handle (from memory) brown and black.[92]

The notes also referenced Arthur's army service, but downplayed the significance by stating, "Definitely not an expert on guns; not expert on forensics."[93]

The second FD 302 on Arthur omits any supporting comments he made about the gun that were noted by the interviewing agent, such as seeing a square handle, which is typical of an automatic pistol. Instead, his official statement reads: "Arthur was of the opinion that if the weapon was in fact a revolver, the cylinder quite possibly could have been covered up."[94] This line in his official statement totally undermines Arthur's clear recollection that the revolver the police say they found in Foster's hand was not the automatic pistol he saw. Through ascribing this opinion to Arthur, it is obvious that one of the interviewing FBI agents had proposed the idea that the gun may have been partially covered by Foster's hand and thus difficult to see.

Arthur was not the only witness to whom agents proffered mitigating scenarios. The FBI suggested to paramedic Todd Hall that he may have seen a car passing in the background, not a person moving away from the body when he arrived at the scene. In a similar manner, CW claimed that FBI agents suggested Foster's head had been tilted to the right (explaining, of course, the strange right-side blood tracks) and that the gun he failed to see when he discovered Foster's body was hidden by foliage.

Other items in the handwritten notes are bothersome. Lisa Foster's official witness statement claims her husband was "fighting depression" before he died. Since, as she acknowledges, she did not notice it at the time, why did she say he was depressed? The handwritten notes for that interview show that Mrs. Foster said her husband was "battling prescription," not depression.[95] Of course "battling prescription" is an odd statement, and one can chalk it up to simple error. But if Mrs. Foster did not observe any signs of it, how could she claim he was "fighting" depression? At another point in her statement, Mrs. Foster said her husband feared taking sleeping pills because they were addictive. We know that Foster's doctor had prescribed Trazodone for insomnia. Is that what the "battling" referred to?

The handwritten notes also suggest that Fiske's investigators tried to narrow the gap between the time the Park Police say they notified the White House of the death and the time the White House says it received word. According to Lieutenant Gavin's FBI statement, he called the White House within ten minutes of learning Foster was an official there. Officer Braun's statement as compiled by the FBI shows that she called Gavin to notify him of Foster's status between 7:30 P.M. and 7:45 P.M. If Gavin called within ten minutes, he would have notified the White House no later than 8:00 P.M. A half-hour gap must be accounted for in order to accept the White House claim that it was not notified until 8:30 P.M.

The handwritten notes show the gap was even longer and was shortened by Fiske's investigators with a little play on the statements. The notes for Braun's interview indicate that she made the call to Gavin by 7:30 P.M. (Braun said she located Foster's identification in his Honda thirty minutes before the Gavin call, making the latest time she learned of his identity 7:00 P.M.)[96] When an FBI agent dictated her official statement onto the FD 302 from the handwritten notes, the agent said that Braun called Gavin between 7:30 and 7:45 P.M. Thus the gap in time was made less obvious by gratuitously adding fifteen minutes.[97]

Even putting aside all the manipulation and fudging of times, the record shows that the White House knew of the death at least a half hour earlier than it claimed. Moreover Lieutenant Gavin told the FBI that five minutes after he had made his notification call to the Secret Service, he was called back by deputy chief of staff Bill Burton.[98] Obviously the higher ranks of the administration were immediately informed.

Handwritten notes also show that Fiske's investigators were concerned about the CNN makeup artist's statement of having overheard a discussion between the president and an unidentified aide in the Map Room as the president was being prepared for the talk show program.

The handwritten notes from the interview with White House aide Bruce Lindsey report that Lindsey was asked about the possibility that the president knew about, or had been informed of, matters relating to Foster's office when Clinton was in the Map Room just before he went on the King show at 9 P.M.

The Lindsey notes read as follows:[99]

> Didn't hear any conversation about finding note that night or look for a note; nor going into Vince Foster's office . . .
>
> Map Room? President never came in. never shut door. never talked about note.

Fiske never indicated in his report that there was any problem with the official time line detailing how and when White House aides and the president were notified of Foster's death. The FBI's handwritten notes, however, give some clues that in fact Fiske and his staff knew that the official story did not jibe with the known facts.

Not every FBI agent working for Fiske was happy with the conduct of the Washington side of their investigation. One FBI agent who had been assigned to work on matters related to Foster's office and the activities of White House aides in the aftermath of the death quit soon after the issuance of Fiske's report in the summer of 1994, to return to his regular duties at FBI's Tysons Corner, Virginia, office.[100]

To all appearances, the agent simply rotated back to his normal FBI duties. But when he spoke with two prosecutors from Kenneth Starr's investigative staff, the agent made it clear that he had left because he wanted out. He told the prosecutors that politics seemed to be guiding the probe.

At the time that the fifty-eight-page Foster report was released, the *New York Times* wrote that Fiske's report on the office matter was due to be issued in the early days of July. A hiccup, however, prevented Fiske from doing so. In July, congressional investigators with the House Oversight Committee, preparing for hearings on the report, asked Fiske's office for permission to conduct preliminary interviews with several White House aides and law enforcement officers assigned there. Fiske begged off, saying he would need more time.[101]

In the end Fiske never issued a public report on the case, since he was not appointed to the newly authorized position of independent counsel. Fiske did issue a secret report to the court, and I am told by a person on Starr's staff who read it that Fiske and his staff cleared all White House officials of any wrongdoing in the immediate aftermath of Foster's death.

The FBI agent who left Fiske's staff, and who has since retired from the bureau and joined IBM, believed that conclusion was not justified. This agent was clearly upset by the handling of the case by Fiske's prosecutors, notably Associate Counsel Mark J. Stein, who had held a third-tier, but pivotal, position in the Washington office.[102]

The agent had better information than most to conclude that officials had engaged in wrongdoing. Based on the same information Fiske had, the Senate Banking Committee voted to recommend several officials for indictments.* Under federal statutes, even if a witness does not lie outright, but gives evasive answers, has memory lapses on critical matters and events, or is deliberately vague and misleading while testifying under oath, the person can be charged with perjury. The Republicans on the Senate committee believed there was ample evidence that key Clinton aides had committed perjury. Fiske was also aware that the index for the Clintons' papers kept in Foster's office was missing. Also, official inventories of documents in Foster's office that had been compiled by White House staff days after Foster's death omitted any mention of files dealing

---

* The preoccupation with the financial scandal of Whitewater led to the curious anomaly of the Senate Banking committee investigating a homicide, something more appropriate to the Judiciary or Government Affairs committees. The House Banking committee had also been probing Whitewater matters but its chairman, Representative Henry Gonzales, decided not to hold hearings on the Foster death. That decision was supported by every Democratic member of the committee while the ranking minority member, Representative James Leach, and all of his fellow Republicans voted to hold hearings.

with controversial matters, though Foster's secretary testified that he kept such files in his office. For example, the inventories showed no files relating to the travel office.[103] Foster was, of course, intimately involved in the travel office affair.* Yet Fiske was willing to accept White House claims that nothing improper had been done by aides in removing files, even with this circumstantial evidence and the eyewitness testimony of Secret Service officer Henry O'Neill, who alleges that Maggie Williams removed papers from Foster's office on the night of the death.

The FBI agent was particularly impressed by O'Neill's testimony and told others he believed O'Neill was "the salt of the earth," as one investigator familiar with the agent's problems related. "You have to understand who Hank O'Neill is," the source said. "For years he worked the graveyard shift at the White House, and his principal job was to make sure confidential trash was disposed of properly and in a timely fashion. He did not hold a management position. He was absolutely not making up that story. He had nothing to gain by doing so, except heartburn."[104]

The O'Neill-Williams imbroglio was one matter that had angered the agent. Another issue was the kid-glove treatment Fiske's staff had afforded Craig Livingstone, the former nightclub bouncer who was now head of White House personnel security.

Livingstone, as it turns out, had been on the radar screen of investigators of the Fiske and Starr probes long before the "Filegate" scandal erupted in 1996.[105] In 1994, several investigators thought Livingstone's testimony might prove to be the "smoking gun" of the cover-up following Foster's death. Livingstone was interviewed by Fiske's investigators, including the FBI agent who quit, because he had been a key player in handling the Foster matter from the outset. Livingstone was among the first to be notified of the death, and he was sent to identify Foster's body in the morgue. Oddly, Mr. Livingstone's FBI statement was not included in the 2,672 pages of the hearings into the death of Vincent Foster.

---

* Though the inventories showed no travel office documents, the White House later claimed that a travel office file was found by Nussbaum in an office briefcase on July 22. Also, a notebook Foster kept regarding the travel office later turned up in Nussbaum's office when his successor, Abner Mikva, turned it over to Congress.

Livingstone has claimed that he was notified of Foster's death at 9 P.M.—a story nicely consistent with White House claims. But other testimony contradicts the Livingstone and White House accounts of when they learned of the death and supports the conclusion that senior aides to the president knew about the death earlier that evening.

Livingstone acknowledges that immediately after hearing the bad news, he called William Kennedy, Foster's friend and White House associate counsel. Livingstone informed Kennedy of the death and asked Kennedy to meet him at Fairfax Hospital morgue to identify the body. Kennedy told the FBI agents working for Fiske that he received Livingstone's call "between 8:15 and 8:30 P.M."

Kennedy's wife, Gayle, had a similar recollection. In 1995 she was called before Starr's grand jury. A confidential source told me that during questioning by Starr's prosecutor Brett Kavanaugh, Gayle Kennedy said she was home with her husband when the call came and distinctly remembered it had come just after she had put their two children to bed, which she did, as usual, at 8 P.M.

The morning after the death, Secret Service officer Bruce Abbott told Park Police that he had spotted Livingstone several times leaving the West Wing's second floor where Foster's office was located. On one occasion, he saw Livingstone carrying a briefcase. Livingstone has said he did carry a briefcase, but never removed documents from Foster's office. Some investigators found that doubtful, since Livingstone later complained to White House staff that he had been "ratted out" by the Secret Service officer—implying that Livingstone had in fact removed the documents as charged.[106]

While being initially interviewed about this and other matters, Livingstone stunned investigators by giving an account about what happened in the days after Foster's death that was completely contradictory to White House claims. As one person familiar with the interview said, it seemed Livingstone was on the verge of "spilling the beans."

As the interview proceeded, with the case unraveling and Livingstone's attorney strongly encouraging his client to tell the truth, "it was clear to everyone in the room, including [Livingstone's] attorney, that he was not telling the truth, or that he was giving half truths, partial statements or false inferences," the source said.[107] At one point Livingstone and his attorney left the room to confer. When the two returned, Livingstone announced he did not want to continue. His lawyer, according to one source on the Fiske investigation, "shrugged his shoulders, he was totally exasperated."[108]

Livingstone underwent a second interview with Fiske's staff, this time with new legal representation and a story more in line with White House claims. Investigators had been focusing on inconsistent times Livingstone had given as to when he and others were notified about the death and his activities immediately thereafter. Livingstone's new attorney, Randall Turk, began by telling the incredulous investigators that Livingstone had been confused about the times, but that he had written a memo-to-file detailing the chronology of his activities.

Livingstone told Fiske's investigators he had no idea what happened to this memo and that he could not find it in his files. He claimed he had sent it to either associate White House counsel William Kennedy or presidential aide David Watkins. When investigators asked for a set of all of Livingstone's memos-to-file, he said that he had never written one before or since. After a warrant was issued seeking Livingstone's memo on White House computer files, it suddenly surfaced.

"If such a memo had existed, [Livingstone] would have mentioned it in his first interview. He didn't when he needed it. The memo was a life jacket; it was a lifeboat," the source said.[109]

Fiske and his staff apparently accepted Livingstone's story at face value, but other investigators found it fantastic. The FBI agent who quit called such stories "very convenient"—including the finding of a so-called suicide note in a previously searched briefcase. The agent believed Stein was not well qualified to handle a complex criminal investigation and had not rigorously pursued the strong evidence that Livingstone, Nussbaum, and Williams had all committed perjury.

By the end of July, the three-judge panel established by the new law to select an independent counsel had something, at least behind closed doors, to judge Fiske by. They no doubt were well aware of the controversy surrounding Fiske's handling of the Foster death case. Already the panel—judges David Sentelle, John Butzner, and Joseph Sneed—had received a letter from ten Republican congressmen asking the panel not to appoint Fiske. According to a source close to the panel, Judge Butzner, the lone Democrat on the panel, wanted to appoint Fiske. His two colleagues, Sentelle and Sneed, wanted a new counsel, but because of the sensitivity of the investigation, all wanted their appointee to be unanimously selected.

As the facts emerged about Fiske's handling of the case—such as his failure to use a grand jury—Butzner's position became untenable. On August 5, this federal judicial panel unanimously appointed Kenneth W. Starr as independent counsel. The judges issued a statement that it was not their "intent to impugn the integrity of the attorney general's appointee [Robert Fiske]," but cited the need to make an appointment in keeping with the spirit of the independent counsel law that a person "not affiliated with the incumbent administration be appointed."[110]

As these events were unfolding in Washington, Vince Foster's family seemed satisfied by the Fiske report and issued a statement:

> Independent Counsel's Report on Vince Foster's death confirms what his family long has believed—that deep depression, which we never will fully understand, caused Vince to take his own life. We also concur that the Whitewater affair had nothing to do with his death.
>
> Vince's family appreciates the sensitive manner in which the Independent Counsel, lawyers working for him, and the FBI handled this investigation. Their efforts to find the truth were thorough and honest, and the family believes that questions as to how and why Vince died are now answered as best they can be. There is now no justification for painful, repetitious examination of those issues. The principal advocates for doing this appear chiefly motivated by mean-spirited partisanship; they certainly care not at all for the feelings of Vince's family, particularly those of his children who have suffered greatly. We are particularly appalled by the shameful statements on the

House floor by a legislator who, in our view, is purportedly employing outrageous innuendo and speculation for political ends. It is so unfair for the family's privacy and emotions to be pawns in a partisan struggle.

Also despicable are the speculations about Vince's death being spread by those calling themselves Christian ministers.

We love Vince and miss him terribly. He was an honorable man and deserves to be treated with respect. On the anniversary of his death, our fervent hope is that this matter now will recede from public view and that the family will be left alone to deal with its loss in private, as we have done for the past year.[111]

Still, the matter was far from closed.

9

Every good story has a hero. In the matter of the death of Vincent Foster, our hero's name is Miquel Rodriguez.

Hired by newly appointed Independent Counsel Kenneth Starr in September 1994, Rodriguez was a Cornell University and Harvard Law School–educated son of a migrant worker. In his early thirties and an assistant U.S. attorney from Sacramento, California, he was a bohemian among law-enforcement types—the only federal prosecutor in the country who wore a ponytail. Though slight of figure and soft-spoken, he had a reputation for being tenacious, intense, and methodical in his work. His background especially suited him to civil rights matters, and he gained some notoriety in that area. He told colleagues that he viewed the Foster assignment essentially as a civil rights case, since the evidence indicated to Rodriguez that Foster had been denied due process.

Starr hired Rodriguez as an associate independent counsel largely on

the recommendation of Paul Cappuccio, Rodriguez's law school room-
mate and a lawyer in Starr's law firm. Soon after Starr was appointed
independent counsel, he succumbed to the Democrats' criticism of him
that he was too partisan. This was evidenced by his staff appointments,
one of which was the appointment of a deputy who was an activist
Democrat with close ties to the Clinton administration.

By mid-September Starr was announcing his key appointments,
which, according to the *Washington Post,* were "designed to quiet fears
that Starr would bring his conservative politics to the investigation. . . ."[1] As evidence that Starr was not departing from the blueprint
created by Fiske, he appointed Fiske staff member William Duffey as his
deputy in Little Rock to handle matters pertaining to the Arkansas side
of his investigation.

As his Washington deputy, Starr hired former District of Columbia
Bar Association president Mark H. Tuohey III. That selection gave Tuohey authority over some of the most sensitive matters involving the
Clintons and Whitewater: the death of Vincent Foster, the handling of
papers after his death, possible efforts by administration officials to
obstruct investigations of the death, and possible illegal interference in
criminal referrals made by the Resolution Trust Corporation relating to
Madison Guaranty Bank, which Starr said he would review.

These largely Washington-oriented issues were especially sensitive
because, unlike the Arkansas matters, which involved relatively stale
allegations, the Washington probe touched on recent matters possibly
involving the president or First Lady directly. Indictments brought here
against aides and associates of the Clintons could quickly turn this case
into a Watergate-level scandal.

At the time of his appointment, Tuohey was a partner at the firm of
Reed, Smith, Shaw & McClay, handling white-collar criminal matters.
A former federal prosecutor, Tuohey had served during the Carter
administration as a special trial counsel prosecuting former Congressman Daniel Flood of Pennsylvania.[2]

Significantly for Starr's critics, Tuohey was a liberal Democrat. The

Washington Post reported that he was "close to some Clinton administration officials, including Associate Attorney General Jamie S. Gorelick, and [in 1993] hosted a party for Attorney General Janet Reno at his Washington home."[3] Not noted in the press at the time was the fact that Tuohey was also a friend of Robert Fiske.

No sooner was Tuohey on the job than he was seen with Webster Hubbell at one of Washington's power restaurants, The Palm, an item that made the *Washington Times*'s gossipy "Inside the Beltway" column. Two journalist colleagues happened to be there on that occasion and noted that the two looked like old friends, laughing and enjoying each other's company. Seeing the two of them alone, and Hubbell without an attorney, struck some people as odd considering Hubbell was a major target of Starr's probe whose indictment was imminent. Three months later Hubbell pled guilty to felony charges.[4]

To further demonstrate how un-Republican he was going to be, Starr hired Sam Dash, another prominent Washington Democrat, to join his staff on a consulting basis. Dash, the former lead counsel to the Senate committee that investigated Watergate, was to serve as Starr's ethics counsel, with the taxpayers paying him $3,200 a week.

Starr's appointment of prominent Democrats Tuohey and Dash quashed, at least temporarily, media criticism that he was too partisan to be independent counsel. Starr may also have believed that the appointments gave him latitude to continue his lucrative private legal practice, representing organizations and corporate interests, such as the tobacco industry, with a known bias against the Clinton administration.

By appointing Dash, Starr was possibly restricting his investigation with an official not required by the law. The questionable wisdom of the Dash appointment became apparent later when Dash was quoted in *The New Yorker* criticizing Starr for not being a full-time counsel, and for suggesting the three-judge panel had made a "mistake" by not reappointing Fiske.[5]

Though the independent counsel law had been enacted after Watergate precisely because it was believed that Justice Department officials and the FBI could not impartially police the executive branch, Starr's selections tended to be insiders who had close ties to either the Justice Department or Washington power circles.

An exception was Starr's choice of W. Hickman Ewing as senior counsel. Starr needed a trial attorney with a Southern twang to replace Rusty Hardin in case it was necessary to go before an Arkansas jury. In Ewing he had a well-qualified candidate who had served for ten years during the Reagan and Bush years as the U.S. attorney in Memphis, where he had earned a reputation for being strictly nonpartisan.[6]

Though Starr's appointments brought an end to the initial criticism and signaled that he was going to follow Fiske's lead, it also meant that he was willing to cede the most critical parts of his investigation, the Washington phase, to the Democrats and the power of the Justice Department, the agency many of his appointees would return to after their work for Starr concluded.

All of this must have been welcome news for the anxious Clinton White House. White House quiescence about Starr abruptly ended in 1996 as the Arkansas side of his inquiry again heated up, when White House officials, and even the president, made critical comments about Starr. The *New York Times* referred to the White House criticisms as "the Johnny Cochran defense"—a reference to O. J. Simpson's defense attorney's strategy to attack the credibility of the prosecution itself rather than a point-by-point rebuttal of the evidence.[7] The White House attacks on Starr appeared to be a preemptive move by the White House to impeach the credibility of Starr's prosecution just in case he tried to move aggressively against the Clintons. After all, it was 1996 and Clinton was up for reelection. There was also a positive flip side to the White House attack—by being critical of Starr it actually bolstered Starr's standing with Clinton's most vociferous critics in Congress and elsewhere. This was especially smart, since if Starr cleared the Clintons of wrongdoing, it would add even more weight behind those conclusions.

AS ASSOCIATE independent counsel, Rodriguez was in a mid-level position. His role was to do the grunt work in building a case before a grand jury that would level indictments; then a trial attorney, like Ewing, could come in and present the case before a jury.*

Rodriguez first reported to Starr's Little Rock office, but it quickly became apparent to Ewing and others that a Hispanic male with a ponytail was not going to be their most effective advocate before an Arkansas grand jury. Starr asked Rodriguez to move to Washington as lead prosecutor under Tuohey in reviewing matters related to Foster's death and the subsequent actions of officials.

At the time of Starr's appointment, Fiske was on the verge of exonerating all White House officials of any charges related to Foster's office search and files. Starr promised that he would "build upon" Fiske's work, taking the time to review it, and would issue his own report on Foster's death.[8]

Rodriguez took Starr at his word and believed, perhaps naïvely, that the review of the case was to be a serious, independent one. Upon coming to Washington, Rodriguez met with Fiske's staff, which was headed up by Mark J. Stein and was turning matters over to Rodriguez and Starr's team. Rodriguez was asked not to change the Fiske conclusions on Foster's death. Rodriguez refused to give such an assurance. Members of Fiske's staff also demanded, without success, to reinterview the CNN makeup artist before he departed. Rodriguez was already aware that some witnesses whose original statements gave indications of foul play in the death had been "reinterviewed," and in the process their statements were made more benign. Clearly, the CNN makeup artist account was a loose end Fiske and his staff would have liked to tie up, especially since it directly contradicted Fiske's conclusions.

Though Rodriguez stopped Stein from reinterviewing the woman, he was quickly disabused of the notion that he, Rodriguez, would be calling all the shots. One such signal was that Starr retained the same agents who had worked for Fiske to review their own work. FBI agent Larry

---

* Much of what I came to learn about the Starr probe and Rodriguez's activities came from several sources close to the probe. I conducted extensive interviews with over half a dozen prosecutors and investigators who worked on the Fiske and Starr inquiries.

Monroe had left the team and then retired (Monroe was subsequently hired by the State Department in their diplomatic security section), leaving William Colombell as the senior agent. Within a week of Rodriguez's arrival in Washington he was told by Colombell in no unmistakable terms that Special Counsel Fiske had concluded the case, and that was how it was going to remain.

Rodriguez did find one sympathizer in his assistant, Lucia Rambusch. In her early twenties, Rambusch had been a paralegal assigned to the Fiske staff. She was immediately impressed by Rodriguez's desire to get to the bottom of the Foster matter and told him that she had observed the previous investigators' attempt to sweep the matter under the rug. Together she and Rodriguez began reviewing over ten thousand pages of documents relating to the case. The documents told a story that impugned both Fiske's handling of the investigation and his conclusions.

Several things stood out. One was the FBI statements of the couple in the park who said they saw two men in and around Foster's Honda. Another was the observations of several witnesses, as noted in the FBI statements, of a briefcase having been seen in Foster's Honda. A review of the Park Police reports showed no mention of this briefcase.

Rodriguez knew that the key to unraveling the case, or confirming Fiske's conclusions, rested in learning if the police had violated Foster's civil rights by issuing fraudulent reports or manipulating evidence. He had to be assured the case was handled properly and no cover-up had taken place.

Rodriguez understood why the briefcase was important and why Fiske's team wanted to smooth over the contradictions. First, if Foster left his office with a briefcase in the middle of the day, it would suggest that he was going to a meeting with persons unknown. Second, if there was a briefcase in Foster's Honda, what happened to it? If it was subsequently turned over to the White House and the police were asked not to mention it in their evidence reports, this could well amount to obstruction of justice. Finally, the briefcase might have contained papers that would shed light on the reasons for Foster's untimely death.

Another cover-up concern that Fiske ignored but Rodriguez wanted to investigate fully was the timeline issue. He found official claims of the time that the Secret Service/White House was notified of the death implausible.

Rodriguez was also disturbed at what he considered Fiske's too-heavy reliance on depression as a motive for Foster's suicide. Given the vagaries of the human mind, no one can say for sure that Foster was not depressed. By the same token it was equally presumptuous to say he was, given the equivocal observations of friends and colleagues.

According to both the Park Police and FBI investigations, many of the people closest to Foster had not noticed anything unusual about Foster's behavior during the time before his death. Rodriguez felt Fiske's work in this area had been sloppy and less than exhaustive. One telling example may have been Fiske's failure to interview key people who were close to Foster in his final days. Syndicated columnist Deroy Murdock, writing in the *New York Post*, revealed that though Fiske's report spent considerable space detailing Foster's state of mind, investigators never interviewed the couple with whom Foster and his wife spent their last weekend together. Murdock called Michael Cardozo, who said neither he nor his wife had been interviewed.[9] Cardozo's wife told the *Washington Post* just days after Foster's death she had observed nothing unusual with Foster and described Foster's relationship with Lisa that weekend as "wonderful."[10]*

Starr's investigation was still in its infancy in the fall of 1994 when Rodriguez began to broach these and many other questions about the

---

* Michael and Harolyn Cardozo were not the only people who spent that last weekend with Foster and were not interviewed.

Curiously, Fiske not only did not interview but made no mention whatsoever of two other guests who spent the weekend at the Cardozos' Eastern Shore vacation home: Nate Landow and nationally famous tennis star Nick Bollettieri. Landow, a Washington D.C./Baltimore-area developer, is Harolyn Cardozo's father, a longtime Democratic National committee fund-raiser, and former Maryland Democratic Party chairman.[11]

Further, Mr. Fiske did not even spell the names of the Cardozos correctly. In his "meticulous" final report, Fiske referred to them as the "Cardozas."[12]

case in meetings with Tuohey and the staff of Starr's Washington office. Tuohey resisted any reopening of the suicide case. Discussions about the problems raised by Rodriguez were punctuated with questions from Tuohey such as, "What's your theory about what happened?" and "What would be the motive for a murder?"

Rodriguez was reluctant to speculate, and Tuohey requested that Rodriguez close the case before any real investigation had taken place.[13] Rodriguez refused to comply, and meetings between the two became adversarial. Many times, Tuohey would raise his voice and challenge Rodriguez's apparent attacks on his friend Robert Fiske.

To Rodriguez, the job was straightforward—examine the evidence. And the evidence cried out for further inquiry. But Tuohey was unwilling to open a door to an unending list of problems in a case he believed to be closed.

Time after time they fought. Rodriguez wanted to explore why the government was claiming they had no set of fingerprints for Foster. Tuohey said no. Rodriguez was incredulous. He thought it imperative that prints be located. For one thing, though no prints had been found on the outer surfaces of the gun found in Foster's hand, the FBI did find two prints of unknown origin on the grip under decorative plates when they were unscrewed.

Rodriguez wanted complete access to Foster's travel, credit card, and phone records. Tuohey said no. The phone records in particular could be crucial to the investigation by identifying whom he talked to and thereby perhaps shedding light on the issues bothering Foster in the closing days of his life.*

When asked, the White House had turned over telephone records for the one office line that was said to have been used by Foster. Rodriguez thought that claim was ridiculous and that Starr's office should challenge the White House and get all of the records. Tuohey nixed any idea

---

* Starr's office had some evidence that Foster tried to call Whitewater figure David Hale a week to ten days before his death. Complete phone records could have confirmed that.

of challenging the White House on this point.* (Nussbaum's personal secretary, Betsy Pond, later testified that Foster had the use of three phone lines.)[14]

To fight and disagree on how to pursue an investigation is one thing—to leak information is quite another. As Rodriguez's work progressed, more and more evidence seemed to suggest that the White House was being tipped off about Rodriguez's work and plans by someone in Starr's office. In the closing days of November 1994, for instance, Rodriguez wrote a memo to Starr outlining his plan to make criminal targets of Nussbaum, Maggie Williams, and Craig Livingstone and identifying the key evidence against each.

At the time Rodriguez was drafting this memo, the White House should have had little inkling of the strategy. Yet a memo compiled by White House associate Jane Sherburne—not two weeks from the date of Rodriguez's memo—laid out plans for dealing with various possible scandals involving the White House.[15] One Starr investigator who has reviewed both memos was stunned that the White House memo matched item for item Rodriguez's proposal to seek indictments against Nussbaum for perjury and obstruction of justice, and against Williams and Livingstone for perjury.[16]

Rodriguez's problems with Tuohey were compounded by problems with the FBI agents who were supposed to be working under him. Rodriguez was at loggerheads with senior agent Colombell, who refused to send out agents to do any of the follow-up investigative work necessary for the probe. At one point, in preparation for grand jury proceedings, Rodriguez asked Colombell if his agents would help prepare a map of Fort Marcy Park. Colombell refused, and grand jury proceedings took place without even a simple sketch of the park.[17] In a normal situation, Rodriguez could have complained about such insubordination

---

* Nor was Tuohey interested in conducting a systematic interview of White House staff and security personnel to question them on matters relating to the investigation. Indeed, it was clear to Rodriguez that the White House thought it could say or do anything with impunity. I contacted Tuohey for comment several times on the various allegations raised in these pages, but each time he declined to do so.

to his boss, but to do so in this situation would have been a waste of time.

The most disturbing problems with the FBI involved the photographic evidence. Rodriguez and his assistant were able to find new information in those "blurry" Polaroids and the 35 mm film the FBI had reported as useless. When Rodriguez presented the evidence, Tuohey reacted angrily and said he did not see anything unusual in the photo.

Consistently, new evidence produced by Rodriguez was met with new objections. If Foster's body had been moved, Tuohey and others argued, why was the body placed so deep in the park? Rodriguez believed this to be a reasonable question, though had the body been dumped at one of the park's entranceways this would surely have raised a red flag. Rodriguez soon found an aerial photo taken of Fort Marcy just months before Foster's death. It showed several park trails that allowed for maintenance vehicles to drive in the area of the cannons. One trail went from the park's rear entrance to the area of the second cannon. As it turned out, park service maintenance vehicles routinely hop the curb in the parking lot and drive on these trails. That finding quickly put to rest the frequently made objection that Foster's body could not have been moved to the back of the park where it was found because it was too difficult to carry.

Rodriguez also questioned the claims of Park Police that they never secured the park's rear entrance because they did not know it existed. Rodriguez later learned that Park Police had regularly been posted at Fort Marcy's rear entrance during the 1991 Gulf War to help protect the Saudi Arabian compound across the street.

Starr and Rodriguez met several times in the late fall and early winter of 1994, but Starr was clearly reluctant to side with Rodriguez. During these conferences, Starr reiterated his significant objection to Rodriguez: "How could so many people be involved in the cover-up?" Rodriguez replied that the evidence did not suggest that all the officials conspired together, just that everyone did what they were told to do, with a number of people fibbing about small matters that together added up to something far greater.

For reasons still unclear, Starr overruled Tuohey and allowed Rodriguez to proceed with limited grand jury proceedings after the New Year in 1995.

JANUARY 5, 1995, the day grand jury proceedings were to start probing the official handling of Foster's death, marked the culmination of three long months of round-the-clock work for Miquel Rodriguez and Lucia Rambusch. Rodriguez's anxieties were summed up in a Scripps Howard News Service story by Lisa Hoffman that was picked up in the next day's *Washington Times*, put on page one, and headlined STARR APT TO SECOND RULING ON FOSTER: NO LINK FOUND TO WHITEWATER. The article reported that "sources familiar with the Starr inquiry" had revealed the new independent counsel, Kenneth Starr, was about to conclude that Vincent Foster "committed suicide for reasons unrelated to the Whitewater controversy."

Who were these "sources"? Rodriguez was the lead prosecutor on the case and had concluded nothing. Rodriguez, in fact, had only just begun the grand jury proceedings by summoning Park Police and county emergency workers who were at Fort Marcy on the evening of Foster's death.

Rodriguez read on with contempt: "The apparent findings of Mr. Starr's team of lawyers and FBI agents mirror those of Mr. Fiske. . . ."

There was one thing in the Scripps Howard wire report that Rodriguez could bitterly assent to. It noted that Starr's team had not conducted a new investigation but had simply "reviewed" Fiske's work.[18]

Prior to grand jury proceedings, Rodriguez had been prevented by his superiors from breaking new ground and had been confined to analyzing and verifying the reports completed during the Fiske investigation. But even the Fiske documents by themselves showed apparent wrongdoing in the case. More worrisome was the effect this front-page story would have on critical witnesses just as they were being summoned before the grand jury. Rodriguez knew it would be hard enough getting people to open up on this matter; now with this report that the supposed findings of the case were all but preordained, it would be nigh unto impossible.

Before the day ended things took a dramatic turn with another news story presenting a sharply different report. The Associated Press reported that Starr had begun probing Foster's death, starting with the summoning of three Fairfax County rescue workers to appear before Starr's Washington grand jury.[19]

Tom Scorza, for one, saw this as a turning point. The former federal prosecutor from Chicago, whom I queried frequently about developments in the case, thought the use of the grand jury signaled that Starr's people had some theory of wrongdoing in the death and had called the grand jury to hand down indictments. According to Scorza, the notion that the grand jury might have been called just to pacify critics or to shroud key evidence in the case behind secrecy rules was unfathomable.

I pointed out to Scorza that the initial Associated Press wire story detailing the grand jury proceedings reported that prosecutors were examining what happened to a briefcase spotted by emergency workers in Foster's Honda found at Fort Marcy Park. The Park Police reports acknowledged no briefcase. Scorza thought the probe of the police, starting at the very bottom, was a sign that prosecutors were trying to work their way up by "flip[ping] the smallest fish"—such as police officers at the scene—who then might cooperate against higher-ups.[20]

It seemed as if Starr's team thought the police may have falsified the record by failing to list such an important piece of evidence as the briefcase. If Starr's team pressed charges against the police on this small matter, Scorza explained, it might just unravel a larger cover-up by higher officials.

By the end of the second day of proceedings, three emergency workers had been called: George Gonzalez and Todd Hall, the first two paramedics to find the body, and EMT worker Richard Arthur, who like Gonzalez had claimed he saw a wound on Foster's neck. Within a week, four emergency workers were acknowledging, under oath, that they had seen a wound or trauma to Foster's neck. The following week Park Police began to testify, beginning with Kevin Fornshill, the first officer on the scene. Other Park Police and emergency workers followed in rapid order.

During that week the *Washington Times* reported that Park Police were becoming irate after questioning by Starr's lead prosecutor, Miquel Rodriguez. This seemed like another good sign.[21] But a week later, it appeared as if the Foster story had fallen off the face of the earth. There were no more press reports about the grand jury, although witnesses were still being called.

Months later, I would learn what had really taken place that stopped Rodriguez from getting to the truth. In March, a colleague in Washington informed me that witnesses relating to the death were no longer being called to the grand jury. Almost on the heels of that news I learned that Starr's lead prosecutor on the Foster case, Miquel Rodriguez, had resigned. The investigation had effectively been shut down.

I spoke to Rodriguez shortly after his resignation in March of 1995, and he understandably declined to discuss the facts of the case. Instead, he told me that he had cited ethical considerations in his resignation letter to Mr. Starr.

"As an ethical person, I don't believe I could be involved with what they were doing," Rodriquez told me coldly of why he left Starr's staff to return as an assistant U.S. attorney in Sacramento.

In the weeks and months after that call to Rodriquez I developed several sources close to the Starr probe and was able to piece together what had happened to Rodriquez and Starr's Foster Investigation.

I learned that although he had been stifled at nearly every turn, Rodriguez had nevertheless developed a within-the-bounds strategy for moving the case. It focused primarily on the possibility of a Park Police cover-up and relied on basic legal tactics: Move the main witnesses, police, and emergency workers efficiently through the proceedings; work overtime; and nail down the testimony quickly before anyone had a chance to compare notes and spin their testimony. If the police had a clear idea what was being focused on, the quest for the truth might be more difficult.

A press that had ignored the case when it desperately needed exposure now threatened to ruin the case by saying too much. On January 6, 1995, an Associated Press wire story was not only reporting on the Washington grand jury proceedings, but revealing highly sensitive information, specifically that Foster's briefcase was a focus of Rodriguez's probe. A "non-government source familiar with the proceeding" was the only identification provided about the leaker.[22]

Rodriguez was astonished and dismayed as he read the report. The whole case was being blown up right before his eyes. Vital and top-secret grand jury information was being leaked to the Associated Press by someone at the highest levels of Starr's Washington office, he believed, to signal the Park Police witnesses who had not yet testified exactly what to be on guard against.

On the next workday after the story appeared, Rodriguez came in to the independent counsel's office angry and bitter. Tuohey, a tall man with salt-and-pepper hair and a rosy complexion, was there to greet him. There were no smiles. Before Rodriguez could open his mouth, however, Tuohey was soon making the laughable allegation that Rodriguez had been the source of the leak.

With the *Washington Times* story suggesting, just as critical witnesses were being called to appear, that the case had been closed, and now the leak about sensitive grand jury testimony, Rodriguez concluded that he was being sabotaged by a real Washington shark. Typically, the lead prosecutor in the case calls the shots. Rodriguez began to fear that he was not going to be able to do this prosecution by the book.

Rodriguez's intense cross-examination of Park Police the following week angered them and drew the ire of Tuohey. Rodriguez knew how to handle a grand jury probe: He would cross-examine for hours, never cracking a smile, giving each witness "the look" from behind his glasses. Using several standard techniques to get to the truth, Rodriguez constantly reminded the officers of the perjury statutes and the harsh penalties for their violation. He was also having witnesses repeat their testimony. Witnesses telling false tales can easily get tripped up on the details in repeating those accounts.*

When Park Police complained that Rodriguez's cross-examination bordered on harassment, Tuohey began to assume more control of the day-to-day affairs of the grand jury proceedings. When Tuohey started dictating how Rodriguez should question Sergeant Edwards—whom Rodriguez considered a possible key to breaking open the case, since Edwards was ranking officer at the park and controlled movement to and from the death scene—the tension between Rodriguez and Tuohey reached a crisis point.

Following a vigorous four-hour session of tough grand jury questioning of Edwards, the proceedings recessed for lunch. Edwards thought, erroneously, that he was finished and gave a wry smile. During the break, Tuohey, Rodriguez, and another prosecutor, John Bates, huddled in another room. Tuohey roared at Rodriguez for questioning Edwards's integrity and that of other officers and demanded that he stop his line of inquiry. With Rodriguez still resisting, Tuohey's anger became physical. He threw a chair to the ground, knocking it across the room.

The afternoon session began, and Rodriguez rose from his seat after having given Tuohey no assurances he was finished. Tuohey sat behind him, anticipating the wrap-up of questioning. Visibly shaking, Rodriguez began by informing Edwards that there were some inconsistencies in his

---

* Rodriguez's techniques had the hearty approval of Tom Scorza, who thought he "was doing exactly what he should be doing." Scorza, who had prosecuted cases involving police corruption in Chicago, said "the police always get upset" but the only way to break through the blue wall of silence is to use the perjury statutes as a constant hammer.[23]

Scorza was surprised by the controversy between Rodriguez and Tuohey. In his ten years as a federal prosecutor in Chicago he could not remember a case where the courtroom prosecutor was interfered with by his superior. The disagreements between Tuohey and Rodriguez were over significant policy issues. For example, Tuohey instructed Rodriguez to allow witnesses to review evidence, including photos, before they entered the grand jury room. He also wanted the witnesses to be called at a slow pace, which Rodriguez believed might allow them to compare notes and spin their stories.

story and that they would have to go back to the beginning. After another four hours—almost eight grueling hours in total—Edwards was allowed off the stand.

The tough questioning by Rodriguez was making its way into the papers. Tuohey was quoted as acknowledging problems but was sticking by Rodriguez as lead prosecutor.[24] Another press report indicated that the police had been assured by Tuohey they were not criminal targets of the probe.[25] Why Tuohey was making even this relatively general sort of information public, given the highly confidential nature of grand jury matters, was baffling to Rodriguez.

Just a week into the grand jury proceedings that January, Rodriguez was continuing to call witnesses. He was seriously disabled by Tuohey's assurances to the Park Police, which he had made without getting any special cooperation in return.

By mid-January Rodriguez concluded that if he continued on what he considered an improperly handled probe, he might actually help foster the cover-up. He could perfunctorily go through a series of witnesses, but no matter what was turned up, the case was going to be written off as a suicide with no criminal wrongdoing on the part of officials.

Rodriguez was also concerned with the FBI's handling of the case. Given the FBI's vested interest in the matter, Rodriguez wanted investigators and experts from outside the bureau to explore the inconsistencies in the case. How could the FBI be entrusted to police itself? Rodriguez sought to impanel a blue-ribbon group of experts—from outside the Washington establishment, and not beholden to the FBI—to take up the serious questions raised by the investigation. It was Rodriguez's consistent plea to Starr that experts from outside the Washington-FBI circle be brought in to the investigation.[26] Tuohey vetoed the idea. Tuohey, when asked to comment about these allegations, claimed they were "absolutely ridiculous."

Even as he was beginning the grand jury proceedings, Rodriguez observed that the FBI agents assigned to Starr, instead of doing any real investigative work, were busy plugging holes and fixing witness statements that did not conform with the official version.

The first statements that required "adjusting" were those of the couple, identified earlier as Mark and Judy, who half a year earlier had told the FBI they each had observed two different men in and around Foster's car as they sat in Judy's Nissan in Fort Marcy's lot. In January 1995, in their second statements to the FBI compiled for Starr's probe, Mark and Judy seemed to have completely forgotten seeing anyone around the Honda, thus eliminating one major obstacle to concluding the case.

The couple's detailed statements in the first interviews were sharply abbreviated in the second. One significant addition was made: Mark, in his later statement, was belatedly able to recall that he may have had a briefcase with him that he used to carry books for night school—thus providing a convenient explanation about the briefcase witnesses had seen in Foster's car: They had simply gotten the cars in the lot mixed up. Curiously, Mark's belated "recollection" precisely coincided with Rodriguez's hard questioning of the death-scene witnesses before the grand jury on the same issue.

With the focus in Washington on "adjusting" witness statements, little genuine progress was being made. Starr was devoting most of his part-time efforts to Little Rock, and his chronic absenteeism was the subject of jokes by his Washington staff. Rodriguez, however, was much more troubled by signals from Starr that he was not going to allow a by-the-book inquiry into the whole Washington side of the Whitewater probe, the Foster death being but one facet.

Upon arriving at Starr's Washington office in late 1994, Rodriguez was startled to learn that almost every White House aide who was an attorney had claimed attorney-client privilege when questioned under oath or subpoenaed for documents before the Fiske and Starr grand jury in Washington. This tactic, he reasoned, surely should have been challenged in every instance as it would be for any other prosecution.

This claim of privilege even extended to Susan Thomases, who was not even on the White House payroll.[27]

In December 1995, Banking Committee chairman D'Amato would do battle, in the course of the committee's Whitewater hearings, on this issue with associate White House counsel William Kennedy III. D'Amato demanded that Kennedy release certain notes relating to a meeting he had had with White House aides on November 5, 1993; Kennedy refused to give them up, citing the privilege. Eventually the White House did relent, but only after making the point that they were not going to concede on their many privilege claims on other matters.

A year before, in the fall of 1994, Rodriguez wrote a memo to Starr pointing out that first Fiske, and now he, Starr, were not following proper procedure in not challenging the claims, including the claim made to withhold Kennedy's notes.[28]

In a normal criminal procedure, a prosecutor will routinely challenge each and every claim of privilege, on the logical grounds that the witness—who may even be a target of the probe—should not be the one to decide if something is privileged. Assuming the witness holds fast in his or her claim, the matter is then brought before an impartial judge, who makes the determination.

Thus it was no surprise that when Senator D'Amato challenged the White House over the Kennedy notes, Starr's team quickly signed a "no-waiver" agreement with the White House, undermining D'Amato's position. In the agreement, Starr consented to a conditional demand that by releasing these particular notes, the White House still had the right to withhold documents and testimony claiming the attorney-client privilege.[29]

Starr's team, which had been quiescent for over a year, did not want to open the floodgates and have the Senate committee challenging the claims and unearthing documents. This could have been embarrassing for Starr, especially if the Senate committee received documents and testimony that showed criminality, when Starr never challenged the White House on the claims in the first place.

Starr eventually did go to court to challenge the attorney-client privilege claims made by the Clintons and their White House attorneys. Starr's legal challenge, however, took place only after the Senate had finished their Whitewater hearings, and after I had reported in a December 1995 article that Starr had consistently failed to challenge such claims.

Starr's legal action on the matter began in the summer of 1996, almost two years after he had been appointed and after perhaps hundreds of claims had been made. In this case, Starr was specifically seeking notes written by White House lawyers during Hillary Clinton's grand jury testimony in January 1996, and during another meeting Mrs. Clinton had with government attorneys in July 1995 discussing matters in the aftermath of Foster's death. Mrs. Clinton had made questionable use of government-paid attorneys in receiving their assistance in her personal affairs—they provided counsel during her own criminal inquiry.

In April 1997, the U.S. Court of Appeals for the Eighth Circuit in St. Louis ruled 2–1 in Starr's favor that the notes should be turned over to his investigation.

The *Wall Street Journal* reported that Starr had asserted that "the unprecedented claims of privilege by the White House had impeded his investigation for months." The harsh truth was that attorney-client privilege had been the shield used by the Clinton White House before Starr even arrived, when the scandal was in its infancy and police and Justice Department investigators sought to review Foster's office papers.

Privilege claims were not challenged then by Fiske, or by Starr during the critical aspects of the Washington side of his inquiry. Late in the game, Starr was more intent on setting a lofty legal principle than using the tools at his disposal to uncover the truth. The Associated Press reported that Starr had bickered with the White House over the name of the case when it was presented to the Supreme Court for final review. The White House filed it as "Office of the President vs. Office of the Independent Counsel." Starr wrote to the Court that the case be renamed the more memorable "Office of the President vs. The United States."

Still another strong indication that Starr was not going to deviate from the blueprint laid out by his predecessor was his handling of the Webster Hubbell plea agreement.

By the fall of 1994, Starr's team had been preparing an indictment listing more than thirty counts against former Associate Attorney General Webster Hubbell. Fiske's chief trial counsel, Russell Hardin, had agreed to stay on with Starr to prosecute the Hubbell case and was put in charge of that. Subsequently there were intimations from Hubbell that he wanted to avoid the embarrassment of a trial and would plea-bargain.

As it became clear that Hubbell would cooperate, Hardin prepared to leave. He told Starr that once the details of the plea agreement with Hubbell were worked out, he would resign in January 1995. Hardin had experience with one plea agreement, that of David Hale, the Little Rock municipal judge appointed by Governor Bill Clinton. Hale, indicted in 1993 on charges of defrauding the Small Business Administration, was the first key witness to turn state's evidence. As he was about to go to trial in March 1994, Hale agreed to a plea bargain, and Hardin success-fully handled that plea.

A prosecutor familiar with the Hale deal told me that before Fiske signed off on any agreement, Hardin spent two weeks holed up with Hale and FBI agents debriefing Hale, finding out "what he knew and what he could give prosecutors." Only then did Fiske agree to a plea agreement.[30]

Starr had no interest in going through any such standard procedure with Hubbell. He was quite willing to sign an agreement without the type of debriefing Hale was obliged to go through and to which similar wrongdoers are routinely subjected.* With Starr's reluctance to pursue Hubbell by the book, Hardin abruptly resigned from Starr's office in October 1994, months before his scheduled departure in January 1995.[31]

In December 1994, Starr's team signed a plea agreement with Hubbell. It was handled by W. Hickman Ewing, Starr's senior trial coun-sel. The list of charges was reduced to only two: mail fraud and tax eva-sion. By signing the agreement, Hubbell believed he was putting to rest any risk that prosecutors would seek new charges relating to wrongdoing under investigation.

Prosecutors on Starr's staff acknowledge that Hubbell broke his plea agreement by not cooperating. At the same time, they also claim that

---

* One Starr associate claimed that Starr thought it improper to press a former judge and Justice Department official in that manner. Hubbell had briefly served as the Chief Justice of the Arkansas Supreme Court.

Hubbell did not get off easy after signing the plea agreement, because he received no actual reduction in jail time. That, like many claims by prosecutors in the case, is half true. Hubbell received no reduction for the time he was sentenced on the two charges brought against him. But Hubbell had already won enormous concessions from Starr when the agreement had been signed: Starr dropped other charges for which Hubbell could have been prosecuted and which, if pursued, could have meant even more jail time for Hubbell. Starr, essentially, gave Hubbell his end of the plea bargain up front, leaving Starr with no leverage to make certain Hubbell followed through on his end of the agreement.

Hubbell, who had agreed to aid the investigation as part of the plea arrangement, never did fully cooperate in the probe of any of his circle. Starr had thus missed a unique opportunity: Hubbell, given his position in Washington, his former position at the Rose firm, and his intimacy with the Clintons and Foster, may have been one of the few who could have tied the whole scandal together.

Starr never did go after Hubbell and seemed little bothered by telltale clues that Hubbell was not going to be overly forthcoming on his own. During the time of his plea agreement, as Hubbell was "cooperating" but had not yet served time in jail, his wife, Suzanna, was rehired to a $60,000-a-year position as special assistant to a public relations unit of the Interior Department (the Park Police are, of course, an agency of the Interior Department), a job given with the approval of the Clinton White House. Mrs. Hubbell had been hired at the Interior Department in the early days of the administration but left after her husband's legal problems arose.[32]

Only after Hubbell was about to be released from prison in early 1997, and only after the press had done the important spadework in exposing why Hubbell may have been motivated not to talk, did Starr revisit Hubbell's lack of cooperation in 1994 and 1995. As a scandal began to break indicating that the Democratic National Committee had received campaign contributions from foreign nationals and other entities, some of which were linked to an Indonesian firm known as the Lippo Group, Starr recalled Hubbell to testify before his Washington grand jury.[33] It had become known that Hubbell, soon after resigning from the Justice Department in 1994, became a consultant to the Lippo Group. Published reports indicate that after resigning from the Justice Department, Hubbell became a Washington lobbyist. With help from top White House officials, Hubbell received fees from several corporations totaling more than $400,000 in the months just before he pled guilty. At least $100,000 was paid to Hubbell from the Lippo Group.[34] Starr was apparently trying to determine if Hubbell had essentially been paid off to stifle his cooperation.

Here again, Starr was a laggard. Hubbell had not cooperated almost two years before, at which time it was known that he was working for Lippo, which had well-known ties to the Clintons going back many years.[35]

The Hubbell controversy that erupted in the press more than two years after Hubbell failed to cooperate with Starr was proof positive Starr had not done his job. An experienced prosecutor knows that witnesses like Hubbell, who break their promise to cooperate, must be dealt with swiftly; a lack of action will send a message to other witnesses that the prosecutor is a patsy. Typically, a prosecutor will try to find out if the witness was paid off or threatened. A prosecutor also usually wants to set an example that this behavior will not be tolerated, as well as open up new lines of inquiry in an attempt to find additional charges that would add jail time to the witness's sentence. Instead of taking these simple and important steps in 1995, Starr rolled over.

Starr's inability to confront the fact that Hubbell had not lived up to his agreement was just one sign to Rodriguez that the whole investigation was tainted. What had been happening with Rodriguez in his grand jury efforts was happening throughout the Starr probe. Sensing this, Rodriguez wrote to Starr in early January offering his resignation effective March 1995. He agreed to stay on for a transitional period, but would no longer be handling the day-to-day grand jury matters.

Starr made no effort to talk Rodriguez out of his decision. Apparently concerned with damage control, Starr quickly dispatched his trial counsel, W. Hickman Ewing, from Little Rock to Washington to serve as Rodriguez's replacement before the grand jury.[36] Starr was doubtless concerned that if the press learned of this key resignation, it might be a major embarrassment. Ewing, with his solid Republican credentials, and fresh from wrapping up the Hubbell plea agreement, would refute any possible criticism that Rodriguez's probe had been thwarted for political purposes.

At the time Ewing went to Washington, neither Rodriguez's resignation nor the problems between Rodriguez and Tuohey appeared in the press. Fearing, however, that Tuohey's handling of the case and his clashes with Rodriguez could later be used by Foster skeptics to argue that a cover-up had taken place, Starr's people tried to make it seem as though Tuohey had been completely removed from the case as it was turned over to Ewing. Yet the facts show that Tuohey continued to play an active, if not dominant, role in the inquiry, handling grand jury interrogations and hiring experts to review the case.

Not only was Rodriguez's resignation potentially embarrassing, but there was speculation among some of Starr's staff that the grand jury might revolt and take some independent action in its wake.

As a technical matter, grand juries have complete control over an investigation and have the power to subpoena, to hand down indictments, and even to question witnesses called before them. In perhaps 99 percent of cases, grand juries serve as lapdogs for prosecutors, willing to "indict a ham sandwich" if the prosecutor asks. Yet there are rare cases where a grand jury chafes under a prosecutor's strong-arm tactics and may even plot its own course.

When Rodriguez came before the Washington grand jury, he found a group that was becoming hostile to the prosecutors. Members of the panel had been irritated by Fiske's prosecutors who kept them in the dark on significant matters and treated them as a rubber stamp. The jurors were particularly upset that never once during the Fiske investigation as they heard countless hours of testimony on Whitewater-related matters did any of the prosecutors inform them about Fiske's investigation of Foster's death. In fact, the panel had to make an official request to get a copy of Fiske's report on the matter.[37]

The man who was to take the baton from Rodriguez, W. Hickman Ewing, was a straitlaced Southerner, a Vietnam veteran, and a devout Baptist whose father was a famous high school football coach in Memphis.[38] Ewing, a conservative, good-soldier type, and Rodriguez, who sported a ponytail and was the free-thinking son of immigrants, were as different as day and night.

Soon after Ewing's arrival in Washington, Tuohey drove him and Rodriguez out to Fort Marcy Park for a tour. The park's terrain was covered with snow and ice, and Rodriguez was confused as to the second cannon site. Trying to find his way, Rodriguez led the three—perhaps unnecessarily—down a berm, at which point Ewing slipped and injured his back.

The injury put Ewing out of commission and meant that he would be the lead Foster prosecutor from his hotel bed. In a peculiar arrangement, prosecutor Kavanaugh would come by Ewing's room each day, with transcripts of questioning led by Tuohey and himself, and discuss the following day's witnesses and what questions should be asked. While lying in bed and poring over documents, Ewing discovered something that would solve the other problem facing Starr, the fear of a runaway grand jury. Ewing noted that the grand jury was set to expire in March 1995, just as the list of witnesses scheduled to appear would come to an end. Ewing notified Tuohey, who was unaware the grand jury was set to expire but undoubtedly realized the significance of the fact.

As it turned out, this Washington grand jury with which Fiske had begun in early 1994 had already been sitting for a year before Fiske arrived, hearing matters unrelated to Whitewater. Fiske, then, inherited a grand jury with a short lease. Since the grand jury had a term of eighteen months, a year of which had already gone by, Fiske would have exclusive use of the panel for only six more months, at which time its term was to expire.[39]

But Fiske was sacked as special counsel just before that date. Thus, Starr was the new counsel when the grand jury came up for renewal in the late summer of 1994. At that point Starr could have seated a new panel, but to keep the continuity of the Fiske probe, he justifiably asked the district court to renew the grand jury for an additional six months, bringing its end date to March 1995.

When that date arrived, the grand jury had been serving for two years and could have been renewed for another six months. That would have seemed the logical thing to do, since the probe was supposed to be near its end. Fiske had found no criminal wrongdoing concerning administration contacts with the Resolution Trust Corporation, and Starr's limited grand jury probe into Foster's death that had begun with Rodriguez came to an abrupt halt by March. The only matters remaining were issues relating to Foster's office search and the handling of his papers after the death.

Mark Tuohey had even given Starr word that he planned to resign as deputy independent counsel effective September 1995, since he believed the major aspects of the case would be completed by then.[40]

Though light was appearing at the end of the tunnel, Starr closed down the original Whitewater grand jury and had a new one impaneled. The effect of this was obvious: The new grand jurors did not have the benefit of any original testimony and simply inherited a paper case. Thousands of pages of documents and testimony heard by the previous grand jury led by Rodriguez were to be distilled by an expert witness, often an FBI agent who has read all of the documents and can detail its significance to the new grand jury. This gives the expert and the prosecution the ability to give their own interpretation of the evidence.

Starr's grand jury, however, was not just any panel. As Jeanine Howard, grand jury administrator for the district court in Washington, told me, "a special grand jury," which she defined as a grand jury assigned to an independent counsel, can be indefinitely renewed for six-month periods as long as the prosecutor and chief judge agree. Howard said that special grand juries are typically renewed three times, giving them lives of about three years. She was able to recall two special grand juries whose terms exceeded two years.[41] Clearly, then, Starr could have renewed the grand jury first used by Fiske, which had heard all the key testimony about Foster's death. He chose not to do so.

The Starr team could do what it wanted because the press was not reporting and not questioning its actions. As for Rodriguez's resignation, most journalists seemed content with the explanation offered by Starr's office—"off the record"—that he left because of his inability to be a team player and his personality conflict with Mark Tuohey.

Tuohey, meanwhile, believing the case had been essentially wrapped up, resigned in September 1995, leaving his handpicked successor, John Bates, a veteran Justice Department lawyer, as Starr's new deputy. Before Tuohey departed, he and Starr took decisive steps to close the Foster case once and for all.

In the wake of Rodriguez's resignation and the report in which two New York homicide investigators, hired by the Western Journalism Center, concluded Foster's body had been moved, Tuohey and Starr hired two forensic experts—Dr. Henry Lee and Dr. Brian Blackbourne, the San Diego medical examiner—to bring the case to closure.[42] Lee, head of the Connecticut state crime laboratory, is perhaps the country's most famous forensic scientist and now best known for his role as O. J. Simpson's defense expert during his criminal trial in 1995.[43]

Lee was born in China, but his family fled to Taiwan in World War II. Once a police captain in Taipei, Lee is something of a Sherlock Holmes to his admirers for his ability to mix the practical and scientific aspects of police work. To his critics, he is a grandstanding opportunist.

Lee first gained stature in 1986 after helping Connecticut police convict a man who had put his wife's body through a wood chipper to destroy her remains. Lee identified tiny pieces of the woman's teeth and bones and other fragments to help police solve the case. He went on to gain national prominence after working as a defense expert on the William Kennedy Smith rape trial, the Robert Chambers preppie murder case, and other controversial cases. (See Appendix V.)

IN A CURSORY inspection of the death scene at Fort Marcy Park in the late spring of 1995, Lee came across what he thought was a human skull fragment.[44] This, of course, was the same area in which Fiske had conducted his extensive survey and "excavation." Before positively identifying the fragment, Lee reported the find to Starr's staff, a signal to them that he was going to be able to pull rabbits out of the hat.

Believing as well that the bullet that had not turned up might still be there, Lee asked the FBI to conduct another search, a third one, in late September 1995. The FBI's two-month search expanded the search area over hundreds of square yards, unearthing most of the park and even bringing in a cherry picker to allow FBI agents to scan tree sides with detectors.* Still no bullet was found.[45]

Whatever hopes Starr and some in the FBI may have had of proving suicide based on Lee's conclusions were dashed after Lee's debacle during the Simpson trial. Though Starr was well aware that Lee was working for Simpson, he could not have foreseen that Lee's credibility would fade so quickly. John Hicks, for one, thought Lee's Simpson testimony had cost him credibility "with a lot of people in the forensic community."[46] Hicks, who retired in 1994 as assistant FBI director for its crime laboratory, is widely respected and pioneered the bureau's efforts in the area of DNA identification. Hicks described Lee's testimony at the Simpson trial as "deceptive and misleading or incompetent. Those are the only two choices you have."

BY DECEMBER 1995, Lee had made significant progress in his own investigation of the Foster case but, in the aftermath of his Simpson case experience, he was apparently gun-shy about releasing a report. Lee did meet with staff from Starr's office in December to review some of his findings. What he revealed elated them, according to one member of Starr's staff.

For one thing, Lee said that after analyzing the Polaroids taken by the police, he had detected blood splatter on the leaves above Foster's head—something twenty or more people at the death scene, including the lead police investigator and Dr. Haut, had not observed.[47] Further,

---

* A reporter for *The Independent,* one of Britain's major daily newspapers, visited Fort Marcy Park as the FBI hunted for the bullet. The newspaper quoted one FBI agent, a twenty-year veteran of homicide cases, as stating, "We're investigating Foster's suicide. And it was a suicide."

the dark specks visible on Foster's face, Lee said, were blood. This was consistent with the use of a relatively high-caliber weapon and seemingly supported the finding of a .38 Colt revolver in Foster's hand. Lee was also substantiating Fiske's conclusion that the blood drainage tracks on Foster's face were consistent with suicide. The large bloodstain on the right side of Foster's face, he concluded, most likely resulted after an emergency worker checked for a pulse of Foster's carotid artery, thereby moving the head all the way to the right and then reorienting the head to its straight-up position. Lee also claimed that the blood track to the area above Foster's ear—seemingly showing blood moving against gravity—was wrongly identified by the FBI. The blood, he said, had actually flowed from the side of Foster's eye to the area above the ear.

Promises by Lee to issue a report in weeks soon turned into months. By June 1, 1996, almost a year after taking the case, Lee was just finishing his report. Lee eventually issued one in 1996, but Starr's office has to date not released it to the public.

As in the Simpson trial, Lee's preliminary and oral findings made to Starr's staff in December 1995 were not without challengers. Fred Santucci, who had analyzed thousands of crime-scene photos for the New York Police Department, was highly skeptical of Lee's finding of blood on the leaves "when no one saw it with their own eyes on the scene." He added that the Polaroid shot on which Lee was basing his analysis "is the worst quality photo for finding small drops of blood."[48]

Pathologist Di Maio also disputed whether the speckled blood found on a decedent's face indicates that a relatively large-caliber weapon, such as a .38, was fired into the victim's mouth. He pointed out that even a .22 caliber gun can cause this effect by way of the blood emanating from the nose in a "nasal spray" fashion after the explosion.[49]

In October 1995, one Washington law-enforcement source told me cryptically not to be surprised if new, highly questionable forensic evidence emerged that would help prove Foster killed himself at Fort Marcy Park. That month, the *Pittsburgh Tribune-Review* published this tip-off. A year later, a book by a prominent pathologist revealed what this "new" evidence Dr. Lee "discovered" actually was.

Though Lee's report has yet to be released, a 1996 book by Dr. Cyril Wecht, entitled *Grave Secrets: A Leading Forensic Expert Reveals the Startling Truth About O. J. Simpson, David Koresh, Vincent Foster and Other Sensational Cases*, offers some hints of possible evidence tampering in the case. Wecht's book, with a foreword coauthored by Wecht's friend Henry Lee, reports that after reexamining Foster's shoes, Lee had found both soil and grass stains on them.

The original FBI reports show no discovery of soil or grass stains—a finding that has been cited as key evidence that Foster's body may have been moved to the park. According to Wecht, Lee chided the FBI for their sloppy work and oversight on this matter and has personally concluded that Foster killed himself at Fort Marcy Park. But Wecht himself is not so sure. Wecht told the *Pittsburgh Tribune-Review* that one of two conclusions can be drawn from Lee's discovery: Either the FBI missed the soil in its original tests, or the shoes were tampered with. "There is no other explanation . . . one of the two. It's not something that would have gotten contaminated in the lab," Wecht stated.[50]

Wecht was not quick to rule out tampering, pointing to allegations made by Frederic Whitehurst, a special agent assigned to the FBI crime lab, who has charged that the FBI altered, tampered with, or fabricated evidence in a number of important cases.[51]

John Hicks, who headed the FBI crime laboratory at the time of the initial testing of the shoes in 1994 and who has since retired, told me it was "very unlikely" that the FBI could have missed soil or grass stains on a pair of shoes it was examining. Hicks said that as a normal procedure, shoes undergo a rigorous inspection in the bureau's microscopic analysis unit, using instruments that magnify "anywhere from 30 to 100 times."[52] The FBI was meticulous enough that the laboratory, while finding no soil on Foster's shoes or clothes, did identify minute particles of mica on them.

Lee's work was not the only point of controversy in Starr's reevaluation of the Fiske inquiry. While Lee was working on the physical evidence, Dr. Brian Blackbourne was reviewing issues relating to the autopsy conducted by Dr. James Beyer. On October 20, 1995, the *Pittsburgh Tribune-Review* broke the news that Starr had hired Blackbourne, San Diego's chief medical examiner, in an apparent attempt to add weight to Lee's findings. In contravention of Rodriguez's departing advice that experts be selected who had no connection with official Washington and the FBI, Starr's choice was a man with close ties to both.

Blackbourne, a Canadian citizen, is a seasoned pathologist with twenty-seven years of experience. He has worked in Washington, Miami, and Massachusetts and has conducted more than five thousand legal-medical autopsies.[53] From 1972 to 1982, Blackbourne served as deputy medical examiner for Washington, D.C. He was also a lecturer at the FBI academy in nearby Quantico, Virginia,[54] and consulted with the FBI on a death-investigation manual. He was also a regular lecturer at the Metropolitan D.C. police department's "homicide school," which trains Park Police as well.

In his tenure as deputy medical examiner in Washington, Blackbourne worked under then–chief medical examiner, Dr. James Luke, who became the lead pathologist for Fiske's investigation. Starr was thus assigning Blackbourne to make a judgment that would have a bearing on his former boss's work.

Just after his appointment, I called Blackbourne for an interview. He declined to discuss the case but, when pressed, did say that he was unaware of any controversy concerning a purported wound or trauma on Foster's neck. He said he had not been given, nor did he ask to receive, any of the enhanced scene Polaroids.[55] In another brief telephone interview in August 1996, Blackbourne said he had finished his report on the Foster autopsy and had sent it to Starr, who sent it back asking for revisions. Blackbourne declined to say what revisions he was asked to make or to discuss his conclusions.[56] As for his friendship with Luke, Blackbourne told me it had not precluded him from offering independent objective findings, even though Luke had already officially ruled on the case for Fiske.

Blackbourne's appointment violates no conflict of interest rules, according to the American Academy of Forensic Sciences. But some argue there are legitimate concerns. "Obviously, one of the things that has to be considered with this kind of work [is] accuracy and validity and also the appearance of accuracy and validity," said a nationally prominent forensic pathologist who asked not to be identified.[57] Since there is "a lot of subjectiveness to these reviews," decision-makers or government agencies with due prudence appoint pathologists who can give an "independent" examination, the pathologist noted. While he agreed there were no rules prohibiting Blackbourne's appointment, he said, it clearly violated common sense.[58] The pathologist reported being told about "concern within Starr's group [about] whom to hire. There was some dissatisfaction initially with Blackbourne because of his relationship with Luke." The pathologist said he was perplexed that with a large field of qualified candidates to choose from, the Starr people stuck with Blackbourne.[59]

STARR'S APPARENT strategy has been a "prevent offense" approach, plugging holes and answering critics as he awaits a propitious moment to close the case. This task has been a Sisyphean one for Starr because each time he was about to close the file, new gaps appeared.

Starr's response to criticism of his handling of the Foster death has been to say, through his spokesperson, that his investigation is "active and ongoing"—this, it should be pointed out, has been said since 1994. Yet during this time Starr has not systematically conducted an active homicide probe. After being criticized for not having done so nine months into his own investigation, Starr sent FBI agents to canvass the neighborhood around Fort Marcy Park—the first time investigators had ever interviewed the many neighbors there.[60]

Given the harsh attacks on Starr from Clinton insiders like James Carville, it is unimaginable to many that Starr is anything but a hard-nosed prosecutor. But the White House may have revealed its true sentiment about Starr when it moved to put two additional scandals—the travel office matter and the Filegate scandal—under Starr's jurisdiction.

If Starr was truly threatening White House interests, it is doubtful that they would have made this request.*

A more careful review of Starr's background shows he is far from being a partisan Republican, let alone a hard-nosed prosecutor. Indeed, Starr had never prosecuted a case before. His reputation was built on Washington deal-making and compromise. "The Clintons ought to be dancing in the streets that they got Ken Starr in charge of this case," Starr's law partner Paul Cappuccio told *Newsweek*. "The guy is just not a no-holds-barred prosecutor. He's a judge."[62]

During the early days of the Reagan administration, Starr had served as counselor to Attorney General William French Smith, and in 1983, at the age of thirty-seven, he was appointed by President Reagan to the United States Court of Appeals for the District of Columbia Circuit, the youngest person ever to be appointed in that circuit. He stayed on that bench until 1989, when President Bush appointed him solicitor general. In that role he became the administration's advocate in arguing cases before the Supreme Court.[63]

With Bush's defeat in 1992, Starr joined Kirkland & Ellis but continued to maintain a high profile in Republican politics. There were reports that he was considering a challenge to Oliver North in the latter's campaign for the Republican nomination for senator of Virginia.

During this period, to the great displeasure of Democrats, Starr assisted a women's organization, the Independent Women's Forum, to help file a brief in support of Paula Jones, a former Arkansas state employee who has charged that while she worked for the state, Governor Bill Clinton tried to get her to engage in a sexual act. Starr's brief countered claims by Clinton's attorneys that he was exempted from civil actions while president.[64] (In May 1997, the Supreme Court ruled in Jones's favor, deciding the president is not exempt from civil suits.)

Had his Democratic critics delved deeper, they might have found that

---

* When Donald Schmalz, the independent counsel probing gifts given to former Agriculture Secretary Mike Espy by Clinton backer Don Tyson, sought to widen the jurisdiction of his inquiry, he was opposed by the White House and Attorney General Janet Reno.[61]

Starr was not the worst choice for their purposes. Starr's association with Kirkland & Ellis should have been one such sign, since the firm is closely connected with the Democratic Party. According to the Leadership Institute, the firm's political action committee (PAC) in the 1993–94 election cycle was one of the highest contributors to Democratic candidates of business PACs studied—having donated 86 percent of its funds to Democrats. Starr himself voluntarily contributed to his firm's PAC.[65]

Another such sign was Starr's position on the thorny issue of abortion. When Reagan took office in 1980, many conservative Republicans argued for a litmus test for judicial appointees, particularly to the Supreme Court. Starr infuriated many antiabortion Republicans in 1981 when, as counselor to Attorney General Smith, he played a role in selecting Sandra Day O'Connor as Reagan's first nominee to the high court. To help her pass muster with antiabortion stalwarts in the White House and Senate, Starr wrote a memo endorsing her, assuring Republican insiders that O'Connor would be a solid conservative vote on the bench. He implied that O'Connor would take an antiabortion stance.

The memo was leaked to the *Washington Post* and helped push the nomination forward—despite the fact that White House conservatives were hearing from Republicans in Arizona, O'Connor's home state, that she had a record as a moderate. Omitted from Starr's memo was the critical fact that as a state legislator O'Connor had supported a liberal abortion-rights law. The *Washington Post* reported that antiabortion groups were calling Starr's memo "a cover-up."[66]

Starr again ran into turbulence when straddling the abortion issue as the Bush administration solicitor general. In 1992, when *Planned Parenthood v. Casey* came before the court, Starr argued on behalf of a Pennsylvania law placing restrictions on abortion. Pro-choice forces saw this as an effort to overturn the 1973 landmark ruling of *Roe v. Wade*. During the course of argument Starr was asked pointedly by Justice John Paul Stevens what position the Justice Department had as to "whether a fetus is a person within the meaning of the Fourteenth Amendment." Starr's response infuriated the antiabortion forces and was cited by the justices in not upholding the full extent of the law. Starr told the court: "We do not have a position on that question. . . . We do not, because we think it would be an extraordinarily difficult and sensitive issue. . . ."[67]

Clinton supporters also seemed not to notice that Starr had a reputation as a conciliator and moderate—not as a tough prosecutor. While Starr had come across as a straight-arrow type who might not comport well with the crowd that surrounded the Clintons, Starr was not known for the kind of aggressiveness that would be essential to challenge a sitting president and his circle.

It is difficult to understand why it has taken Starr so long to make some decision on the Foster case, considering Fiske had finished the death investigation and was within days of closing the Foster office inquiry before Starr came on board. With the same resources as Fiske, Starr has been a laggard.

On the Arkansas side, Starr had apparently been diligent in bringing over half a dozen indictments and winning several high-level convictions. By focusing his efforts in Arkansas, Starr has effectively limited his inquiry to the stale, old financial scandal that the Clinton White House prefers and pretty much adhered to the blueprint laid out by Fiske and his predecessors. Starr did indict and win convictions against the McDougals and Jim Guy Tucker, but it should be remembered that even Fiske, who so poorly handled the White House side, planned as much, and sooner than when Starr got around to it (see Appendix VII.)

THE APPARENT coziness between Starr, the Washington establishment, and the White House was further underscored when Starr quietly allowed Mark Tuohey, upon leaving as his Washington deputy in 1995, to take a position with the Washington law offices of Vinson & Elkins. Vinson & Elkins is the same firm that has been representing the Rose Law Firm in Whitewater-related matters before Starr's own office, including matters relating to Vince Foster's death.

Phil Carroll, a senior litigator with the Rose firm who was represented by Vinson & Elkins when interviewed by FBI agents for the Fiske probe of Foster's death, told me that Rose "retained them as our lawyers to give us advice, about how to handle all these subpoenas and all this investigation. . . . You know there are thousands of pages of files. . . . Even lawyers need lawyers."[68] Rose, of course, was a key principal in the Whitewater matter since it had represented Madison Guaranty Bank, had been the law firm where Hubbell committed the fraud prosecuted by Starr, and was the firm that Foster, Hillary Clinton, and William Kennedy hailed from—the same firm where two couriers claimed they had spent a day shredding all of Foster's files soon after Fiske was appointed.

Rose has never been charged with any crimes. Of all the law firms in Washington, Tuohey obviously believed there was no impropriety in joining a firm that represented Rose in its dealings with the independent counsel and the Senate committee that investigated Whitewater—even as these investigations were still active.

There is no indication that after leaving Starr's office, Tuohey assisted Vinson & Elkins with information about the independent counsel's office. "We definitely had a client-screening process at the time Mr. Tuohey joined the firm," explained Angela Anthony, who handles media relations for Vinson & Elkins. As a result, she continued, Mr. Tuohey's work would be kept separate from any work the firm did for Rose. A legal agreement would codify this "walling off" of a partner from such a potential conflict.[69]

Even so, experts in the field are not sure this matter has been put to rest. No one says that Tuohey did anything illegal or even technically unethical. "It doesn't violate capital 'E' Ethics rules that govern lawyers, but there are other considerations," said Professor Geoffrey Hazard of the University of Pennsylvania Law School, one of the nation's authorities on legal ethics. Hazard suggests Tuohey's move and Starr's acquiescence "raises serious questions" since it violates "good sense and standards of prudence." He was surprised that Starr did not simply tell Tuohey to go to another firm. Hazard said the move "creates suspicions" that hurt all parties involved as the inquiry continues.[70]

However, with so many other aspects of the case, including the inconsistencies at the death scene, the irregularities of the Park Police, and the problems of Robert Fiske, Starr and Tuohey escaped examination by the press. After all, Foster's death was nothing more than a tragic suicide with no apparent connection to the swirling Whitewater scandal.

10

There are few facts of the "official" Foster case that are not in serious dispute. Almost four years after Vince Foster died, we have few answers about where he died, where he was found, or how he died. Much evidence has either been mysteriously lost or simply altered. Testimony on which the case is supposedly based is frequently contradictory, occasionally blatantly false. And those tasked with the burden of finding answers seem strangely complacent.

Since Miquel Rodriguez's departure from the independent counsel's office, it is increasingly apparent that Starr's investigation has actually helped thwart an investigation that might reveal a cover-up. One especially strong indication of Starr's aversion to such a probe is his staff's unusual handling of witness Patrick Knowlton, the motorist said to have spotted what Fiske claimed was Foster's Honda in Fort Marcy Park. Knowlton, an affable small-business man who sports a "Clinton-Gore" campaign bumper sticker on the wall of his Washington apartment, has claimed the FBI "lied" on his FD 302, the official witness statement.

At first Starr's office seemed genuinely interested in Knowlton's charges. When the allegations surfaced in the *Sunday Telegraph*, Starr had Knowlton summoned to appear before his Washington grand jury. The calling of Knowlton in November 1995 was the first time in months that the grand jury had heard any matters relating to Foster's death.

On the day Knowlton received his subpoena, he and his girlfriend went out for a drive and believe they were followed by two men in a black sedan. The couple took down the Maryland plate numbers, which a subsequent check by (London) *Telegraph* reporter Ambrose Evans-Prichard traced back to the federal government.

Knowlton claimed that the next day he was harassed and followed on his morning walk along Pennsylvania Avenue from his apartment to a nearby newsstand. He reported that about a dozen men passed him from behind or walked toward him from another direction and as they passed gave him a hard "intimidating stare."

When I learned of this, my immediate reaction was that Knowlton was under stress and perhaps paranoid, so I volunteered to walk with him the following day to the newsstand. Parking in front of his building on a Friday I noted the neighborhood seemed quiet. I picked him up at his apartment, and we began walking along Pennsylvania Avenue. What happened next was not so much frightening as astonishing. Pedestrian traffic picked up abruptly, and two men passed, giving Knowlton just the sort of look he had described. At first I ascribed this to mere happenstance, but then I saw a man across the street spot us and abruptly change direction to cross the street and make a diagonal beeline to intercept us at the next intersection. He, too, gave Knowlton the "look" and shook his head in an awkward gesture.

Similar encounters took place at least two dozen times. Two men in a white Honda gave us intense looks, tailed us as we walked along the avenue, and even circled back around a traffic circle in a conspicuous effort to let us know we were being watched. (I subsequently traced the plates to the home of a Virginia man. Within a day the plates were switched to another car that sat outside the man's home.)

All of this was having a debilitating effect on Knowlton. At one point he sat down on a concrete ledge housing some plants and put his hand on his stomach, indicating he was nauseated. Upon returning to his building, we decided to get in my car and drive around, when a young man sporting a military haircut, wearing earphones, and carrying a gym bag pointedly checked my front and rear license plates. Knowlton snapped a photo of this man.

When Knowlton appeared before the grand jury the following week, Brett Kavanaugh, one of Starr's prosecutors who (according to his official biography) had never prosecuted a case before, was doing the interrogation. Kavanaugh, a Yale graduate, was seen as one of the rising stars on the team: extremely bright, an establishment man in his late twenties with Harrison Ford looks and a demeanor to match. Knowlton would later recount that during the proceedings he "was treated like a suspect," with Kavanaugh focusing more on his character than on the potentially valuable information he had to offer. Kavanaugh asked a series of questions about Knowlton's encounter with the Hispanic-looking man, including one of a graphic sexual nature.

Tough questioning of a witness is not unusual; prosecutors have to establish credibility. The sexual question may have been another matter, however. Jerris Leonard, a former assistant attorney general for civil rights in the Nixon administration and now a prominent Washington attorney, suspects that, assuming such a question was indeed asked, it was for one reason: to falsely paint Knowlton as a homosexual before the grand jury. Leonard was baffled that Starr had allowed a novice prosecutor to serve as the lead interrogator on such an important case.

As reports of Kavanaugh's treatment of Knowlton leaked out, Starr's office vigorously denied that Kavanaugh had asked a graphic sexual question. Knowlton was then recontacted by Starr's staff and told that a good-faith effort was under way to review his statement. He was asked to revisit the independent counsel's office, which he did. There he was asked by three investigators, including FBI special agent James Clemente, if he would join them in visiting the park to go over his story. To this, Knowlton also agreed.

They went to the park that same day, arriving at about 4:30 P.M., the same time Knowlton said he had arrived at the park on the day of Foster's death. Acting surprised, one of the agents noted the presence of Robert Reeves, the unofficial "keeper" of the park, and asked Knowlton to join him in saying hello. It was now clear to Knowlton why he had been brought there: to see if Reeves could identify Knowlton as a gay cruiser or other park habitué, something Knowlton has denied.

After the Reeves encounter, a series of young men seemed to pass by, sizing him up, said Knowlton. Upon leaving the park the four men pulled into the gas station nearby, where it was obvious to Knowlton the agents were setting him up for a possible identification as a regular customer by the attendants.

"It infuriated me, unnerved me," Knowlton complained soon after the incident. "It's not right. I'm just a citizen here to cooperate. Why should I be treated like I did something wrong?"[1] Knowlton, through his lawyer, called the independent counsel's office to protest the treatment. The office denied he had been set up for identification and said that Reeves's presence was a coincidence.

Contradicting that claim was none other than Reeves himself, whom I interviewed at his Alexandria home. He told me that the FBI had contacted his wife by phone and requested that he come to the park "to help identify if someone was a regular visitor at the park."[2] Like any good citizen, Reeves showed up. His account of events matches Knowlton's.

In Reeves the investigators had a potential warehouse of information that could lead to any number of revelations in the case. But the only interest shown in him seemed to be as a potential debunker of someone else with potentially valuable information. In fact, Starr's office had never interviewed Reeves during their "active and ongoing" two-year investigation.

Jerris Leonard, for one, was puzzled by this inordinate focus on discrediting Knowlton instead of checking out his leads. He thought that Knowlton's lead on the briefcase was especially promising and that Park Police should have been vigorously pressed on it.

With Knowlton, Starr's office had moved from a simple prevent-offense strategy, which might have entailed calling him before the grand jury, treating him civilly, and letting him go, thereby ending the matter, to a more aggressive approach where it was deemed necessary to undermine his credibility.

Was Knowlton's testimony about the manipulation of his FBI interview statement threatening to someone? Did the fact that he saw at Fort Marcy a Honda with Arkansas plates—but one very different from the official description of Foster's Honda—have greater significance than we know? Does Knowlton's unshakable recollection of a briefcase in Foster's car put the integrity of the Park Police in question? Could the Hispanic-looking man have taken part in some operation that might relate to the movement of the body? Are some officials upset that Knowlton has been steadfast in his story and, like many others, has not changed it through FBI "reinterviews"?

In March 1996, the Memphis *Commercial Appeal* reported that a local federal prosecutor, Steve Parker, had been recruited by Starr to review Foster's death. This seemed a promising sign: Parker was a trained homicide prosecutor. Starr's deputy, Hickman Ewing, was quoted as saying: "There remain questions about Foster's death. . . . Was it a murder? Or was it a suicide? Either way, why?"[3] But any hopes of a proper investigation were dashed when, just weeks later, the *New York Times* reported that Starr was set to conclude that the case was closed as a suicide.[4] How could Parker's review have been concluded so quickly?

Obviously it was not, but the *Times* report showed that Parker's appointment did not mean there would be any attempt to actually investigate the case. Parker's background is also enlightening: He is a protégé of Ewing. Since Ewing had sided with Tuohey in the Rodriguez controversy, it is doubtful Parker was brought in to unravel the case. To be sure, Starr had, once again, picked an "outsider"—but one like Dr. Lee and Dr. Blackbourne, who was a known commodity and could presumably be trusted.

Starr's team seemed immune from criticism, with neither Congress nor the press willing to demand answers to the questions in the case. D'Amato's Banking Committee was also eager to accept the Fiske conclusions and apparently unwilling to explore the possibility of a cover-up. This became manifest when the committee called Helen Dickey in February 1996 to testify about the time she called Perry in Arkansas. Dickey said that she called Perry in Arkansas after 10 P.M., contradicting both Perry and Patterson who have claimed she called hours earlier. D'Amato and his fellow senators were happy with that response and asked no serious follow-up questions.

Dickey had apparently been brought in at the request of the Democratic counsel on the committee, Richard Ben-Veniste. Her testimony was needed to quell murmurings about the contradictory accounts of Perry and Patterson. As for the one-sidedness of that arrangement, Ben-Veniste said that the troopers had declined to testify. Both troopers said they would have happily done so and told the *Washington Times* they had never been asked, let alone informed that Dickey was called to testify.[5]

Even assuming that the troopers did decline to testify, the committee has the power to subpoena them. Why was the committee unwilling to use this most basic and effective law-enforcement tool?

The White House had initially claimed that no call had been placed by Helen Dickey to the Arkansas governor's mansion on July 20, 1993.

There were two mechanisms by which Helen Dickey could have placed that call: the private lines in the executive residence or the White House signal switchboard. On September 30, 1995, the White House told the committee that "no such call was made from the private telephone lines in the executive residence."[6] On October 13, 1995, the White House told the committee that they had "obtained records of long-distance calls placed through the signal switchboard, and have confirmed that no call to the Governor's mansion was made . . . on July 20, 1993."[7]

Helen Dickey testified under oath in February 1996 that she did, indeed, call the Arkansas governor's mansion and speak with Roger Perry on July 20, 1993, contradicting the White House claims.[8] The only disputed fact was the timing of the call, and committee attempts to place this were met with unusual stumbling blocks.

Did the call go through the signal switchboard as Dickey later testified it did? While asserting they had determined that no such call had been made through the switchboard on July 20, 1993, the White House advised, in the same breath, that Sprint—the provider of the signal switchboard long-distance service—did not retain records of individual long-distance calls.

The committee discovered the White House was mistaken and that indeed Sprint retained some such records. They subpoenaed these records on November 20, 1995.

Sprint responded to the committee by asserting that the records detailed the destination number to which a call was placed, but did not reflect the extension in the White House from which the call originated. Sprint then backtracked and claimed that, oddly, the records showed only the first six digits of the destination number—the area code and the prefix. Without the last four digits of the destination number, the committee later asserted, it was impossible to determine which call(s) had been placed specifically to the governor's mansion in Arkansas.

One has to wonder how the White House could have unequivocally asserted that no calls were placed to the governor's mansion when the records the White House obtained from Sprint in response to the initial committee request were ostensibly missing the identifying last four digits.

Was the call placed through the private line in the executive residence? Dickey testified that her call to the Arkansas governor's mansion was one of several she placed shortly after she called her father with the news of Foster's death. The White House informed the committee eleven days after the Dickey testimony that they had "confirmed that a call to Ms. Dickey's father . . . was made at 10:06 P.M. on July 20, 1993, from one of the private lines in the residence."[9] No corroborating evidence was given to the committee to support the White House claims.

Did Dickey call her father from the residence line, then place her next calls through the signal switchboard, as she testified? Or did Dickey continue to use the private line in the residence to make the call to the governor's mansion? The White House continued to maintain that no call was placed to the governor's mansion on a private line from the residence. The committee never pursued the residence phone records, taking the White House on their word.

Despite these machinations, pinpointing the exact time that Dickey called the Arkansas governor's mansion should have been easily resolved. A simple question was asked: What time did Dickey call the governor's mansion on July 20, 1993? A simple answer, which should have been easily obtainable and would have put an end to the speculation, was something the committee chose not to pursue.

In the Senate committee's final report on Whitewater issued in June 1996, a footnote mentions that three forensic experts had declared the Foster suicide note a forgery. The footnote states that the committee was unable to review the matter because the family would not turn over the note. Again, what happened to their subpoena power?

THERE ARE indisputably dozens of problems associated with the physical, circumstantial, and forensic evidence involving Vincent Foster's death. Serious issues have been raised about the possibly criminal behavior of White House officials in the aftermath of Foster's death. And, as this investigation further demonstrates, the official inquiries have been fraught with ineptness, inadequacy, and even possible complicity.

In February 1997, Starr's office leaked word to the Associated Press and other media that a memo had been completed stating that Starr would decide whether or not his inquiry would bring indictments against the president or First Lady on matters relating to the Whitewater scandal. How could any such decision be made when Starr never received the cooperation of key witnesses such as Webster Hubbell and former Arkansas governor Jim Guy Tucker?

On the Foster side of Starr's inquiry, his office has fed the press a steady diet of leaks that his investigation was all but closed and a report was due shortly. Those reports began with the Scripps Howard story of January 1995 that appeared on the front page of the *Washington Times*.[10] Similar leaks and false news reports continued for more than two years. Finally, some four years after Foster died of what the police said was an "obvious" suicide, Starr closed his case.

On July 15, 1997, in a brief two paragraph statement, Starr concluded that "Mr. Foster committed suicide by gunshot in Fort Marcy Park, Virginia, on July 20, 1993." At the completion of this manuscript, the Starr report was still unavailable for public scrutiny. The decision to release, or forever seal, the report lay in the hands of the three-judge panel who had appointed Starr.

Part of the problem has been the absolute refusal of the establishment media to report on this case. The Foster matter testifies, on the one hand, to the power of the American media to set the nation's public agenda and, on the other, to the way in which policymakers, Congress, and even independent counsels set their course based on the media's agenda.

Readers of this book have gotten a glimpse of the bizarre manner in which this case has been reported by several major media outlets: ABC *World News Tonight*, *Nightline*, and the *Wall Street Journal*, to name a few. The press's attitude might best be exemplified in the *60 Minutes* segment that Mike Wallace conducted with me. Here again, rather than focusing on the many contradictions and inconsistencies of the case, Wallace applied himself to attacking the messenger.

The twenty-minute segment, which aired in October 1995 and was then rebroadcast in July 1996, was based on more than three hours of taped interview. It quickly became apparent during this interview with Wallace that he knew little about the case. He admitted during the course of the interview that there seemed to be serious problems with the investigation into Foster's death.

Following a morning session, we broke for lunch, and Wallace went back to CBS. Upon our return, he said as the cameras rolled that he had seen Andy Rooney during the break and told him about me "and what you had been saying." Wallace recounted that Rooney commented: "Well, I think [Foster] committed suicide but there's something strange there. There's something that doesn't seem quite right." Wallace added, "And I think that's what the American people feel."[11]

Wallace also agreed with me on camera that Robert Fiske had erred: "I confess that when people say that one reason that Fiske didn't call a grand jury was because it would take him such a long time and so forth, I think that also is dead wrong. If it is worth investigating at all, it's worth putting it in front of the grand jury."[12] Wallace's misgiving about the Fiske probe never aired, nor did any other real criticism of Fiske (a friend of Wallace's) or of the Park Police for that matter.

On camera, I encouraged Wallace to look at the evidence and suggested he take the same simple test the New York detectives had conducted: walking the 700 plus feet through Fort Marcy to see if any soil adhered to his shoes. He told me he had already done so and acknowledged he had found soil on his shoes. That never aired on the show, either.

When the segment appeared, I barely recognized myself. Apparently 60 Minutes was more intent on showing my mistakes, such as my "error" in reporting that Foster had been left-handed and the gun had been found suspiciously in the right hand. Wallace and his staff knew well that this story had been promulgated first by the Boston Globe. They knew it was a mistake because I pointed it out to Wallace's producer, Ty Kim, and reported it in my own newspaper. Wallace went on to insinuate that I had made out of whole cloth my report that Dr. Haut, the medical examiner who viewed Foster's body at Fort Marcy, saw little blood on the ground. This was significant because Fiske had claimed otherwise. When Wallace interviewed Dr. Haut, he gave another story, which Wallace said proved me wrong. Even though he knew I had a tape recording of my conversation with Haut, as well as Haut's FBI interview statement, Wallace went with the story.

During the course of my investigation I have heard all the arguments against pursuing the case, not only from media colleagues, but from leading political and law-enforcement figures as well. Here are several of the most common:

The Foster case is the Kennedy assassination redux. While both share similarities—such as the fact that the first investigations into their deaths were not considered thorough—there are major differences. To begin with, there is a tremendous amount of forensic, circumstantial, and physical evidence that contradicts the official ruling on Foster's death, not to mention the mountain of evidence that contradicts the official account of what happened in its aftermath. And, of course, much more is known about Foster's death than with Kennedy's, where the facts trickled out over years.

This can't happen in America. A death, possibly a murder, and a cover-up concerning a high official could not happen in this country. This sentiment is a highly emotional premise that asks any reasonable person to ignore the evidence in forming a conclusion.

It would be bad for the country. This argument is made by people who agree that there are problems with the suicide scenario or the handling of the case by Park Police and Fiske. Such people argue that if the truth came out, it would weaken public faith in the presidency, Congress, and the justice system. The stock market might even fall.

While I agree it would be bad for the country and for the institutions involved if this scandal should erupt, it will be far worse for the country and the civil liberties of each citizen if the strange death of a high-ranking government official can be swept under the rug and not properly investigated because of the political implications.

Such a conspiracy would require too large a number of officials from different agencies who would have had to be in on it. This view is slightly more reasonable than the "it can't happen here" argument. However, many of the irregularities and inconsistencies in the case—though they do point to possible wrongdoing—need not have been the result of any real conspiracy.

Like Ted Koppel, many in the media have framed the issue of a cover-up with pejoratives like "collusion" and "conspiracy." These terms serve to marginalize legitimate criticisms of the handling of the case. Rare indeed is a major cover-up conducted by a group of secret participants meeting in a smoke-filled room. "Complicity" would be a far more appropriate term.

A major cover-up, rather than being an active effort by a tight-knit group of conspirators, may be simply the result of a number of people—acting on their own, for any number of reasons—whose interests would be threatened by disclosure of some part of the truth. These individuals become "compliant" with a tendency to conceal information or misdirect investigators. Perhaps a bureaucrat is aware of chicanery but does not want to jeopardize promotion possibilities. Maybe a factory supervisor in a small community knows of rampant petty theft in the shop, but does not want to risk the opposition of neighbors who might take the side of any dismissed employees.

In the Foster case, this tendency could work in several ways. Witnesses or associates with vital information about Foster might tell a "white lie" or two. Imagine, for example, that a White House staffer is asked—at the earliest stage before anyone thought there would be significant probes into the matter—to tell the Park Police that he had lunch with Foster in his office on the day of Foster's death. He might have been asked by someone who told him it would embarrass the administration and Foster's family if it were revealed where Foster really was that afternoon. The staffer tells the Park Police this "little fib," thinking he is doing a noble service to Foster's family, his superiors and colleagues, even his country. To others, that little fib is one of inestimable importance: It conceals the fact that Foster perhaps did not eat lunch at his office, but somewhere else. It might also help explain why Foster's autopsy found a full meal of meat and potatoes in his stomach.

Months later, when the staffer picks up the paper or turns on the TV and learns that there is more than something "embarrassing" here, it is too late to change his story. If he does not realize that on his own, sufficient hints will surely be dropped that he and his family could possibly be harmed by any change in his testimony.

There is no implication here that any such person ever actually lied about Foster's whereabouts on the day of his death. The example is purely theoretical, as is this one: Imagine a Park Police beat officer, not known for being particularly meticulous, is asked to sign off on a police report without checking to see that all the facts are accurate. When he later learns there is something "seriously" wrong in the report, it is too late. Even if he is inclined to be honest, he might, at this point, fear to venture forth with the truth.

Any number of such relatively innocent people can come to be involved in a cover-up. They have no idea they are part of a giant web of duplicity. Indeed, it is safe to say that if they did know, they never would have taken the fateful first step.

It is also likely that some of the key people in a cover-up do not have a complete picture of what is going on. White House officials, for example, might have different reasons for suppressing certain facts about Foster's death than do, say, the Park Police. Their seemingly common goal might be no more than an unlucky coincidence, occurring without meaningful contact between the parties.

That is why those who posit only two possibilities—either Foster's death took place as officialdom said, or there has been a mass conspiracy to suppress the truth—have, inadvertently or otherwise, fallen into an intellectual trap.

If we accept the logic that "too many had to be in on it, therefore it couldn't have happened," then the Watergate cover-up could not have taken place, either. There were, after all, more than enough official probes to make the concept of "collusion" and "conspiracy" in the Watergate matter look impossible. Had not Nixon's Attorney General Richard Kleindienst stated that the FBI had conducted "one of the most intensive, objective and thorough investigations in many years," completing no less than 1,500 interviews? In the Foster matter, only 125 people were interviewed before issuing a similar clean bill of health. And were we not also assured, following this exhaustive process, that there was no indication of wrongdoing at high levels of the Nixon administration?

Indeed, a grand jury investigation turned up nothing involving Nixon higher-ups for well over a year. In the Foster case, Special Counsel Fiske did not even employ a grand jury. Congressional hearings into Watergate, for a substantial time, turned up little evidence of wrongdoing. Remember, too, that a major turning point in the Watergate scandal occurred when judge John Sirica handed down an extremely harsh sentence to Watergate burglar James McCord. After sentencing, McCord agreed to cooperate, but appealed in writing directly to Sirica: "Since I cannot feel confident in talking with an FBI agent, in testifying before a grand jury whose U.S. Attorneys work for the Department of Justice, or in talking with other government representatives."[13]

The Foster family has accepted the suicide verdict and does not want further investigation. This argument fails for several reasons. For one thing, Foster was a high official who died during the workday. The public has a right to know the full facts of the case. Also, families do not dictate death investigations for good reason: Family members often are suspects or have other motives for not wishing a suspicious death looked into. If the person was murdered, fear or intimidation could prevent the family from pressing for a full inquiry. Some family members may themselves be involved in wrongdoing and fear this will be exposed. The family may also fear disturbing disclosures about their loved one. In the Foster case, the Park Police spread stories early on about Fort Marcy being a homosexual cruising park in a possible effort to discourage the Foster family from seeking a further inquiry.

Still other concerns might have influenced the Foster family. For one thing, published reports claim or intimate that Vince Foster and Hillary Clinton had a romantic affair. Because of such complicating factors, Foster's wife may not want the matter further examined. The family's willingness to accept the suicide verdict should be no surprise, even though families typically do not wish to do so for obvious emotional reasons. Nevertheless, while Foster's family has publicly stated that they have no doubt about the verdict, both Foster's son and daughter have reportedly told classmates at their respective college campuses in Texas and Arkansas that their father did not commit suicide.

The Republicans themselves agreed that Foster committed suicide. This argument postulates that because Republicans and Democrats agree on something, it must therefore be true. In a day and age where image outweighs substance, this notion sells well even if it falls short as good reasoning.

Who are the Republicans signing off on the suicide verdict? One is

William Clinger of Pennsylvania. Clinger first became involved with the case in the early days of 1994, just after Fiske was appointed. At the time I interviewed Clinger, then-ranking minority member of the House Government Operations committee, he told me that while he believed wrongdoing had occurred relating to Foster's office, he had no doubt that Foster committed suicide and said he had no plans to investigate Foster's death. In the summer of 1994, when Fiske's own report was coming under some criticism, Clinger released the results of his own investigation. The Clinger report, as it turned out, was nothing more than a few pages of the Fiske report refashioned and presented as an independent inquest. Clinger's was not a committee report, or even a minority committee report, but the report of a single congressman whose investigation amounted to having some of his aides (with no police experience) conduct a few interviews.

Most frequently cited is the Republican minority's acquiescence to the Senate Banking committee report of 1994, which concluded Foster killed himself at Fort Marcy Park. The Senate investigation involved only one day of hearings, with some review of the documents from the Fiske inquiry, and several depositions of officials involved in the case. So lacking was the Senate's inquiry that they never deposed the Confidential Witness, a key part of Fiske's report, who was then claiming that Fiske and the FBI had essentially manipulated his statement.

Senator D'Amato, the ranking minority member on the committee when the report was issued, later recanted or challenged some of the report's conclusions. In August 1995, as chairman of the committee, D'Amato told PBS's Charlie Rose, commenting on the Park Police probe, "There is no doubt the initial investigation was botched."[14] That same week D'Amato appeared on New York's WABC's Bob Grant talk radio program and recited to Grant the problems: "Did [Foster] die in that position? Was he dragged there? Was he carried there? What about grass stains and other kinds of evidence that might be found on his clothing or on his shoes? More particularly what about the powder burns? What about the gun? And the manner in which the gun was held? And the manner in which the gun was found?"[15]

D'Amato did a great job of summing up the problems in the case. He was apparently less successful in having any of these questions addressed by his committee.

D'Amato was not the only Republican to question the death. House Speaker Gingrich also stated in July 1995 that after having read an *Investor's Business Daily* article by Thomas McArdle about the case, he believed the public was "entitled to a full airing" of the case with congressional hearings. "When you look at it, there's just too much there to not try to find out what really happened," Gingrich said.[16] Soon after making those comments, Gingrich offered even stronger sentiments to a group of reporters. "I just don't accept it," he said of the suicide verdict, adding, "I believe there are plausible grounds to wonder what happened and very real grounds to wonder why it was investigated so badly." Gingrich came under widespread press criticism for having raised the issue, and hearings never did take place.

THE HANDLING of the official investigations into Foster's death has raised the very serious question of whether authorities were simply uninterested in investigating evidence of wrongdoing or, worse, refused to do so. It is, after all, more than four years since Foster's death. Starr has been at work for more than three years, and still, basic tasks such as a second autopsy have not been performed.

Police typically can open and close a death investigation in weeks. In this case, which everyone claims is an open-and-shut case of suicide, years have passed. Several possible conclusions may be drawn from this delay. One is that the investigators are lazy and incompetent. Second is that the authorities believe the case is not as claimed and are seriously on the trail looking for new suspects. Third, the authorities may be fully aware that there is much more to the case—that it may have been murder or that a cover-up took place—but instead of bringing this out, the authorities feel, for various compelling reasons, that the matter can never be revealed. In this case, the investigators may simply be waiting for a politically opportune moment to close it as a suicide.

Frankly, the handling of the case by official investigators—including claims of evidence manipulated or destroyed, and the many allegations of official tampering with witness statements—seems to point to this last scenario.

If the third explanation were not true, investigators would be seriously concerned about why the Park Police were given exclusive jurisdiction of this investigation in the first place. Further, after they had so mishandled it—recall their malfeasance regarding photographic evidence, their failure to canvass the neighborhood, their wrongful reports about Foster's briefcase, their apparent misidentification of the death scene, and so forth—why has no one held them accountable?

The Park Police's malfeasance has generally been written off by arguing that they are, after all, just Park Police. But the later investigations by Special Counsel Fiske and Independent Counsel Starr—which had the benefit of what is arguably the most proficient, sophisticated, investigative unit in the world, the FBI—cannot be so easily excused.

At first glance Fiske's failure to get to the bottom of the matter can be chalked up to his team's overanxiousness to accept the Park Police probe. But such charitable explanations seem unwarranted given Fiske's decision to exempt Foster's death from his grand jury proceedings and his questionable handling of evidence and testimony.

Gross misrepresentations on significant issues proliferate in the Fiske report. Fiske's claim that park visitors Mark and Judy saw nothing unusual in the park seems inexcusable, given their prior account to Fiske's own FBI agents. As evidence of Foster's supposed depression, Fiske cited Foster's weight loss, which he said was noticeable to "many." The medical records show the weight-loss statement was wrong, and the FBI statements compiled by his own staff cannot substantiate that this loss was observed by "many."

Fiske's selective withholding from Congress of key documents that contradict the account he presented to the public is equally troublesome. It is a solid indication that Fiske's team knew it was playing with the facts. Fiske never mentioned in his report that White House aide Thomas Castleton saw Foster leave on his last day with a briefcase, though that is what Castleton told Fiske's investigators.[17] Castleton's statement was never turned over to the Senate Banking committee, nor was that of the CNN makeup artist.

Starr's inquiry to date has been no better. His investigators and prosecutors—with the notable exception of Miquel Rodriguez—have apparently been intent on confirming Fiske's conclusions, even to the point of forcing the evidence to fit them. The consistent pattern of witness statement manipulation and the finding of key evidence as destroyed, missing, contaminated, or altered supports the conclusion that the whole investigative process into Foster's death was, as William Sessions put it so succinctly when speaking of the FBI's role, "compromised from the beginning."

The process began when Foster's body was found dead at Fort Marcy Park. A violent and suspicious death, the Park Police violated the most elementary rule in police procedure by immediately declaring it a suicide. All of their investigative work fit that conclusion.

The unusual haste of White House officials to get into Foster's office and to stymie police and Justice Department investigators, the Clintons' preposterous claims that they expressed no concern to aides about the personal papers kept in Foster's office, and evidence that key documents such as the index of papers relating to the Clintons' business dealings are now missing are strong clues that Foster's death may have been related to the matters he was working on at the time, including matters involving the Clintons' business dealings.

Even if Foster's death was a suicide, police should have been more diligent in establishing a motive. Instead, they accepted flimsy evidence that several *Wall Street Journal* editorials had led to Foster's death.

Later, when questions were raised about the actions of officials in Foster's office, the press was remiss in jumping to the conclusion that Whitewater was linked to Foster's death. The press should have examined the broader picture. Since the strange actions in the office were precipitated by the death, legitimate questions should have been asked about the death's circumstances.

Those questions were not asked. Instead, through the power of the press, a rather specific criminal inquiry was initiated, first headed by

Fiske, and later Starr, not to investigate specifically Foster's death or his office, but Whitewater and related business dealings. Foster's death and the office matter thus became tangential to a scandalous business deal that may or may not have had anything to do with the death.

This returns us to square one. The Park Police never conducted an open-ended homicide investigation. The FBI, kept out of the original investigation, quickly signed off on the Park Police conclusions and by doing so became a party to them. Later, both Fiske and Starr would conduct a deeper investigation, but still fail to conduct a by-the-book homicide inquiry. Fiske and Starr turned to the FBI for their investigative work, and during the course of both inquiries agents acted as if the FBI had a vested interest in containing the scandal.

Like Miquel Rodriguez, I believe that Vincent Foster has been denied his most fundamental civil rights. Many who have sworn an oath to serve and protect have, for whatever reasons, failed to do so in the case of Vincent Foster. If such a disregard for oath, law, procedures, and even good sense is ignored and condoned, then we have all begun to walk down a very dangerous path.

ANYONE WHO chooses to stand silent in that old garrison at the center of Fort Marcy Park can hear the rush of the Potomac whisper through the trees and feel the venerability of the republic itself. Little has changed there in over a hundred years.

On most days one has no trouble finding a space to park at Fort Marcy Park, despite the smallness of the lot. The visitor cannot help but wonder how Mark and Judy could have forgotten who they saw in and around Foster's car, so close to theirs.

The visitor can trace Foster's supposed final steps, up the path from the parking lot, through the main clearing, to the second cannon site. The paths, as they will see, are wide enough for a small truck. By chance, the visitor might see one in the rear of the park, with park service workers in tow as they cut the lawn or tend to the landscape.

On the way through the park's clearing—once the center of the old fort—the visitor can glance to the left and see the first cannon, secured as it is by a metal-concrete anchor. It had been removed from the park a year or so after Foster's death, soon after I reported that the body had likely been found closer to it, and as abruptly returned to its spot in late 1996. This is the same cannon that Gonzalez and others said they passed en route to finding the body just off to the left.

The visitor continues to walk deep into the less accessible rear of the park to find the elusive second cannon, the one that never shows up in any of the Park Police photos with the body. Standing on the crest of the berm that the cannon overlooks, the visitor can see the homes through the park's woods just across Chain Bridge Road. The voices of children and the barking of a dog can be clearly heard from that direction. The visitor wonders why, by the same laws of physics, the thunderous sound of a .38 revolver was not heard over there, or why nobody bothered to ask the residents if they had heard such a noise.

The visitor may then take the dirt path down the berm to the point directly in front of the cannon and note the old, exposed, and worn root stems that have etched that trail for many years. The visitor can pace ten feet from the cannon's barrel to where Fiske said the body was found, or eighteen feet to where the Park Police say it was found: Take your pick. In either spot one may sit, as one theory has Foster doing, on one of the root stems that is not supposed to be there anymore, having been purportedly removed by Fiske's forensic excavation.

At this point the visitor may check his shoes for soil or grass stains. And when, as is almost inevitable, the visitor sees such material with the naked eye, he or she may wonder how it was possible for FBI microscopes not to detect the same on Foster's shoes.

Getting up, the visitor will have to shake the seemingly indelible soil from the back of his or her pants. The visitor can only wonder how Foster, too, sat there and yet no soil came to be on his clothes. The visitor might also want to see where Foster's eyeglasses landed, counting off nineteen feet from where Foster's head was said to be found, and wonder how anyone could claim they "bounced" that far.

Turning around, the visitor can take a short hike down a path running alongside Chain Bridge Road leading to the rear entrance of the park, the one the Park Police said they never knew about and which Fiske said only pedestrians use—but which is, in effect, a miniature parking lot that vehicles can use as casually and unnoticed as the regular parking lot. With a short walk back to the lot, the visitor has come full circle.

A visit to Fort Marcy—built on President Lincoln's orders—takes one back to a critical period in our history when rivers of blood were spilled in order to preserve this unique experiment of ours—this government where justice would reign supreme, and no man, no group of men, no matter how powerful or highly placed, would be exempt from public accountability. With the "investigations" of the Park Police, the FBI, Fiske, and Starr, this tiny square of land may yet become the symbol of a cover-up conducted by people who have, with the help of the press, placed themselves above the law.

APPENDIX I

1993

January 20	William J. Clinton inaugurated forty-second president of the United States. Foster joins White House staff as deputy White House counsel.
January 23	Clinton withdraws his nomination of Zoe Baird for the post of attorney general. Shortly after, his second choice, Kimba Wood, is also withdrawn from consideration.
May 8	Foster gives commencement address at University of Arkansas.
May 19	Clinton administration fires longtime employees of the White House travel office.
June 4	Lani Gunier, Clinton's choice for assistant attorney general for civil rights, is withdrawn, She was vetted by Foster.
June 17	*Wall Street Journal* editorial, WHO IS VINCENT FOSTER?, appears.
June 24	A second *Wall Street Journal* editorial entitled VINCENT FOSTER'S VICTORY appears.
July 3	White House management review of the travel office firing released. Associate counsel William Kennedy is criticized.

July 15	Senator Robert Dole calls for appointment of special counsel to investigate the travel office firings.
July 16	Foster and wife, Lisa, leave for weekend on Eastern Shore of Maryland.
	Freeh offered job as FBI director at White House meeting with Clinton.
July 17	Early morning meeting at Justice Department with FBI director William Sessions. Attorney General Reno, Nussbaum, and Hubbell tell Sessions to resign or be fired. Sessions refuses.
July 18	Foster calls Clinton attorney James Lyons. They agree to meet on Wednesday, July 21.
July 19	Hubbell meets with Chief of Staff McLarty to talk about Foster's state of mind.
	Hubbell meets with Foster.
	President Clinton fires FBI director William Sessions. Deputy director Floyd Clarke named acting director.
	Clinton calls Foster at home and invites Foster to join him, Hubbell, and Bruce Lindsey for a private White House showing of the movie *In the Line of Fire*. Foster declines but agrees to meet Clinton on Wednesday.
July 20	Freeh nominated as FBI director at Rose Garden ceremony.
	Foster makes repeated efforts to speak with William Kennedy by phone but fails.
	Warrant issued for offices of David Hale's Capital Management Services in Little Rock.
	Foster found dead at Fort Marcy.
July 21	Secret Service officer Bruce Abbott observes Craig Livingstone suspiciously carrying documents from the area of Foster's office.
	Park Police investigators arrive at White House but are denied access to Foster's office or the right to conduct interviews.
	Autopsy conducted on Foster by deputy medical examiner for Northern Virginia.

July 22   White House counsel Nussbaum conducts search of Foster's office.

                 Williams and counsel aide Thomas Castleton remove Clinton's papers from Foster's office and store them in closet located in Clinton's residential quarters.

July 23   Foster buried in Hope, Arkansas.

July 26   Associate White House counsel Stephen Neuwirth finds torn note in Foster's office briefcase.

July 27   Lisa Foster views note at 2:30 P.M.

                 Susan Thomases and the Clintons' personal attorney Robert Barnett arrive at the White House. Barnett takes possession of the Clintons' personal papers that were found in Foster's office.

                 6:29 P.M. Webster Hubbell arrives at White House residence and meets with Hillary Clinton. Susan Thomases is already in the residence. Both Hubbell and Thomases leave together at 8:20 P.M.

                 7:00 P.M. Reno and Deputy Attorney General Philip Heymann arrive at White House and are informed of note.

                 8:00 P.M. Park Police notified of note.

July 29   Park Police interview Lisa Foster for first time.

August 5   Park Police conclude investigation, rule death a suicide.

August 9   FBI concludes investigation into the torn note.

August 10   Justice Department press conference chaired by Heymann. Park Police chief Robert Langston and FBI special agent in charge for Washington Robert Bryant announce results of inquiries. Contents of torn note revealed to press. Officials decline to release Park Police report.

August 15   *Washington Post* reveals that Park Police report says that Nussbaum, Williams, and Thomasson conducted late-night entry into Foster's office on the night of the death.

August 16	Park Police hand-delivered the Colt revolver found in Foster's hand to the ballistics laboratory of the Bureau of Alcohol, Tobacco and Firearms. This is the first time the gun is tested.
December 20	*Washington Times* reports that Clinton aides removed Whitewater papers from Foster's office on night of death.

1994

January 9	Senator Daniel Patrick Moynihan calls for appointment of special counsel to probe Whitewater.
January 20	Robert Fiske appointed special counsel by Janet Reno.
January 27	*New York Post* report by Christopher Ruddy details doubts of paramedics at the death scene about Foster's "suicide."
January 28	*Wall Street Journal* files lawsuit against the Justice Department for not releasing the Park Police report completed on August 5, 1993.
February 2	William Sessions issues a statement to *New York Post* that his firing by President Clinton "compromised" the FBI's role in the Foster death case.
February 23	Special Counsel Fiske's investigators begin interviewing first paramedics at the death scene.
March 5	White House Counsel Bernard Nussbaum tenders his resignation.
March 14	A page one *New York Daily News* story by Mike McAlary entitled CASE CLOSED reports that Fiske had concluded Foster's death a suicide at the park.
	Webster Hubbell offers his resignation as associate attorney general.
April 4	The FBI begins a search and "excavation" for the missing bullet at Fort Marcy.
	Wall Street Journal story by Ellen Joan Pollock reports that Fiske has concluded Foster committed suicide.

May 9	Fiske's investigators interview Lisa Foster for the first time.
	First significant FBI laboratory and forensic reports relating to death case completed. Others completed by mid-June.
June	A team of four independent pathologists reviews Foster case for Special Counsel Fiske.
June 30	Fiske releases his report on Foster's death, concluding that Foster killed himself at Fort Marcy.
	President Clinton signs re-authorized Independent Counsel law.
July 29	Senate Banking Committee holds one day of hearings into Foster's death.
August 5	Three-judge panel created by newly authorized independent counsel statute selects Kenneth W. Starr as independent counsel. Fiske inquiry ends.
September	Starr hires Mark H. Tuohey III as Washington deputy, as well as assistant U.S. attorney Miquel Rodriguez to be the lead prosecutor reviewing matters relating to Foster's death.
October	Prosecutor Russell G. Hardin resigns from Starr's Little Rock office over matters relating to Webster Hubbell.
December 6	Hubbell pleads guilty to fraud and tax evasion charges and agrees to cooperate with Starr.
December 13	Associate White House counsel Jane Sherburne writes White House "Task List" memo identifying White House concerns over scandals, including Foster's death.

1995

January 3	Senate Banking Committee releases report agreeing with conclusions made by Fiske.
January 5	Starr's office begins grand jury proceedings into Foster's death.
January 6	A Scripps Howard wire story by Lisa Hoffman appears on the front page of *Washington Times* claiming that Starr has closed his review of

	Foster's death and has concluded the death a suicide.
March	Rodriguez and his assistant resign.
April 27	The Western Journalism Center releases report prepared by two former New York City police homicide experts. The report concludes that murder cannot be ruled out and Foster's body had been moved to the park.
May 3	Christopher Ruddy's story in *Pittsburgh Tribune-Review* reports that Rodriguez resigned over policy dispute in Foster case.
June	Starr hires O. J. Simpson defense expert Henry Lee and the San Diego medical examiner Dr. Brian Blackbourne to review Foster's death.
June 28	Hubbell sentenced to twenty-one months, of a possible ten-year sentence, for fraud and evasion charges. Starr admits Hubbell reneged on his agreement and failed to cooperate.
July	White House publishes and distributes a 331-page file called "Communication Stream of Conspiracy Commerce." The file deals largely with issues pertaining to Foster's death.
July 6	House Speaker Newt Gingrich publicly states there will be hearings on Foster's death.
July/August	Senate Banking Committee now chaired by Senator D'Amato holds hearings into actions of White House aides involving Foster's office.
August 14	Senator D'Amato publicly states that questions remain on the Foster death.
August 22	Dr. Lee testifies as defense expert for O. J. Simpson.
September 1	Starr's deputy Mark Tuohey resigns and joins Washington law firm representing the Rose Law Firm before Starr's office and Congress.
September 3	Profile of Lisa Foster appears in *The New Yorker*. Lisa states that she accepts official conclusions.
Mid-September	Starr begins two-month FBI search for the bullet at Fort Marcy Park.

October 8	Mike Wallace segment on *60 Minutes* reports the Foster case is closed.
October 22	Ambrose Evans-Prichard reports in the London *Sunday Telegraph* that Fort Marcy witness Patrick Knowlton claims the FBI falsified his testimony in their report.
October 25	Strategic Investment and James Dale Davidson hold press conference announcing the findings of three handwriting experts that the torn note is a forgery.
December	Banking Committee threatens to hold White House in contempt for not turning over notes written by William Kennedy.

1996

January 1	Lisa Foster marries U.S. District Court Judge James Moody, a Clinton appointee.
March	Starr hires Memphis federal prosecutor Steve Parker to review Foster death case.
March 25	Starr's most cooperative witness, David Hale, pleads guilty to lying to the SBA and is sentenced to twenty-eight months, of a possible fifty-seven-month sentence. Hale receives stiffest sentence to date for any sentenced in the scandal.
April 21	*New York Times* reports that Starr will soon be releasing report concluding Foster committed suicide.
May 28	Little Rock jury convicts Jim and Susan McDougal and Arkansas governor Jim Guy Tucker of bank fraud and conspiracy charges.
July	Internal Revenue Service begins audit of the Western Journalism Center.
July 28	*60 Minutes* re-airs October 1995 segment on Foster. Wallace states that Starr will issue report closing the case by the end of the summer.
October 22	*USA Today* reports that Starr's Foster report delayed due to "several unforeseen complications."

November 5	Clinton reelected to second term.
November 12	Witness Patrick Knowlton files suit in federal court alleging the government violated his civil rights.
November 21	Hubbell appears before Starr's grand jury in Little Rock, which begins investigating various payments made to Hubbell shortly before he signed a plea agreement with Starr's office.
December 2	Starr appears on *Newsweek* cover and gives exclusive interview. Magazine reports Starr had concluded Foster killed himself at Fort Marcy.
December 4	*Washington Post* reports that James Carville has launched a grassroots campaign "to discredit Kenneth W. Starr."

1997

February 13	Hubbell exits prison after seventeen months and defiantly says he will not cooperate with Starr or inquiries into campaign financing abuses.
February 17	Pepperdine University announces Starr will step down as independent counsel by August 1 to become dean of its law school.
February 21	Starr says he made a mistake by giving a resignation date of August 1 and will stay on as independent counsel.
February 23	Jack Nelson reports in *Los Angeles Times* that Starr had completed a "voluminous report" on Foster's death, concluding suicide.
April 25	Court of Appeals for the Eighth Circuit rules against White House claims of attorney-client privilege involving notes taken by government lawyers assisting Hillary Clinton.
May 12	White House appeals circuit court ruling to Supreme Court.
June 23	Supreme Court refuses to hear Clinton administration appeal on notes made by government lawyers during their conversations with Hillary Clinton.

APPENDIX II

8:00 A.M.	Foster leaves home for work. Drives daughter to work and son to Metro station.
9:00 A.M.	Foster attends counsel's office daily staff meeting.
9:27 A.M.	Foster attends Rose Garden ceremony. President Clinton introduces Louis J. Freeh, his nominee for the directorship of the FBI.
9:40 A.M.	Rose Garden ceremony ends.
9:50 A.M.	Deborah Gorham states Foster arrived at counsel suite.
10:30 A.M.	Foster leaves his office for unknown location.
Approx. 11:30 A.M.	Foster returns to the office and stops in at Nussbaum's office. Nussbaum offers congratulations for the apparent success of the nominations of Louis Freeh and Ruth Bader Ginsburg to the Supreme Court.
12:00 P.M.	Linda Tripp, Nussbaum's assistant, says that Foster asked her to get his lunch from the White House cafeteria.
Approx. 12:30 P.M.	White House claims Foster eats lunch in office.
1:00 P.M.	Foster leaves White House counsel's office.

Approx. 1:00 P.M.	Secret Service officer John Skyles sees Foster exit West Wing. Last sighting of Foster alive.
Approx. 4:30 P.M.	Motorist Patrick Knowlton drives into Fort Marcy's parking lot and sees dark brown Honda with Arkansas plates.
Approx. 5:15 P.M.	A couple, identified as Mark and Judy, drive a white Nissan into Fort Marcy's lot. The couple observes two men in and around the Honda.
5:30 P.M.	Confidential Witness claims he entered the parking lot driving a white utility van. Witness said he found Foster's body in front of the second cannon. Witness then drove to nearby parkway headquarters to notify authorities.
5:59 P.M.	Park service employee Francis Swann calls Fairfax County 911 notifying them of a possible dead body in Fort Marcy.
6:03 P.M.	Swann makes second call to Park Police.
6:10 P.M.	Fairfax Fire and Rescue personnel and Park Police officer Kevin Fornshill arrive at Fort Marcy.
Approx. 6:15 P.M.	Dead body located in park. Fornshill radios Park Police headquarters and notifies them of a "suicide" in the park.
Approx. 6:30 P.M.	Park Police investigators and supervisors begin to arrive at park.
6:37 P.M.	Fairfax personnel leave park to return to firehouse.
7:40 P.M.	Fiske reported that Dr. Donald Haut, the medical examiner, arrived at Fort Marcy Park to view the death scene.
8:02 P.M.	Fairfax ambulance arrives at park to pick up body and bring it to morgue.
8:17 P.M.	Ambulance leaves Fort Marcy.
8:30 P.M.	White House claims that Secret Service is first notified of Foster's death.
	Ambulance arrives at Fairfax Hospital.
	Hillary Clinton's plane makes unscheduled stop in Little Rock returning to Washington from West Coast trip.

Approx. 8:45 P.M.	Park Police investigators Cheryl Braun and John Rolla clear scene at Fort Marcy and exit park.
8:45 P.M.	Park Police "Evidence/Property Control Receipt" shows police investigator Braun retrieved two rings of keys from Foster's front pocket. (Braun states she was at morgue at the time.)
9:00 P.M.	President Clinton appears on CNN's *Larry King Live* program from White House Library.
Approx. 9:00 P.M.	Senior White House aides claim to be first notified of the death.
Between 9:00 and 10:00 P.M.	Craig Livingstone and William Kennedy identify Foster's body at morgue.
	Park Police investigators Rolla and Braun drive to morgue to retrieve Foster's car keys.
9:25 P.M.	Foster's Honda towed from Fort Marcy Park.
9:45 P.M.	White House claims Hillary Clinton first notified of death.
9:55 P.M.	White House claims it confirmed Foster was dead.
10:00 P.M.	Clinton leaves King program, takes elevator to White House residential quarters. Mack McLarty informs Clinton of Foster's death.
	Park Police arrive at Foster's Georgetown home and notify family of death.
10:13 P.M.	Hillary Clinton calls Maggie Williams and informs her of death.
10:45 P.M.	Nussbaum arrives at White House counsel's suite.
10:48 P.M.	Patsy Thomasson arrives at White House. Thomasson, Nussbaum, and Williams enter Foster's office. Williams observed by Secret Service officer Henry O'Neill exiting Foster's office with documents.
11:00 P.M.	Clinton arrives at Foster home.
11:41 P.M.	Officer Henry P. O'Neill sets security alarms in the White House counsel's suite after Thomasson, Nussbaum, and Williams have left.
11:45 P.M.	Clinton leaves Foster home.

APPENDIX III

1:00 P.M.	Foster last seen alive exiting White House West Wing.
Approx. 5:45 P.M.	Confidential Witness claims he discovered Foster's body in park.
5:59 P.M.	Park service employee Francis Swann calls Fairfax County 911 to notify them of a possible dead body.
Approx. 6:00 P.M.	Arkansas Trooper Larry Patterson arrives in his Little Rock apartment and receives a phone call from Trooper Roger Perry informing him of Foster's death. Patterson said the call came no later than 6:00 P.M. EST.
6:03 P.M.	Swann, after calling 911, hangs up and notifies Park Police.
Approx. 6:15 P.M.	Body of unknown male found in Fort Marcy Park. Park Police officer transmits radio call of "suicide" in park.
Approx. 6:35 P.M.	Paramedics return from death scene to parking lot. Paramedic Richard Arthur claims he saw Park Police entering Foster's car in search of identification.

6:40 P.M.	Fairfax Fire and Rescue workers exit park to return to station house.
Approx. 6:45 P.M.	Fairfax Fire and Rescue workers arrive at station house. Rescuers report to station supervisor Lieutenant William Bianchi that a White House official was found dead in park.
7:00 P.M.	Latest possible time former state police commander Lynn Davis claims he was notified of Foster's death by Trooper Perry.
Approx. 7:00 P.M.	Park police senior investigator Cheryl Braun claims she first entered Foster's Honda in search of identification. She claims she was still unaware of deceased's name. After finding Foster's White House identification, Braun asks Lieutenant Watson to call shift commander Lieutenant Gavin to notify him of death.
Approx. 7:15 P.M.	According to a *New York Post* report, White House administrative chief David Watkins is paged at Georgetown theater and notified of death.
Approx. 7:30 P.M.	Braun discovers that Lieutenant Gavin was not called by Watson. She calls Gavin herself to notify him of Foster's death.
Approx. 7:40 P.M.	Gavin calls White House and notifies Secret Service of Foster's death.
Approx. 7:50 P.M.	Deputy Chief of Staff Bill Burton calls Gavin to confirm death.
8:00 P.M.	Latest possible time Trooper Roger Perry claims he was notified of Foster's death by Helen Dickey at the White House. Perry says call likely came earlier.
Approx. 8:00 P.M.	According to grand jury testimony, Gayle Kennedy put her two children to bed when call came notifying her husband William Kennedy of Foster's death.
Approx. 8:15 P.M.–8:30 P.M.	According to his FBI statement, William Kennedy first was called by Craig Livingstone and notified of Foster's death.

Approx. 8:30 P.M.	Lead Park Police investigator testified under oath that for the first time he enters Foster's Honda in search of Foster's identification and only then was White House notified.
8:30 P.M.	According to a Secret Service memo and the White House, this is the exact time when the Park Police in the person of Lieutenant Gavin first notified the White House of Foster's death. According to the Secret Service, the first official notified by the Secret Service was David Watkins sometime after 8:30.
Approx. 8:45 P.M.	CNN makeup artist preparing president for *Larry King Live* overhears the president being informed about the finding of a document in Foster's office.
9:00 P.M.	*Larry King Live* begins.
Approx. 9:05–9:15 P.M.	Senior White House aides, including McLarty, Lindsey, Livingstone, and Gearan, first claim they learned of Foster's death.
9:55 P.M.	White House claims that Livingstone and Kennedy made positive identification of Foster at morgue.
10:00 P.M.	Clinton departs King program and takes elevator to residential quarters. Once there McLarty informs him of Foster's death.
10:06 P.M.	Dickey claims she made call to her father, after which she called Arkansas governor's mansion and spoke to Perry informing him of death.

APPENDIX IV

CASE HISTORIES OF DR. JAMES BEYER

On March 8, 1994, the *Washington Times* and the *New York Post* (my byline) published stories detailing concerns about Dr. James Beyer's handling of previous cases involving possible suicide. The *Times* focused on the 1989 slaying of twenty-one-year-old Timothy Easley. Beyer ruled that Easley died of a self-inflicted wound—he had stabbed himself in the chest. Easley's family found that difficult to believe and became concerned that Beyer noted the young man's hair as "gray" when it was dark brown. "I made a mistake . . . the hair color is not altered after death," Beyer apologized in a letter to the family.

But that was trivial compared to what the family noticed and photographed on the body: cut marks on the back of Easley's right hand.

The family had their photos examined by Dr. Harry Bonnell, the deputy chief medical examiner for San Diego. "The cut on the hand is definitely antemortem [before death] and I cannot understand how any competent forensic pathologist would miss it. It is a classical 'defense' wound, suffered while trying to avoid the knife," Bonnell concluded. Bonnell also found the knife's entry point and trajectory into Easley's chest inconsistent with suicide. Beyer claimed he did not note the cuts because they were "consistent with a needle mark," which he believed resulted from first aid administered by rescue workers.

Forensic pathologists say in a legal-medical autopsy the pathologist must note anything unusual on the body, even if it may be caused by medical personnel. A needle mark would also be important in a possible suicide case because it might indicate that the victim was drugged before death.

The controversy would have been moot had it not been that Easley's girlfriend confessed to the murder several years later. At that time an investigator, while reviewing the original polygraph taken by the young lady just after the death, noted it had been inaccurately analyzed; she had failed, though the examiner had passed her.

In his Senate deposition, Beyer described the *Times* report as "typical media reporting with gross inaccuracy" and then went on to explain why he believed it to be a suicide. Beyer said the girl had passed the polygraph administered by the police. If it was known that the first one had been wrong, Beyer explained, "then further investigation might have been conducted by the police." None of the Senate investigators followed up on that statement by asking why a polygraph exam should have any bearing on his autopsy examination of Easley's body.

My *New York Post* article not only examined the Easley case, but the tragic death of Tommy Burkett, also a college-aged Virginia man. Beyer ruled that death "consistent with a self-inflicted wound." Young Burkett was found dead in December 1991 in his bedroom at his parents' suburban Virginia home. Like Foster, he was found with a revolver in his hand, and police quickly determined suicide. In lieu of any real police investigation, Fairfax County authorities relied heavily on Beyer's autopsy as supporting evidence. Beyer found a perforating gunshot wound to the head through the mouth and noted no signs of a struggle.

Again, the family would not accept the results of the police inquiry and noted several inconsistencies, including blood outside their son's bedroom. The family commissioned a second autopsy by Dr. Erik Mitchell, the former chief of pathology for Syracuse, New York. Mitchell found possible signs of a struggle that were never noted on Beyer's autopsy: Tommy's ear had suffered trauma, his jaw had been broken, and abrasions were found on his chest. As in the Foster case, Beyer took no X-rays. Mitchell also discovered that Beyer had not dissected Tommy's lungs, though his report claimed he had completed that procedure.

There is no way of telling if these were isolated cases, or if the Foster case fits a pattern of Beyer's recent work. It does suggest, however, that legitimate questions can be raised about the Foster autopsy and that Beyer's ruling is less than certain since he was dead wrong before.

APPENDIX V

CASE HISTORIES OF DR. HENRY LEE

In the 1991 trial of William Kennedy Smith, the nephew of Senator Edward Kennedy, Smith was accused of having raped a young Florida woman one spring night outside the Kennedy's oceanfront estate in Palm Beach. As the defense's chief witness, Henry Lee played a key role in convincing the jury that the woman was lying.

During his testimony he dramatically pulled out his handkerchief soiled with grass stains and said he had rubbed it on the same area of grass where the young lady claimed she first struggled with Smith and then was raped. Since Lee found no grass stains on the woman's pantyhose or clothing, he concluded the woman had not struggled, suggesting the sex was consensual. Critics say the method was faulty: Lee should have used the same material as that used in the clothing of the woman and also ensured that the atmospheric and ground conditions were the same.

Other controversial cases Lee has been involved with include New York's "preppie murder" case and the death of journalist Danny Casolaro. The former never came to trial because the accused Manhattan prep student, Robert Chambers, confessed to the accidental killing by strangulation of young Jennifer Levin during a sexual tryst in New York City's Central Park. Lee was to have been Chambers's defense expert.

In 1991, Lee reviewed the death of Casolaro, a freelance reporter found dead of an apparent suicide in the bathtub of a West Virginia hotel room. Casolaro's family contested the ruling, citing the large number of cuts on the man's wrist and the fact that his papers were missing from his hotel room.

Lee reviewed the case and bolstered official claims that the death was a suicide, based on blood-splatter analysis. The finding is still disputed by the family.

Lee has worked on numerous government cases and boasts to colleagues of his close relationship with Attorney General Janet Reno. He will sometimes take high-profile private cases for nothing or donate his fee to charitable enterprises while bolstering his image and enhancing his credibility.

Some colleagues suggest that Lee's desire for publicity outweighed any ethical or moral concerns that might have prevented him from working for accused murderer O. J. Simpson. At the trial, Lee's interpretation of bloodstains found on the grounds of Nicole Brown Simpson's condominium enabled Simpson's defense lawyers to argue that the murders were accomplished by more than one individual. Lee, for example, argued that one blood pattern found on an envelope, perhaps a piece of litter found on the ground near the bodies, could have been made from a shoe different from the one prosecutors claim Simpson wore on the night of the slayings. On the stand, Lee hedged his testimony, however, explaining that his judgment was not definitive as to whether the pattern was a shoe print.

Soon after Lee testified, two FBI experts took the stand to rebut Lee's findings. One expert said the bloodstains were more likely the result of fabric impressions than of a shoe. He said Lee's work was "inadequate" and suggested it had been "irresponsible" to draw any inferences about the bloodstains.

Lee declined to testify again to rebut the FBI. Instead, he called a press conference back in Connecticut to defend his testimony. He said he had drawn no specific conclusions about the stains and that Simpson's defense attorneys may have exaggerated the significance of his testimony. He said that his appearance was "not worth it" and refuses to discuss the case with the press or at the seminars he conducts on prior cases.

Some of his colleagues were not happy with Lee's testimony at the Simpson trial and suggest it represents the type of work he does in other cases. "I think [Lee] is definitely a hired gun," John Hicks, a former head of the FBI laboratory, explained. "Henry is a very personable individual, and it's easy to be sort of drawn in by Henry, he's full of . . . stories . . . very enjoyable, and sort of an exciting person to listen to. But unfortunately some people may not be able to sort through the B.S. he's laying out. He's a salesman selling a little snake oil."

The famed Charles Manson prosecutor Vincent Bugliosi, writing in his bestselling book *Outrage: The Five Reasons Why O. J. Simpson Got Away with Murder*, chided the prosecution for not having "exposed Lee so the jurors could see the emperor without his clothing on."

As Bugliosi explains, Lee's testimony was one of the key factors cited by jurors in their decision to let Simpson off. As one juror told the *Los Angeles Times* after the verdict, the jurors considered Dr. Lee "the most credible witness," and that his "something wrong" testimony "had a lot of impact on a lot people." Bugliosi, of course, viewed Lee quite differently, suggesting Lee's Simpson testimony indicated he "was nothing short of incompetent" and that his reputation was "bloated"—in reality, says Bugliosi, Lee fits Mark Twain's definition of an expert: "Just some guy from out of town."

APPENDIX VI

PARK POLICE CASE HISTORIES

Congressman Wilbur Mills, the chair of the influential Ways and Means Committee, saw his career take a nosedive in 1974 when he was found at the Washington Tidal Basin with a stripper named Fanne Fox. Fox had fallen into the basin, which was under Park Police jurisdiction. The Park Police like to point to their handling of the Mills incident to prove they are willing to go toe-to-toe with powerful Washington figures.

A careful examination of the facts, however, shows the Park Police were reluctant to pursue the case, and did so days after the incident and only after television footage of the incident surfaced.

On the night of the Mills-Fox incident, Larry Krebs, a cameraman working for a local Washington television station, went to the tidal basin after hearing of a problem there on his police scanner. Upon arriving, he heard a woman scream and saw a Park Police officer, who was soaking wet, being assisted out of the basin. As he was filming the dripping officer, Krebs noticed out of the corner of his eye a Park Police officer escorting another man.

Turning his camera toward the two, Krebs realized the man with the officer was Mills. Krebs recalled the Park Police officer quickly turning

MIlls around to hide his face from the camera. Immediately following the incident, as rumors began to swirl, the Park Police denied that Mills was found at the basin, as did Mills's office. Their stories changed after the film surfaced.

Another, less-well-known case involving the Park Police suggests they can be less than candid with the facts, even in a death investigation. This is the case of Robert Groves.

Robert Corley Groves, a twenty-nine-year-old ABC News producer, was at the top of his profession in December 1988 when he was killed in a car accident involving a Park Police officer. Groves, who had a particular interest in stories involving official corruption, organized crime, and drug trafficking, was considered a rising star at ABC News the day he lawfully drove his BMW into a Washington intersection to make a fatal left turn. As Groves did so, court records show a Park Police car ran a red light at "an excessive rate of speed."

The nightmarish accident was worsened for the Groves family by the questionable actions of the Park Police after the death. The Groves family, a surviving passenger, and other witnesses have accused the police of fabricating a witness statement, withholding statements from a critical witness, altering the crime-scene diagram, destroying crime-scene evidence, and even attempting to smear Groves's character by suggesting the straight-arrow newsman was on drugs.

By doing these things, critics charge, the Park Police reduced their officer's negligence by making it look as if he had not sped and that he had his flashing lights on (one witness said he did not) as he entered the intersection. Also apparently of concern to the Park Police was the fear that the case might go before a grand jury to review whether vehicular homicide had taken place. The Park Police then made "changes" to the crime-scene diagram of the skid marks found at the intersection— changes that reduced the officer's reported speed. After that, the matter did not have to go before a grand jury.

Eventually the Groves family brought a civil suit against the Park Police and won a $1.25 million settlement. While working on the Groves story in March 1995, I spoke with a producer for ABC News who told me, off the record, that "nothing the Park Police did [in the Groves case] would surprise me."

That case was ignored by the press—despite the questionable actions of the police—largely because it appeared to be nothing more than a traffic accident. But what about the Park Police handling of the "suicide" of Terry Todd Wright, a twenty-year-old Army soldier? Young Wright, then assigned to the National Security Agency, had been found dead on park land near Fort Meade, Maryland.

The 1991 case was destined for oblivion were it not for the report of Pulitzer Prize–winning journalist David Zucchino of the *Philadelphia Inquirer*. Wright's alleged suicide was one of a number of questionable military suicides Zucchino investigated in 1993 for his paper. Zucchino told me (it sounded like déjà vu) that the Park Police were "very, very unprofessional" in handling the case: "They didn't bother to gather crucial evidence. They assumed it was a suicide from the very beginning." The Army investigator who worked with the Park Police on the Wright case told Zucchino flat out, "The investigation does not support a suicide."

The "suicide" was similar to Foster's, though police said Wright killed himself by firing a .22 caliber rifle into his head. The first person to find the body, Eugene Hyatt, a civilian who was out hunting, found the suicide questionable because the rifle did not look like it had been fired by Wright, the position of the body was neat, eyeglasses and a baseball cap were still perfectly situated on the victim's head, and the young man was wearing thick gloves, which would have made it difficult for him to put his finger into the trigger guard.

Hyatt told me that after the Park Police arrived and he pointed out the neat arrangement of the hat to them, an Army photographer went over to the body and partially removed the hat, making it look disheveled. The photographer did this before he took pictures of the scene, and in the presence of Park Police, including a ranking officer. As Gene Wheaton, a former Army investigator, told me, the alteration of the scene before taking photos is "a crime."

Wright's parents, Sydney and Carlos Wright of Albertville, Alabama, found it difficult to believe that their son, who had no history of instability, had killed himself. Their suspicions were aroused when Park Police could never tell them exactly where their son had been found and gave the family several varying accounts as to the body's location and position. The family had no idea why the Park Police handled the case the way they did.

APPENDIX VII

Perhaps the most telling element of the Starr inquiry into the Arkansas side of Whitewater is that Starr's key cooperating witnesses, David Hale and James McDougal, have received the harshest punishments of anyone linked to the Whitewater scandal. Hale received twenty-eight months with no chance of parole, and additional fines and restitution due of over $2 million; McDougal received a three year prison term with equally heavy restitution due. While Starr himself did not hand down those sentences, he has been publicly silent about this strange form of justice. Only after the Tribune-Review and others pointed out the unusual sentence for Hale, did Starr tepidly ask the court to review his sentencing.

In August 1995 I reported in the *Tribune-Review* that, based on sources close to the Starr investigation, it was highly unlikely that Starr would be able to indict the Clintons on any wrongdoing related to Whitewater, because Hale was the only credible witness they had to implicate Clinton in the bank fraud, and "Hale versus the president is not going to fly," one prosecutor told me, indicating Starr would need much more corroboration to indict the president.

Both Jim and Susan McDougal have serious credibility problems that

285

make them practically useless as prosecution witnesses. Also in that August piece, I noted that Governor Tucker would be a powerful witness, but it is likely he would never testify against Clinton under any circumstances.

Starr finally had the long-sought lever over the McDougals and Tucker when an Arkansas jury convicted the trio on federal charges in May 1996, but Starr again missed his opportunity, specifically with Tucker. Federal Judge George Howard, noting Tucker's need for a liver transplant, gave Tucker an extremely light sentence of home arrest and probation. However, health reasons, under federal guidelines adopted in 1987, are not an acceptable reason for a reduction in jail time (Tucker's crimes were committed before the 1987 guidelines, but judges like to follow the new, stricter guidelines). Federal prisons have extensive medical facilities, and any leniency based on health did not extend to David Hale, who has suffered two serious heart attacks, undergone bypass surgery, and is on life-sustaining medication.

The weakness of Starr's prosecution was brought home by a *Washington Times* report about the pre-sentencing hearing for Tucker. At that hearing, Starr's prosecutor did little to argue against Tucker's receiving a reduced sentence. The *Times* reported that Starr's prosecution "offered no witnesses, no statistics on how many such (liver transplant) operations had been performed on inmates and no opposition to the defense witnesses' often evasive answers on cross examination."

Instead of strenuously pursuing a key credible witness like Tucker, Starr accepted Jim McDougal's cooperation. As someone put it, McDougal's usefulness is diminished "because he has lied so many times," not to mention his erratic and unstable personality. Starr, after having given a pass to Tucker, was then intent on proving his prosecutorial manhood by hammering Mrs. McDougal, to the point of having her publicly shackled, though Starr knows she has questionable value to his prosecution. Susan McDougal has also been charged in California for defrauding Zubin Mehta.

Starr's close ties with the Justice Department, which have so infected the Washington side of his probe, have also made their way to Arkansas in his hiring of Ray and LeRoy Jahn for the Little Rock office. The Jahns, a husband-and-wife team of federal prosecutors, had previously gained some notoriety as prosecutors in the Waco case. The Jahns headed up the government case against the eleven surviving members of the siege of the Branch Davidian compound in Waco. The Waco prosecution had been a sensitive one for the Clinton administration, and the Jahns had been specifically selected for that task.

NOTES

CHAPTER 1

1. *Time*-CNN poll, Associated Press, "Foster's Suicide in Doubt," 8 August 1995.
2. Christopher Ruddy, "Wecht Advised Second Autopsy to End Foster Case Speculation," *Pittsburgh Tribune-Review,* 15 November 1996.
3. Associated Press, "Questions about Foster Suicide," 27 January 1994.
4. United States Park Police Report, *Hearings Before the Committee on Banking, Housing and Urban Affairs on the Death of Vincent Foster,* 29 July 1994, 2441.

CHAPTER 2

1. Press conference with Philip Heymann, Robert Langston, Robert Bryant. "Report on the Death of Vincent Foster," 10 August 1993. Federal News Service Transcript. *Hearings Before the Committee on Banking, Housing and Urban Affairs on the Death of Vincent Foster,* 29 July 1994, Senate Hearing #103–889, vol. 2, 1847–48.
2. FBI Statement of Kevin B. Fornshill, 29 April 1994. *Hearings,* vol. 2, 1582.
   Senate Deposition of Kevin B. Fornshill, 12 July 1994. *Hearings,* vol. 1, 916–17, 923.
   FBI Statement of Franz Josef Ferstl, 2 May 1994. *Hearings,* vol. 2, 1628.
3. Fairfax County, Virginia, Memorandum, 24 February 1994. *Hearings,* vol. 2, 1392.
   Fairfax Fire and Rescue Incident Report, 20 July 1993. *Hearings,* vol. 2, 1416.
4. Senate Deposition of Kevin B. Fornshill, 12 July 1994. *Hearings,* vol. 1, 923.
5. FBI Statement of Kevin B. Fornshill, 29 April 1994. *Hearings,* vol. 2, 1583.
6. Vincent J. Scalice Associates, "Independent Report in Re: The Death of Vincent Foster, Jr.," 27 April 1995, Western Journalism Center.
   Christopher Ruddy, *Vincent Foster: The Ruddy Investigation* (Western Journalism Center, 1995), 202.
7. FBI Statement of Donald David Haut, 12 April 1994. *Hearings,* vol. 2, 1660.

8. Transcript of 911 call at 17:59:59 hrs., 20 July 1993, Fairfax County Public Safety Communications Center, 9 March 1994. *Hearings*, vol. 2, 1430–32.
9. United States Park Police Report, transcript of call to Park Police at 18:02:35 hrs., 20 July 1993. *Hearings*, vol. 2, 2119.
10. FBI Statement of "Judy," 7 April 1994. *Hearings*, vol. 2, 1470.
11. FBI Statement of "Mark," 5 April 1994. *Hearings*, vol. 2, 1474.
12. FBI Statement of "Judy," 7 April 1994. *Hearings*, vol. 2, 1471.
13. United States Park Police Report, Supplemental Incident Record by Cheryl Braun, 2 July 1994. *Hearings*, vol. 2, 2564.

CHAPTER 3

1. Senate Deposition of Richard M. Arthur, 14 July 1994. *Hearings Before the Committee on Banking, Housing and Urban Affairs on the Death of Vincent Foster*, 29 July 1994, Senate Hearing no. 103–889, vol. 1, 886–89.
2. FBI Statement of Richard M. Arthur, 29 April 1994, *Hearings*, vol. 2, 1565.
3. Senate Deposition, Arthur, *Hearings*, vol. 1, 886–87.
4. FBI Statement of Corey Ashford, 23 February 1994, *Hearings*, vol. 2, 1347.
5. Christopher Ruddy, "Doubts Raised over Foster's 'Suicide,' " *New York Post*, 27 January 1994, 5.
6. Fairfax County Fire and Rescue Department, "EMS Incident Report," 20 July 1993, *Hearings*, vol. 1, 1097.
7. Senate Deposition of Cheryl A. Braun, 23 July 1994, *Hearings*, vol. 1, 522.
8. U.S. Park Police Criminal Investigations Branch, "Death Investigations Guidelines," *Hearings*, vol. 1, 1322–23.
9. Senate Deposition, Braun, *Hearings*, vol. 1, 501.
10. Ibid., 502.
11. Robert B. Fiske, Jr., "Report of the Independent Counsel in Re Vincent Foster, Jr.," 30 June 1994, *Hearings*, vol. 1, 229.
12. Interview with George Gonzalez, 16 January 1994.
13. Interview with Kevin Fornshill, 21 January 1994.
14. Fiske, Report, *Hearings*, vol. 1, 227–28.
15. Vernon J. Geberth, *Practical Homicide Investigation: Tactics, Procedures, and Forensic Techniques*, 2d ed. (Boca Raton, FL: CRC Press, 1993), 259.
16. FBI Statement of Donald David Haut, 14 April 1994, *Hearings*, vol. 2, 1658.
17. FBI Statement of Donald David Haut, 12 April 1994, *Hearings*, vol. 2, 1659–60.
18. Ibid., 1660.
19. Senate Deposition of John C. Rolla, 21 July 1994, *Hearings*, vol. 1, 401–2.
20. FBI Statement of Richard M. Arthur, 16 March 1994, *Hearings*, vol. 2, 1383.
21. FBI Statement of Richard M. Arthur, 29 April 1994, *Hearings*, vol. 2, 1564–65.
22. Ibid., 1564.
23. U.S. Park Police Report, Letter from John C. Sloan to Captain Charles Hume, *Hearings*, vol. 2, 2169.
24. U.S. Park Police Report, *Hearings*, vol. 2, 2170–72.

25. FBI Statement of Lee Foster Bowman, 28 June 1994, *Hearings*, vol. 2, 1807.
26. Congressmen Burton, Mica, and Rohrbacher; interview with "Confidential Witness," "In Regards to Discovery of Vince Foster's Body on July 20, 1993," 28 July 1994, *Hearings*, vol. 2, 2660.
27. Fiske, Report, Exhibit 8: Report of Autopsy, *Hearings*, vol. 1, 365.
28. Fiske, Report, *Hearings*, vol. 1, 220.
29. Ruddy, Doubts Raised.
30. Associated Press, "Questions About Foster Death," 28 January 1994.
31. Vincent J. Scalice Associates, "Independent Report in Re: The Death of Vincent Foster, Jr.," 27 April 1995, Western Journalism Center.
32. Christopher Ruddy, "Cops Made Photo Blunder at Foster Death Site," *New York Post*, 7 March 1994, 9.
33. U.S. Park Police Report, Mobile Crime Lab Report Supplement, 29 July 1993, *Hearings*, vol. 2, 2141.
34. Senate Deposition, Rolla, *Hearings*, vol. 1, 426.

CHAPTER 4

1. Senate Deposition of John C. Rolla, 21 July 1994, *Hearings*, vol. 1, 473.
2. U.S. Park Police Report, Interview with Bernard Nussbaum, 21 July 1993, *Hearings*, vol. 2, 2129.
3. U.S. Park Police Report, Interview with Ms. Betsy Pond, 22 August 1993 (*sic*), *Hearings*, vol. 2, 2130.
4. U.S. Park Police Report, Interview with Deborah Gorham, 22 August 1993 (*sic*), *Hearings*, vol. 2, 2132–33.
5. U.S. Park Police Report, Interview with Thomas Castleton, 22 July 1993, *Hearings*, vol. 2, 2134.
6. U.S. Park Police Report, Interviews with Drs. Hedaya, Pasternak, and Allen, 22 July 1993, *Hearings*, vol. 2, 2135.
7. U.S. Park Police Report, Interview with Beryl Anthony, 27 July 1993, *Hearings*, vol. 2, 2146.
8. U.S. Park Police Report, Interview with Lisa Foster, 29 July 1993, *Hearings*, vol. 2, 2152–53.
9. Frank J. Murray, "Victim of Washington?" *Washington Times*, 24 July 1993, sec. A, 1.
10. Robert B. Fiske, Jr., "Report of the Independent Counsel in Re Vincent Foster, Jr.," 30 June 1994, *Hearings*, vol. 1, 202.
11. U.S. Park Police Report, 5 August 1993, *Hearings*, vol. 2, 2114.
12. U.S. Park Police Report, Supplemental Criminal Investigation Incident Record Re: CIA Witness, 26 July 1993, *Hearings*, vol. 2, 2145.
13. FBI Statement of "CIA Witness," 18 April 1994, *Hearings*, vol. 2, 1529.
    Handwritten notes of FBI interview with CIA witness, 18 April 1994.
14. Christopher Ruddy, "Cops: Foster Gun Was Never Tested," *New York Post*, 28 January 1994, 5.
15. Interview with Dr. Vincent DiMaio, 10 February 1994.

16. U.S. Park Police Report, Mobile Crime Lab Report Supplement, 24 July 1993, *Hearings*, vol. 2, 2140.
17. FBI Field Report on Fort Marcy Excavation, 4 April 1994, *Hearings*, vol. 2, 1905–12, 2039.
18. Senate Deposition of Peter J. Simonello, 14 July 1994, *Hearings*, vol. 1, 662.
19. Ibid., 661–63.
20. Senate Deposition, Rolla, *Hearings*, vol. 1, 429.
21. Senate Deposition, Simonello, *Hearings*, vol. 1, 663.
22. Fiske, Report, Exhibit 3, Forensic Pathology Report, *Hearings*, vol. 1, 336.
23. Christopher Ruddy, "Did Vincent Foster Fire the Gun?" Special Report, *Vincent Foster: The Ruddy Investigation*, Western Journalism Center, 1995, 49.
24. Christopher Ruddy, "Forensic Experts Doubt Foster Suicide Finding," *Pittsburgh Tribune-Review*, 18 January 1995, sec. A, 1.
25. Ruddy, "Did Vincent Foster Fire the Gun?" 45–59.
26. Ruddy, "Forensic Experts Doubt Foster Suicide Finding."
27. Ibid.
28. Ibid.
29. Fiske, Report, Exhibit 1, *Hearings*, vol. 1, 250.
30. Fiske, Report, *Hearings*, vol. 1, 218.
31. Fiske, Report, *Hearings*, vol. 2, 2061–67.
32. U.S. Park Police Report, *Hearings*, vol. 2, 2123.
33. FBI Laboratory Report, 9 May 1994, *Hearings*, vol. 2, 241–42.
34. Fiske, Report, Exhibit 1, *Hearings*, vol. 1, 245.
35. Fiske, Report, *Hearings*, vol. 1, 231.
36. FBI Laboratory Report, 9 May 1994, *Hearings*, vol. 2, 245–46.
37. Fiske, Report, Exhibit 1, *Hearings*, vol. 1, 234, 244.
38. Melinda Henneberger, "First Lady, in Blue, Opens Refurbished Blue Room," *New York Times*, 18 February 1995.
39. Fiske, Report, Exhibit 1, *Hearings*, vol. 1, 235, 243.
40. FBI Statement of "Confidential Witness," 14 April 1994, *Hearings*, vol. 2, 1543.
41. Christopher Ruddy, "Aide Saw Foster Leave with Briefcase: Contradicts Official Claims," *Pittsburgh Tribune-Review*, 4 February 1996, sec. A, 1.
42. U.S. Park Police Report, Interview with Linda Tripp, 22 July 1993, *Hearings*, vol. 2, 2134.
43. FBI Statement of Patrick Knowlton, 15 April 1994, *Hearings*, vol. 2, 1526.
44. FBI Statement of George O. Gonzalez, 23 February 1994, *Hearings*, vol. 2, 1351.
45. Christopher Ruddy, "Missing Briefcase Could Be Key in Solving Vince Foster Mystery," *Pittsburgh Tribune-Review*, 13 June 1995, sec. A, 1.
46. Senate Deposition, Rolla, *Hearings*, vol. 1, 393.
47. Senate Deposition, Braun, *Hearings*, vol. 1, 501.
48. Ibid., 507.
49. Interview with confidential source.
50. U.S. Park Police Report, Supplemental Criminal Incident Record, Autopsy of Vincent Foster, 21 July 1993, *Hearings*, vol. 2, 2128.

51. Ibid., 2123.
52. Christopher Ruddy, "Fiske Probe Leaves Trail of Unanswered Questions," *Pittsburgh Tribune-Review,* 29 March 1995, sec. A, 7.
53. United States Government Memorandum, U.S. Secret Service, 20 July 1993, *Hearings,* vol. 2, 2551.

CHAPTER 5

1. Senate Deposition of John C. Rolla, 21 July 1994, *Hearings,* vol. 1, 411, 413, 414.
2. Senate Deposition of Robert Allen Rule, 26 July 1994, *Hearings,* vol. 1, 1298.
3. Senate Deposition, Rolla, *Hearings,* vol. 1, 418.
4. Christopher Ruddy telephonic interview with Dr. Beyer, 16 January 1994.
5. Senate Deposition, Rule, *Hearings,* vol. 1, 1301.
6. Christopher Ruddy, "Pathologist, FBI Go Way Back," *Pittsburgh Tribune-Review,* 10 December 1995.
7. U.S. Park Police Report, *Hearings,* vol. 2, 2128.
8. Christopher Ruddy, "Foster Coroner Has Been Dead Wrong on Suicide Before," *New York Post,* 8 March 1994.
9. Senate Deposition of James C. Beyer, 13 July 1994, *Hearings,* vol. 1, 592, 593.
10. U.S. Park Police Report, *Hearings,* vol. 2, 2128.
11. Christopher Ruddy, "Fumbling Feds Change Story on Foster 'Suicide,' " *New York Post,* 10 February 1994.
12. Ibid.
13. FBI Statement of Donald David Haut, 12 April 1994, *Hearings,* vol. 2, 1659, 1660.
14. Senate Deposition, Rolla, *Hearings,* vol. 1, 401.
15. Robert B. Fiske, Jr., "Report of the Independent Counsel in Re Vincent Foster, Jr.," 30 June 1994, *Hearings,* vol. 1, 211.
16. FBI Statement of Julian Orenstein, 14 April 1994, *Hearings,* vol. 2, 1656–1657.
17. Interview with Joe Purvis at his Little Rock, Arkansas, office, March 1994.
18. Fiske, Report, *Hearings,* vol. 1, 212.
    Senate Deposition, Beyer, *Hearings,* vol. 1, 94, 97.
19. U.S. Park Police Report, *Hearings,* vol. 2, 2128.
20. Ambrose Evans-Pritchard, "White House Death: Murder Theory Comes under Scrutiny," *Sunday Telegraph* (London), 11 June 1995.
21. Fiske, Report, *Hearings,* vol. 1, 371.
22. U.S. Park Police Report, *Hearings,* vol. 2, 2114.
23. Interview with Dr. James C. Beyer, 31 March 1994, *Hearings,* vol. 1, 611, 614.
24. Christopher Ruddy, "Foster's Death Discrepancies Are Abundant: Did His Neck Suffer Trauma?" *Pittsburgh Tribune-Review,* 16 June 1995.
25. FBI telephonic interview with Wayne Johnson, 10 June 1994, *Hearings,* vol. 2, 1772.
26. Mike Wallace, "What About Vince Foster?" *60 Minutes,* CBS, 8 October 1995.
27. Christopher Ruddy, "Top Docs Cast Doubt on Foster 'Suicide,' " *New York Post,* 17 February 1994.

28. Ibid.
29. Telephonic interview with Dr. Richard Mason, July 1994.
30. Ruddy, "Top Docs."

CHAPTER 6

1. Remarks by the President on *Larry King Live,* 20 July 1993.
2. Ibid.
3. White House press briefing by McLarty and Gearan, 21 July 1993.
4. Howard Fineman and Bob Cohn, "The Mystery of the White House Suicide," *Newsweek,* 2 August 1993.
5. Robert B. Fiske, Jr., "Report of the Independent Counsel in Re Vincent Foster, Jr.," 30 June 1994, *Hearings,* vol. 14, 4212, 4213.
6. Christopher Ruddy, "Foster's Death: What and When Did the White House Know?" *Pittsburgh Tribune-Review,* 15 June 1995.
7. Ambrose Evans-Pritchard, "When Did White House Learn of Aide's Death?" *Sunday Telegraph* (London), 9 April 1995.
8. FBI Statement of Richard Arthur, 16 March 1994, *Hearings,* vol. 2, 1383.
   FBI Statement of William Joseph Bianchi, 17 March 1994, *Hearings,* vol. 2, 1365.
   FBI Statement of Jennifer Morgan Wacha, 11 March 1994, *Hearings,* vol. 2, 1355.
   FBI Statement of James Atwater Iacone, 11 March 1994, *Hearings,* vol. 2, 1358.
   FBI Statement of Todd Stacey Hall, 18 March 1994, *Hearings,* vol. 2, 1388.
9. Exhibit 3, Handwritten notes of John C. Rolla, 20 July 1993, *Hearings,* vol. 1, 488.
10. Christopher Ruddy, "Make-up Artist Links Clinton to Possible Cover-up," *Pittsburgh Tribune-Review,* 14 February 1996.
11. Affidavit of Roger L. Perry, 28 March 1995.
12. Affidavit of Larry Patterson, 28 March 1995.
13. Affidavit of Lynn A. Davis, 24 March 1995.
14. John Crudele, "White House Lying on Foster Death," *New York Post,* 7 February 1996.
15. John Crudele, "Foster Death: Aide's Slip May Be Showing," *New York Post,* 8 August 1995.
16. Senate Deposition of John C. Rolla, 21 July 1994, *Hearings,* vol. 1, 446, 447.
17. Peter J. Boyer, "Life After Vince," *New Yorker,* 11 September 1995.
18. Senate Deposition, Rolla, *Hearings,* vol. 1, 448.
19. Ibid., 457.
20. Senate Testimony of Bernard Nussbaum, 9 August 1995, *Final Report of Special Committee to Investigate Whitewater Development Corporation and Related Matters,* 17 June 1996, Senate Report no. 104–280, 52.
21. Senate Testimony of Patsy Thomasson, 25 July 1995, Special Committee to Investigate Whitewater Development Corporation and Related Matters, *New York Times,* 27 July 1995.
22. DEA Document.

23. Senate Testimony of Henry P. O'Neill, 26 July 1995, Special Committee to Investigate Whitewater, *New York Times*, 27 July 1995.

24. Senate Testimony, O'Neill, *Final Report*, 54.

25. Senate Testimony of Maggie Williams, 26 July 1995, Special Committee to Investigate Whitewater Development Corporation and Related Matters, *New York Times*, 27 July 1995.

26. Senate Testimony, O'Neill, Special Committee to Investigate Whitewater, *New York Times*, 27 July 1995.

27. Senate Deposition of Charles W. Hume, 22 July 1994, *Hearings*, vol. 1, 708–9.

28. Senate Deposition of Robert H. Hines, 25 July 1994, *Hearings*, vol. 1, 1186–87.

29. Senate Deposition, Hines, *Hearings*, vol. 1, 1221, 1222.

30. David Johnston, "Investigators to Seek Ex–White House Aide's Files on Clinton Land Dealings," *New York Times*, 22 December 1993.

31. *Investigation of the White House Travel Office Firings and Related Matters, Fifteenth Report by the Committee on Government Reform and Oversight*, 26 September 1996, House Report no. 104–849.

32. Ibid.

33. Senate Deposition, Hume, *Hearings*, vol. 1, 723.

34. Christopher Ruddy, "Foster File Shocker," *New York Post*, 9 March 1994.

35. Christopher Ruddy, "Fiske Probe Leaves Trail of Unanswered Questions," *Pittsburgh Tribune-Review*, 29 March 1995.

36. Senate Deposition of Betsy Pond, 26 June 1995, Special Committee to Investigate Whitewater.

37. Senate Deposition, Hume, *Hearings*, vol. 1, 723–27.

38. Senate Testimony of Roger C. Adams, 27 July 1995, Special Committee to Investigate Whitewater, *New York Times*, 28 July 1995.

39. Senate Testimony of Philip Heymann, 2 August 1995, Special Committee to Investigate Whitewater, *New York Times*, 3 August 1995.

40. Senate Testimony, Heymann, 2 August 1995, *Final Report of Special Committee to Investigate Whitewater*, 68.

41. Senate Testimony of David Margolis, 10 August 1995, *Final Report of Special Committee to Investigate Whitewater*, 69, 71.

42. Senate Testimony of Scott Salter, 27 July 1995, *Final Report of Special Committee to Investigate Whitewater*, 72–73.

43. Senate Testimony, Nussbaum, 8 August 1995, Special Committee to Investigate Whitewater, *New York Times*, 10 August 1995.

44. Senate Testimony, Margolis, Special Committee to Investigate Whitewater, *New York Times*, 11 August 1995.

45. Senate Testimony, Heymann, *Final Report of Special Committee to Investigate Whitewater*, 83.

46. Bernard Nussbaum, "What I Did and Why I Did It," *New York Times*, 8 August 1995.

47. Interview with Thomas Scorza, 20 June 1995.

48. Christopher Ruddy, "Grand Jury Examines Foster Matters," *Pittsburgh Tribune-Review*, 28 June 1995.

49. *Final Report of Special Committee to Investigate Whitewater,* 105–6.

50. Senate Testimony of Susan Thomases, 8 August 1995, Special Committee to Investigate Whitewater, *New York Times,* 9 August 1995.

51. *Final Report of Special Committee to Investigate Whitewater,* 65–66.

52. Senate Testimony of Stephen Neuwirth, 10 July 1995, *Final Report of Special Committee to Investigate Whitewater,* 65.

53. Associated Press, "Whitewater Testimony Conflicts," 3 August 1995.

54. Senate Testimony, Williams, *Final Report of Special Committee to Investigate Whitewater,* 79–80.

55. Senate Testimony of Thomas Castleton, 3 August 1995, Special Committee to Investigate Whitewater, *New York Times,* 4 August 1995.

56. Senate Testimony of Carolyn Huber, 3 August 1995, *Final Report of Special Committee to Investigate Whitewater,* 81.

57. *Final Report of Special Committee to Investigate Whitewater,* 91–92, 116.

58. White House press briefing by Dee Dee Myers, 27 July 1993.

59. Ibid.

60. Fred Barnes, "Spinning Grief," *New Republic,* 23–30 August 1993.

61. Remarks by President Bill Clinton in the Rose Garden, 21 July 1993.

62. Fred Barnes, "Spinning Grief."

63. "Suicide Motive Not Part of Probe," *Washington Times,* 27 July 1993.

64. White House press briefing by Dee Dee Myers, 27 July 1993.

65. Senate Testimony, Neuwirth, 10 July 1995, Special Committee to Investigate Whitewater, *New York Times,* 4 August 1995.

66. *Final Report of Special Committee to Investigate Whitewater,* 84.

67. Ibid., 88–89.

68. Susan Schmidt, "Whitewater Counsel Probes Question of Foster Documents Removal," *Washington Post,* 20 April 1995.

69. Christopher Ruddy, "Experts Say Foster 'Suicide' Note Forged," *Pittsburgh Tribune-Review,* 25 October 1995.

70. David Johnston, "New Gap Arises in Inquiry into Death of Clinton Aide," *New York Times,* 14 August 1993.

Justice Department Document FBI-00000079, *Final Report of Special Committee to Investigate Whitewater,* 97.

71. Ruddy, "Experts Say."

72. Press conference, 25 October 1995, with James Davidson, Vincent Scalice, Reginald Alton, and Ronald Rice; Willard Hotel, Washington, D.C.

73. Ibid.

74. Ruddy, "Experts Say."

75. FBI Lab Report, 13 June 1994, *Hearings,* vol. 2, 2046–47.

76. Ruddy, "Experts Say."

77. Mike McAlary, "The Unfostered," *New York Daily News,* 14 March 1994.

78. *Final Report of Special Committee to Investigate Whitewater,* 97–98.

79. Senate Deposition, Simonello, *Hearings,* vol. 1, 692, 693, 684, 685.

80. Ibid., 694.

CHAPTER 7

1. *Facts on File, 1994,* 20 January 1994, 31.
2. "Fiske Named as Clinton Whitewater Prosecutor," Reuters, 20 January 1994.
3. Jerry Seper, "Clinton Papers Lifted After Aide's Suicide," *Washington Times,* 20 December 1993.
4. James Ring Adams, "The Obstructionists," *American Spectator,* April/May 1994.
5. FBI Statement of Webster Lee Hubbell, June 7, 1994. *Hearings,* vol. 2, 1746.
6. Maureen Dowd, "Lessons on Covering-up at the White House," *New York Times,* 17 December 1995.
7. Ibid.
   "Clinton Got Whitewater Advice," Associated Press, 15 December 1995.
8. White House Press Release, Office of the Press Secretary, 6 December 1995.
9. Sam Vincent Meddis, "Special Counsel Called as 'Honest as They Come,' " *USA Today,* 21 January 1994.
   Robert L. Jackson, "GOP Lawyer Picked to Probe Whitewater," *Los Angeles Times,* 21 January 1994.
10. Wayne Barrett, "Freedom to Steal," *New York* magazine, 4 February 1980.
11. Ibid.
    James Carney, "The Squeaky-Clean G-Man," *Time,* 2 August 1993.
12. Wayne Barrett, "Freedom to Steal."
13. Jane Fullerton and Terry Lemons, "Whitewater's No. 1 Investigator," *Arkansas Democrat-Gazette,* 15 May 1994.
    Kim Masters, "Over Whitewater," *Washington Post,* 4 April 1994.
    Arnold Lubasch, "Lead Candidates for Fiske's Post," *New York Times,* 9 January 1980.
    Dennis Cauchon, "Walsh's Ex-Partner Called Likely Whitewater Counsel," *USA Today,* 20 January 1994.
    "The Fiske Hangout," Review & Outlook, *Wall Street Journal,* 26 July 1994.
14. "The Fiske Hangout."
    "Who is Webster Hubbell?" Review & Outlook, *Wall Street Journal,* 14 February 1994.
15. "Too Much Baggage," Review & Outlook, *Wall Street Journal,* 21 January 1994.
16. "The Fiske Coverup," Review & Outlook, *Wall Street Journal,* 9 March 1994.
17. "Reno OKs Faster Access to Death Report on Foster," *Los Angeles Times,* 4 February 1994.
18. "The Fiske Coverup."
19. Jerry Seper, "Rose Firm Shreds Whitewater Records," *Washington Times,* 9 February 1994.
20. Robert L. Bartley, "What Mr. Fiske Can't Do with the Facts," *Wall Street Journal,* 30 March 1994. "The Fiske Coverup."
21. Robert B. Fiske, Jr., Letter to Steven Froot, Assistant U.S. Attorney, regarding *Dow Jones & Co.* v. *U.S. Department of Justice,* 28 February 1994.
22. Interview with Russell Hardin, 24 July 1995.
23. Interview with Maurice Nadjari, 22 July 1996.

24. Jerry Seper, "Fiske Brings 8 Aboard His Whitewater Team," *Washington Times,* 24 February 1994.

25. Mike McAlary, "The Unfostered," *New York Post,* 14 March 1994.

26. Ellen Joan Pollock, "Fiske Is Seen Verifying Foster Killed Himself," *Wall Street Journal,* 4 April 1994.

27. Dennis Cauchon and Judy Keen, "Special Counsel's Task Tougher Than Expected," *USA Today,* 19 April 1994, sec. A, 9.

28. James Vicini, "Whitewater Counsel to Report Foster Killed Himself," Reuters 4 May 1994.

29. FBI Report, Fort Marcy Excavation, 4 April 1994, *Hearings,* vol. 2, 1905.

30. FBI Report, Foster autopsy, 6 April 1994, *Hearings,* vol. 1, 610–614.

31. FBI Statement of Donald David Haut, 12 April 1994, *Hearings,* vol. 2, 1659.

32. FBI Statement of John S. Skyles, 20 April 1994, *Hearings,* vol. 2, 1546.

33. FBI Statement of John C. Rolla, 27 April 1994, *Hearings,* vol. 2, 1600.

34. FBI Statement of Elizabeth Braden Foster, 9 May 1994, *Hearings,* vol. 2, 1633.

35. Fiske, Report, Exhibit 1, FBI Lab Report, 9 May 1994, *Hearings,* vol. 1, 234.

36. Fiske, Report, Exhibit 3, Forensic Pathology and Medical Examiner-Related Findings, undated, *Hearings,* vol. 1, 333–36.

37. Fiske, Report, Exhibit I, FBI Lab Report, 9 May 1994, *Hearings,* vol. 1, 242.

38. Fiske, Report, *Hearings,* vol. 1, 219.

39. FBI Statement, Haut, 14 April 1994, *Hearings,* vol. 2, 1658.

40. Fiske, Report, Exhibit 1, FBI Lab Report, 9 May 1994, *Hearings,* vol. 1, 242.

41. Report of Interview between G. Gordon Liddy and the "CW," 22 March 1994, *Hearings,* vol. 2, 1464.

42. Ibid.

43. Robert D. Novak, "No Foster Gun?" *New York Post,* 18 April 1994, 25.

44. FBI Statement of Confidential Witness, 14 April 1994, *Hearings,* vol. 2, 1514.

45. Ibid., 1517.

46. Fiske, Report, *Hearings,* vol. 1, 205.

47. Christopher Ruddy, "Foster's Death Site Strongly Disputed," *Pittsburgh Tribune-Review,* 25 January 1995.

48. Fiske, Report, *Hearings,* vol. 1, 206.

49. Ruddy, "Foster's Death Site Strongly Disputed."

50. FBI Statement of Chuck Stough, 21 June 1994, *Hearings,* vol. 2, 1785.

51. Ruddy, "Foster's Death Site Strongly Disputed."

52. FBI Statement, Confidential Witness, 14 April 1994, *Hearings,* vol. 2, 1517.

53. Report of Interview between Liddy and the "CW," *Hearings,* vol. 2, 1461.

54. Fiske, Report, *Hearings,* vol. 1, 184.

55. Fiske, Report, *Hearings,* vol. 1, 233.

56. Fiske, Report, *Hearings,* vol. 1, 214.

57. Christopher Ruddy, *Vincent Foster: The Ruddy Investigation,* United Publishing, 1996, 35.

58. Christopher Ruddy, "Opposites Join Call for Starr to Probe Foster's Death," *Pittsburgh Tribune-Review,* 19 December 1994.

59. Ruddy, *Vincent Foster: The Ruddy Investigation,* 35.

60. Interview with Christopher Ruddy by Mike Wallace, New York, August 1993.

61. Fiske, Report, *Hearings,* vol. 1, 233.

62. Senate Testimony of Dr. Charles Hirsch, 29 July 1994, *Hearings,* vol. 1, 63.

63. Fiske, Report, Exhibit 3, Forensic Pathology and Medical Examiner-Related Findings, undated, *Hearings,* vol. 1, 336.

64. Senate Testimony, Hirsch, *Hearings,* vol. 1, 65.

65. Ibid.

66. Christopher Ruddy, "New Face Emerges in Probe of Foster's Death," *Pittsburgh Tribune-Review,* 20 October 1995.

67. Fiske, Report, *Hearings,* vol. 1, 222–23.

68. Christopher Ruddy, "Fiske Probe's Excavation Challenged," *Pittsburgh Tribune-Review,* 5 April 1995.

69. FBI Report, Fort Marcy Excavation, 4 April 1994, *Hearings,* vol. 2, 1910.

70. Ibid., 1906.

71. Ruddy, "Fiske Probe's Excavation Challenged."

72. Ibid.

73. Fiske, Report, *Hearings,* vol. 1, 182.

74. FBI Statement of Robert Arthur Denning, 20 April 1994, *Hearings,* vol. 2, 1607. FBI Statement of Roger George Bailey, 20 April 1994, *Hearings,* vol. 2, 1608.

75. Fiske, Report, *Hearings,* vol. 1, 203.

76. Ibid., 218.

77. Ibid., 208.

78. Christopher Ruddy, "Foster's Death Discrepancies Are Abundant: Did His Neck Suffer Trauma?" *Pittsburgh Tribune-Review,* 16 June 1995.

79. Fiske, Report, *Hearings,* vol. 1, 183.

80. Ibid., 210.

81. Christopher Ruddy, "Other Witness Still Unexplained," *Pittsburgh Tribune-Review,* 14 June 1995.

82. Christopher Ruddy, "Aide Saw Foster Leave with Briefcase," *Pittsburgh Tribune-Review,* 4 February 1996.

CHAPTER 8

1. Christopher Ruddy, "Ex-Chief: Politics Kept FBI Off Foster Case," *New York Post,* 3 February 1994.

2. Press conference with Philip Heymann, Robert Langston, Robert Bryant; Report on the Death of Vincent Foster, 10 August 1993, *Hearings,* vol. 2, 2635.

3. *Investigation of the White House Travel Office Firings and Related Matters,* 26 September 1996, House Report 104–849, 733.

4. Transcript of Note Found in Foster's Briefcase, *Hearings,* vol. 2, 2023.

5. Interview with Phillip Heymann.

6. Ruddy, "Ex-Chief: Politics Kept FBI Off Foster Case."

7. Ibid.

8. "Remarks by the President on Larry King Live," 20 July 1993.

9. "What's the Rush?" Review & Outlook, *Wall Street Journal,* 19 July 1993.

10. Fiske, Report, *Hearings*, vol. 1, 214–15.

11. Senator Lauch Faircloth, Senate Hearings, 29 July 1994, *Hearings*, vol. 1, 63.

12. Testimony before the Senate, 29 July 1994, *Hearings*, vol. 1, 55.

13. Ibid., 56.

14. Ibid., 60–61.

15. Senate Testimony of William Colombell, 29 July 1994, *Hearings*, vol. 1, 60–61.

16. Senate Hearings, 29 July 1994, *Hearings*, vol. 1, 52.

17. Ibid., 55.

18. Ibid., 52.

19. Ibid., 53.

20. Ibid., 54.

21. Ibid., 53.

22. Fiske, Report, *Hearings*, vol. 1, 182.

23. Ibid., 184.

24. Final Report, Senate Whitewater Committee, 17 June 1996, 104–280, 100.

25. Ibid., 67.

26. Ibid., 68.

27. FBI Statement of Wayne Johnson, 10 June 1994, *Hearings*, vol. 2, 1772.

28. Hearings before the Senate, 29 July 1994, *Hearings*, vol. 1, 45.

29. FBI Statement of Deborah L. Gorham, 19 and 26 April 1994, *Hearings*, vol. 2, 1444, 1448, 1449.

30. FBI Statement of Dr. Larry S. Watkins, 16 May 1994, *Hearings*, vol. 2, 1675, 1676.

31. Fiske, Report, *Hearings*, vol. 1, 186.

32. FBI Statement, Dr. Larry S. Watkins, *Hearings*, vol. 2, 1676.

33. Fiske, Report, Exhibit 8, Report of Autopsy, 28 July 1993, *Hearings*, vol. 1, 364.

34. FBI Statement of Elizabeth Braden Foster, 9 May 1994, *Hearings*, vol. 2, 1633.

35. James B. Stewart, *Blood Sport: The President and His Adversaries* (New York: Simon & Schuster, 1996), 281.

36. Fiske, Report, *Hearings*, vol. 1, 196.

37. Ibid., 197.

38. FBI Statement of Psychiatrist #1, 11 May 1994, *Hearings*, vol. 2, 1654.
    FBI Statement of Psychiatrist #2, 11 May 1994, *Hearings*, vol. 2, 1655.

39. Confidential source.

40. Confidential source.

41. Confidential source.

42. FBI Statement of psychiatrist Dr. Robert Hedaya, 17 May 1994, *Hearings*, vol. 2, 1662.

43. FBI Statement, Hedaya, *Hearings*, vol. 2, 1662, 1663.

44. FBI Statement, Elizabeth Braden Foster, *Hearings*, vol. 2, 1640.

45. FBI Lab Report, 13 June 1994, *Hearings*, vol. 2, 2046–47.

46. FBI Statement of Webster Lee Hubbell, 7 June 1994, *Hearings*, vol. 2, 1745.

47. FBI Statement of William H. Kennedy, 9 June 1994, *Hearings*, vol. 2, 1758.

48. FBI Statement of Loraine Wolfe Cline, 18 May 1994, *Hearings*, vol. 2, 1730.

49. Fiske, Report, *Hearings*, vol. 1, 187–88.

50. FBI Statement, Hubbell, 13 and 15 April 1994, *Hearings*, vol. 2, 1482.

51. Ibid., 1478.
52. Fiske, Report, *Hearings,* vol. 1, 186.
53. Senate Deposition of Deborah Gorham, 23 June 1995, before the Special Committee to Investigate Whitewater Development Corporation and Related Matters.
54. FBI Statement, Hubbell, 13 and 15 April 1994, *Hearings,* vol. 2, 1479.
55. FBI Statement, Hubbell, 7 June 1994, *Hearings,* vol. 2, 1744.
56. Ibid., 1744, 1745.
57. Ibid., 1745.
58. Fiske, Report, *Hearings,* vol. 1, 188.
59. FBI Statement of W. David Watkins, 22 June 1994, *Hearings,* vol. 2, 1791.
60. Fiske, Report, *Hearings,* vol. 1, 195.
61. *Investigation of the White House Travel Office Firings and Related Matters,* 26 September 1996, House Report 104–849, Section X[E], 120.
62. Ibid., 109.
63. Christopher Ruddy, "Which Webb Hubbell Was Telling the Truth?" *Pittsburgh Tribune-Review,* 23 July 1995.
64. Ibid.
65. Ibid.
66. Ibid.
67. FBI Statement, Elizabeth Braden Foster, *Hearings,* vol. 2, 1637–38.
68. Peter J. Boyer, "Life After Vince," *The New Yorker,* 11 September 1995.
69. Ibid.
70. Howard Fineman and Bob Cohn, "The Mystery of the White House Suicide," *Newsweek,* 2 August 1993.
71. Paul Bedard, "Foster Troubled by Travelgate Firings," *Washington Times,* 28 July, 1995.
72. Ibid.
73. Ibid.
74. Ibid.
75. Gregory Jaynes, "The Death of Hope," *Esquire,* November 1993.
76. FBI Statement of John Phillip Carroll, 17 May 1994, *Hearings,* vol. 2, 1724–28.
77. Jaynes, "The Death of Hope."
78. Interview with John Phillip Carroll, 27 June 1996.
79. FBI Statement, Carroll, *Hearings,* vol. 2, 1727.
80. Reed Irvine interview with Confidential Witness.
81. Ambrose Evans-Prichard, "Death in the Park: Is This the Killer?" *Sunday Telegraph* (London), 22 October 1995.
82. FBI Statement of Patrick Knowlton, 15 April 1994, *Hearings,* vol. 2, 1526.
83. FBI Statement of Todd Stacey Hall, 18 March 1994, *Hearings,* vol. 2, 1387.
84. Christopher Ruddy, "Other Witness Still Unexplained," *Pittsburgh Tribune-Review,* 14 June 1995.
85. FBI Statement, Hall, 27 April 1994, *Hearings,* vol. 2, 1551.
86. Ruddy, "Foster Case: Starr Investigator Sought Testimony Changes," *Pittsburgh Tribune-Review,* 11 February 1996.
87. Stewart, *Blood Sport,* 284–85.
88. FBI Statement of Susan T. Thomases, 14 June 1994, *Hearings,* vol. 2, 1778.

89. "Hillary's Enforcer," *Wall Street Journal,* 8 April 1996.

90. FBI Handwritten Notes of interview with Richard M. Arthur.

91. FBI Statement of Richard M. Arthur, 16 March 1994, *Hearings,* vol. 2, 1383, 1384.

92. FBI Handwritten Notes of interview with Richard M. Arthur.

93. Ibid.

94. FBI Statement, Arthur, 29 April 1994, *Hearings,* vol. 2, 1565.

95. FBI Handwritten Notes of interview with Lisa Foster.

96. FBI Handwritten Notes of interview with Cheryl Braun.

97. FBI Statement of Cheryl Ann Braun, 28 April 1994, *Hearings,* vol. 2, 1625.

98. FBI Statement of Lieutenant. Patrick Steven Gavin, 28 April 1994, *Hearings,* vol. 2, 1555.

99. FBI Handwritten Notes of interview with Bruce Lindsey.

100. Christopher Ruddy, "Security Chief Livingstone Played Central Role After Foster's Suicide," *Pittsburgh Tribune-Review,* 29 September 1996.

101. Letter from Robert Fiske to the Committee on Banking, Housing, and Urban Affairs, 15 July 1994, *Hearings,* vol. 1, 168.

102. Ruddy, "Security Chief Livingstone Played Central Role After Foster's Suicide."

103. *Investigation of the White House Travel Office Firings and Related Matters.*

104. Confidential source.

105. Confidential source.

106. *Investigation of the White House Travel Office Firings and Related Matters,* Section XI[E], 131–33.

107. Ruddy, "Security Chief Livingstone Played Central Role After Foster's Suicide."

108. Ibid.

109. Ibid.

110. "Text of Order Appointing Starr," *Los Angeles Times,* 6 August 1995.

111. "Statement of Vince Foster's Family," *Hearings,* vol. 1, 154.

CHAPTER 9

1. Susan Schmidt, "Whitewater Counsel Assembles Team," *Washington Post,* 13 September 1994.

2. Press release from the Office of the Independent Counsel, 12 September 1994.

3. Schmidt, "Whitewater Counsel Assembles Team."

4. John McCaslin, "Interesting Pair," *Washington Times,* 19 September 1994.

5. Jane Mayer, "How Independent Is the Counsel?" *The New Yorker,* April 1996.

6. Press release, Office of the Independent Counsel.

7. Stephen Labaton, "Prosecutor Accused of Partisanship," *New York Times,* 21 April 1996.

8. Ronald J. Ostrow and John M. Broder, "Starr to 'Build Upon' Fiske Probe," *Los Angeles Times,* 11 August 1994, sec. A, 10.

9. Deroy Murdock, "Some Unanswered Questions in the Vince Foster Case," *New York Post,* 15 August 1994.

10. Ann Devroy and Michael Isikoff, "Foster Depression Called Job-Related," *Washington Post,* 30 July 1994.

11. FBI Statement of Webster Lee Hubbell, 13 and 15 April 1994, *Hearings*, vol. 2, 1481.
    "2 Tribes Look to DNC for Land," Associated Press, 10 March 1997.
    "The Golden Gore Touch Turns to Velcro," *Wall Street Journal*, 13 March 1997.
12. Fiske, Report, *Hearings*, vol. 1, 197–98.
13. Christopher Ruddy, "Ex-Prosecutor Can Show Apparent Cover-up in Foster Death Probe," *Pittsburgh Tribune-Review*, 19 June 1995.
14. Senate Deposition of Betsy Pond, 26 June 1995, before the Special Committee to Investigate Whitewater Development Corporation and Related Matters.
15. *Investigation of the White House Travel Office Firings and Related Matters*, 26 September 1996, House Report 104–849, Section XV[F], 760.
16. Christopher Ruddy, "White House Memo Suggests Tipoff on Prosecutor Tactics," *Pittsburgh Tribune-Review*, 29 September 1996, sec. A, 1.
17. Ruddy, "Ex-Prosecutor Can Show Apparent Cover-up in Foster Death Probe."
18. Lisa Hoffman, "Starr Apt to Second Ruling on Foster," Scripps Howard News Service, *Washington Times*, 6 January 1995.
19. "Starr Reviewing Foster Death," Associated Press, 6 January 1995.
20. Christopher Ruddy, "Clinton Indictments Unlikely," *Pittsburgh Tribune-Review*, 6 August 1995.
21. Jerry Seper, "Foster Probe Grilling Stirs Police Complaint."
22. "Starr Reviewing Foster Death," Associated Press.
23. Christopher Ruddy, "Prosecutor's Resignation Comes at Crucial Point in Foster Probe," *Pittsburgh Tribune-Review*, 6 April 1995.
24. "Foster Suicide Witnesses Irate," Associated Press, 13 January 1995.
25. Jerry Seper, "Foster Probe Grilling Stirs Police Complaint."
26. Christopher Ruddy, "Policy Dispute Led to Shakeup in Foster Probe," *Pittsburgh Tribune-Review*, 3 May 1995.
27. Christopher Ruddy, "Starr's Probe Failed to Challenge Privilege Claims," *Pittsburgh Tribune-Review*, 24 December 1995.
28. Ibid.
29. Ibid.
30. Ruddy, "Clinton Indictments Unlikely."
31. Ibid.
32. Christopher Ruddy, "Senator Questions Hubbell Hiring," *Pittsburgh Tribune-Review*, 2 March 1995.
33. "W'Water Eyes Hubbell Payments," Associated Press, 22 November 1996.
34. Jeff Gerth and Stephen Labaton, "Two Clinton Advisers Knew of Hubbell's Plight," *New York Times*, 5 May 1997.
35. L. J. Davis, "The Name of Rose," *New Republic*, 4 April 1994.
36. Christopher Ruddy, "Starr's Grand Jury," *Pittsburgh Tribune-Review*, 3 May 1995.
37. Interview with confidential source.
38. Glenn R. Simpson, "Southern Edge: A Veteran Prosecutor of Political Corruption Steers Whitewater Case," *Wall Street Journal*, 31 July 1996, sec. A, 1.
39. Christopher Ruddy, "Starr Terminated Washington Grand Jury, but Why?" *Pittsburgh Tribune-Review*, 29 December 1995.
40. Ibid.

41. Ibid.
42. "Scientist Helps in Whitewater," Associated Press, 11 June 1995.
Christopher Ruddy, "New Face Emerges in Probe of Foster's Death," *Pittsburgh Tribune-Review*, 20 October 1995.
43. "Simpson Expert Profiled," Associated Press, 22 August 1995.
44. Christopher Ruddy, "Foster Death: Lee's Findings Questioned," *Pittsburgh Tribune-Review*, 13 November 1995.
45. "FBI Re-Seeks Foster Bullet," Associated Press, 14 September 1995.
Jim Keary, "FBI Fires Shot in Search of Foster Bullet," *Washington Times*, 16 September 1995. Ruddy, "Foster Death: Lee's Findings Questioned."
46. Christopher Ruddy, "Controversial Lee to Issue His Report," *Pittsburgh Tribune-Review*, 24 November 1995.
47. Ruddy, "Foster Death: Lee's Findings Questioned."
48. Ibid.
49. Ibid.
50. Christopher Ruddy, "Foster Case: Book Says There's 'New' Evidence," *Pittsburgh Tribune-Review*, 29 October 1996.
51. David Johnston, "FBI Chemist Says Experts Are Pressured to Skew Tests," *New York Times*, 15 September 1995.
52. Christopher Ruddy, " 'New' Evidence in Foster Case Would Strain Credibility," *Pittsburgh Tribune-Review*, 26 October 1995.
53. Christopher Ruddy, "New Face Emerges in Probe of Foster's Death," *Pittsburgh Tribune-Review*, 20 October 1995.
54. Christopher Ruddy, "New Expert with Old Ties Reviews Foster Report," *Pittsburgh Tribune-Review*, 14 August 1996, sec. A, 1.
55. Ruddy, "New Face Emerges in Probe of Foster's Death."
56. Ruddy, "New Expert with Old Ties Reviews Foster Report."
57. Ibid.
58. Ibid.
59. Ibid.
60. Susan Schmidt, "Two Years After Foster's Death, Conspiracy Theories Thrive," *Washington Post*, 4 July 1995.
61. "Tyson's Corner," Review & Outlook, *Wall Street Journal*, 14 April 1995.
62. Michael Isikoff and Mark Hosenball, "A Gentlemanly Lawyer Plays Political Hardball," *Newsweek*, 19 February 1996.
63. Background of Kenneth W. Starr, Office of the Independent Counsel.
David Lauter, "Fiske's Successor Is Active GOP Partisan," *Los Angeles Times*, 6 August 1994, sec. A, 19.
64. Jane Mayer, "How Independent Is the Counsel?" *The New Yorker*, April 1996.
65. "1993–94 Election Cycle: Business and Association PAC Study," Leadership Institute.
66. Fred Barbash and Lou Cannon, "Tactics of O'Connor Foes Irritate Sen. Humphrey," *Washington Post*, 10 July 1981.
67. Ruth Marcus, "High Court at Abortion Juncture," *Washington Post*, 23 April 1992.
68. Interview with John Phillip Carroll, 27 June 1996.

69. Christopher Ruddy, "Prosecutor Moved to Firm with Whitewater Ties," *Pittsburgh Tribune-Review,* 7 August 1996.
70. Ibid.

CHAPTER 10

1. Christopher Ruddy, "Grand Jury Witness in Foster Probe Taking Aim at FBI Tactics," *Pittsburgh Tribune-Review,* 8 February 1996.
2. Ibid.
3. Chris Conley, "Parker on Team to Investigate Foster Link," *[Memphis] Commercial Appeal,* 23 March 1996.
4. Stephen Labaton, "Prosecutor Accused of Partisanship," *New York Times,* 21 April 1996.
5. Jerry Seper, "Arkansas Troopers Prepared to Testify," *Washington Times,* 19 February 1996.
6. Letter from White House Counsel Jane Sherburne to Robert Guiffra, 30 September 1995; Final Report, 17 June 1996, 49.
7. Sherburne to Guiffra, 13 October 1995; Final Report, 17 June 1996, 49
8. Senate Testimony of Helen Dickey, 14 February 1996, 48–49.
9. Letter from Sherburne to Viet Dinh, 25 February 1996; Final Report, 17 June 1996, 50.
10. Lisa Hoffman, "Starr Apt to Second Ruling on Foster," *Washington Times,* 6 January 1995.
11. Mike Wallace interview with Christopher Ruddy, August 1993, the Meridien Hotel, New York.
12. Ibid.
13. Carl Bernstein and Bob Woodward, *All the President's Men* (New York: Simon & Schuster, 1974), 275–76.
14. Charlie Rose interview with Alfonse D'Amato, 14 August 1995.
15. Alfonse D'Amato on the *Bob Grant Show,* WABC, New York City, August 1995.
16. Newt Gingrich on the *Bob Grant Show,* WABC, New York City, 6 July 1995.
17. Christopher Ruddy, "Aide Saw Foster Leave with Briefcase; Contradicts Official Claims," *Pittsburgh Tribune-Review,* 4 February 1996.

INDEX